D1068710

Solutions

Tools and Strategies for Schools

Allen Salowe
Leon Lessinger

A SCARECROWEDUCATION BOOK

The Scarecrow Press, Inc.
Lanham, Maryland, and London
2002

MT

A SCARECROWEDUCATION BOOK

Published in the United States of America
by Scarecrow Press, Inc.
4720 Boston Way
Lanham, Maryland 20706
www.scarecrowpress.com
4 Pleydell Gardens, Folkestone
Kent CT20 2DN, England

British Library Cataloguing in Publication Information Available

Library of Congress Cataloging-in-Publication Data Available

ISBN 0-8108-4286-6 (alk. paper)
ISBN 0-8108-4285-8 (pbk. : alk. paper)

∞™ The paper used in this publication meets the minimum requirements
of American National Standard for Information Sciences—Permanence of
Paper for Printed Library Materials, ANSI/NISO Z39.48-1992.
Manufactured in the United States of America.

Contents

Foreword xi

It Integrates What Is Known—Research-
and Performance-Based Concepts and
Tools—To Define and Make Education in
the United States Work xi

It Is Easy to Read xii

If Followed, One Could Transform Schools
from Places Where Kids Simply Go to Places
Where Kids Learn and Perform xiii

**The First Day of School: From the Business
World into the Classroom** xv

Introduction 1

Through the Looking Glass 1

Quality: An Idea Whose Time Has Finally Come 2

Framing the Issues 4

Solutions for Our Time 7

Why This Dismal Picture? 8

Talk—A Solutions Tool 12

A Case Study: The Florida Governor's Commission   14

A Historical Perspective   15

Putting the Focus on Schools   16

Can Schools Change?   17

What's Coming?   18

Notes   19

1   **Follow the Money Trail**   20

The Illusion of a Monopoly   24

Finding New Approaches to Financing Schools   27

How Does the School District Follow the Money?   29

Putting School Results on the Line   30

From the Desk of the Principal   32

Toward Actions   32

Notes   33

2   **Student-Centered School Management
    and Technology**   34

Teacher Education for K–12 Student-Centered
Classrooms   36

Problem-Based Learning   36

What Is Problem-Based Learning?   37

The Payoffs?   38

Where Does Technology Fit in Student-Centered
Schools?   39

Logistical Support for the Teaching and
Learning Process   41

Data Drives School Improvement   45

The Stage Is Set   46

Notes   47

3   Why Student-Center the School?   48

Focus on School Accountability   49

To Achieve System Improvement   50

To Gauge Reliability   52

Why Are We So Sure Classroom Teaching Is
Often Unreliable?   53

General Measurement Considerations   54

Performance Measurement   54

The Nature of Measurement   54

Why We Find Unreliable Classroom Teaching
Distressing   56

Student-Centered Schools Where Unreliability
Is Not a Problem   57

Can "Expert Instruction" Be Clearly Defined?   57

Stakeholders Know Reliable Classroom Teaching
When They See It   58

To Strengthen Educational Systems   59

To Reinforce Instructional Systems   60

To Remove System Constraints   60

To Clear up Perplexing Systems   63

Fostering Student-Centered Improvement   64

Notes   65

4   Performance Management   66

The Backdrop to Change   66

Parents Are Running out of Patience   67

The Likely Future Scenario   72

Good Practice, Poor Practice, and
Malpractice in Education   73

Using the Right Tools to Do the Right Job   75

The Meaning of Tools   76

Tools for Teamwork   76

Starting with the Balanced Scorecard   78

Measurement-Based Performance Management   79

Outcome Metrics   80

Management by Fact   81

Processes Lead the Way   83

The Measurement Processes   84

Responses to Objections for Deploying the
BSC and Quality Processes   84

Dealing with Common Mistakes   87

A Short Story Worth Repeating   88

Summing up the BSC   89

Notes   90

5 **Customer Relationship Management in Education**   92

Who Is the School Customer?   92

Breaking down Barriers and Building Relationships   93

New Challenges Need a Proven Approach   94

Relying on the Experts   94

What Is Not CRM?   95

Lessons Learned in CRM   97

CRM Case Studies   98

Using Technology   103

A Monopoly Agency Restores the Trust   105

Serving the Public Can Only Get Tougher   109

Notes   111

**6 The Right Data Guides Student-Centered
Decision Making   112**

Data Warehousing for School Improvement   112

Raise the Ceiling Not Lower the Floor—Data
Expectations for Students   113

Clear and Explicit Goals   113

What Is Data Warehouse and What Are Its Intentions?   114

Summary of DW Benefits   114

DW Components   115

The Enterprise-Wide Strategic Data Approach   119

User Needs   122

Concerns for Security   122

User Interfaces   123

Implementing the DW   124

Blueprints for Building a DW   124

Notes   125

**7 The College of Engineering Helps Bring Education
into the Twenty-First Century   126**

Applying Engineering Principles to Classroom Teaching   126

Insights into the Nature of Engineering   128

The Engineering Way of Thinking   128

Changing Toxic Assumptions about Schooling   129

An Engineering Mind-Set Approach to Aptitude   130

Modifying Educator Expectations through the
Engineering Mind-Set   132

Changing Student Expectations   135

Changing Public Expectations   135

Engineering for Greater Capability in the
Public Schools   136

Benefits of an Educational Engineering Mind-Set   137

Student Benefits   137

Teacher Benefits   138

Benefits for School Administrators   139

Benefits of the Educational Engineering Frame
of Reference   140

Case Studies in Engineering and Education
Collaboration   141

The Challenge to Public Education   144

School Performance Management through
Engineering Thinking   145

Notes   146

8 **Quality and Performance Management Initiatives
around the Globe**   148

The Pros and Cons of ISO 9000 for Schools   150

American Schools Follow Gradually   151

Tangible Benefits   151

A Matter of Judgment—True Story   153

Maybe We're Starting the ISO Campaign at the
Wrong End   154

A Whole Town Earns ISO 9000 Certification 155

Quality Starts with Caring 158

Notes 159

9 Benchmarking for World-Class Schools 160

What Is Benchmarking for Schools? 160

Why Benchmark a School? 161

What School Benchmarking Is 161

What School Benchmarking Is Not 163

Details of the Benchmarking Process 165

Where to Look for Benchmark Models 167

Possibilities for Improving Education 168

On the Subject of Change 168

Conducting the Benchmarking Site Visit 169

Benchmark: Good Research 170

Benchmark: Reliable Teaching and School
Effectiveness 171

Benchmark: Processes That Drive Performance 172

Benchmark: Essentials of Effective Schools 172

The Spirit of Organizational Change 173

Identifying Low-Performing Schools 175

Benchmark Principles for Reliable Schools 177

Benchmarking Case Studies 178

U.S. Schools Accept Singapore Math Books 180

Policy Voids Blocking School Improvement 181

Notes 187

10 Conclusion: Education and the Future of the Nation   188

   Precipitating Change: Starting an Epidemic   190

   Notes   191

Afterword   192

**Appendix A: Benchmarking the Comer School
            Improvement Process**   197

**Appendix B: State of Hawaii Act 272 Student-Centered
            Schools: Summary**   212

**Appendix C: Minneapolis Public Schools' School-Based
            Management and School Improvement Plans**   215

Appendix D: The School Benchmark Principles   231

**Appendix E: New Jersey Permanent Statutes Title
            18A 7A14.4: Level I District May Apply
            for Alternative Program of Monitoring,
            Evaluation**   236

**Appendix F: State of Washington Quality Initiative 97-03
            Executive Order: Quality Improvement**   238

**Appendix G: State of Washington Balanced Scorecard
            Application: Department of Personnel
            Scorecard—Overall Priorities FY 2001**   241

Appendix H: Eighth-Grade Final Exam—1895   244

Bibliography   247

About the Authors   252

Foreword

This book has several flaws:

First, it integrates what is known—research- and performance-based concepts and tools—to define and make education in the United States work. Second, it is easy to read. Third, if followed, one could transform schools from places where kids simply go to places where kids learn and perform.

Why are these flaws? The answer is simple. Let's examine these three "flaws" in turn.

IT INTEGRATES WHAT IS KNOWN—RESEARCH- AND PERFORMANCE-BASED CONCEPTS AND TOOLS—TO DEFINE AND MAKE EDUCATION IN THE UNITED STATES WORK

The conventional wisdom about education includes:

1. It cannot be fixed with new concepts, understandings, and tools; it can be helped only by raising the investment in order to improve it and people won't pay more money.
2. It takes specialists—read "educationists"—to diagnose and fix whatever is wrong; outsiders don't and cannot understand the world of education, and parents can help but they can't really define what should be used, done, accomplished, and delivered.
3. Research doesn't reflect the "real world," and the mysteries of education are best left to teachers and educators.

4. We cannot measure education or its impact—we can only improve the process.

5. Evaluation is basically limited (if not evil), for the tests are not valid and one cannot put pressure on the kids that high-stakes testing visits on them.

6. The lessons and practices of business, industry, and the balance of the public sector cannot be generalized to education—you can't run education with the same concepts and tools that work in other sectors.

7. What is really important for education lies beyond simple definitions of goals, objectives, curriculum design and development, and evaluation. Education is intangible and is a continuous process that is disrupted if one sets objectives and uses performance criteria and measures, designs, and delivers continuous improvement.

Of course, these allegations are widely agreed on, but they are also nonsense. And they have been deeply held by many educators and those they have influenced—in classrooms and in political meetings—for many years. The resistance is there, a resistance that says let's violate what management guru Peter Drucker has told us for years, that "we are getting better and better at doing that which should not be done at all," and that is spending money, especially on what we know doesn't work and is counterproductive.

This book takes on these misunderstandings—or myths—by exploring them and showing what to do to deliver predictable success. Dangerous stuff: defined and delivered educational success!

IT IS EASY TO READ

In order to be really useful, such text should be dense and complex. After all, if it "was that easy we would have already done it." We lay out our hypotheses, rationales, and methods with clarity and data. This book is clean, simple, and understandable. Why is this a flaw? We don't usually think that straightforward ideas and tools can be useful. They can be, and in this book they are.

IF FOLLOWED, ONE COULD TRANSFORM SCHOOLS FROM PLACES WHERE KIDS SIMPLY GO TO PLACES WHERE KIDS LEARN AND PERFORM

We have come to believe that *our* schools are fine while everyone else's are failing. Thus, we tend to support the schools where we live and where our kids (or grandchildren) go. Transforming (not just changing, as suggested by quality-management inventor W. Edwards Deming) schools means accepting that there are real and important gaps between what we are producing now and what is required to be productive citizens and good neighbors in the future. And change is painful for most of us.

What would happen to those on both sides of current arguments about education if there were proven methods for defining and delivering measured educational success? Those critics would have no role left in being the adversaries of education. And on the other side, the defenders of the status quo (just give us more money and resources) would have their role taken away because it could be proven that we can define and deliver measurable educational success.

This thoughtful and pragmatic book is not another searing indictment of public schools, nor is it a quick fix, feel-good pronouncement of magic bullets. It is a thoughtful, research-based, and rational way for us to make our schools the incubators for tomorrow's citizens.

If people dare to try what is provided here, they will define and deliver educational success. But using this book, people should proceed at their own risk for it is sensible, sensitive, and practical.

Roger Kaufman

The First Day of School: From the Business World into the Classroom

Not long ago I received a story from a retired business associate. She wanted very much to teach public school following an eleven-year career in business. Her experience went something like this:

As I entered the teacher's lounge, I was reminded about the educational humor I'd heard during my practice teaching assignment. Then a colleague remarked, "School would be great if it wasn't for the kids!" Laughter resonated throughout the room. I entered the room and they looked at me. I was a bit different than the rest of the faculty. I was coming into the classroom after 11 years in the business world. I was an outsider. I was qualified and certified, but I had done other things rather than spend 20 years in the classroom. Nevertheless, I smiled, walked to the coffeepot, poured my cup, in a mug that had been on sight since the 1960s. It read, "make love, not war." And then I retreated to my classroom.

Unlocking the door, I was greeted with educational "state of the art technology." Unfortunately, state of the art in the classroom is about 10 years late. There were 3 Apple II computers, with outboard 5¼ floppy drives. (The media specialist told me proudly, "We never throw anything away.") I had a PC on my desk, attached to the Internet and a telephone with no speaker functions.

What did I need to do my job that was missing? When I compare it with the business world, a great deal.

I was driven to produce in the business world; billings, signings, revenue, expense controls, customer satisfaction, performance reviews by my peers, employees and management. If I needed software applications to achieve my objectives it was given to me. In education, I was given a spreadsheet, word processor and storyboarding software.

Let's see, what were my objectives in the high school business classroom?

MISSION: To provide a quality education for all students in a safe and positive setting.

To achieve this mission I need the following information from the educational system:

1. Attendance tracking and enrollment daily software.
2. A grade book.
3. Remote wireless tools to capture those fleeting student "eureka" moments that I could document their unique, individual successes; real time grading through observation.
4. Discipline history software.
5. Health data for each student, so I could tell if that starry look in Sammy's eyes were a result of his anti-seizure medicine and not smoking pot during his lunch break.
6. A historic business intelligence system, a data warehouse. An information system where I could see his history from head start to high school. I need to analyze data and get historical reports about the educational strengths and weakness of my kids, just like I used to with my clients.

During my interview with the district recruiter, I was told to stop dreaming. "This is a public school, not a business." I wondered if the recruiter understood that the public school system is one of the largest employers in the county, the largest provider of food, transportation, health services and social services, in addition to teaching and learning. Public schools have the third largest business budget in the country.

Anyway, the recruiter said he couldn't even imagine that type of information being provided to teachers. Real time reporting on history of each child. It now takes him weeks to get reports and then they are usually not valid.

Why did I have access to the Internet? When I discussed using it to teach, I was told, I needed it to do research and provide the students with real time learning based upon the most current information. Of course, I did not have an attachment to project my computer screen; basic Business 101 seemed to be missing in my classroom. Back in the 1960s, when I was in high school, my algebra teacher proudly used a projection device to demonstrate large group instruction, but that tool was missing. I had an isolated computer, hooked up to the web, and a network that I could use for small groups of kids, but not the option to use it for the entire classroom of 30 kids.

Oh, well, I will make the best of it. I want excellence, but it's the lowest common denominator theory that is pervasive in the schools. It is the pervasive attitude of negligence: "What makes you think you should have the best? We never have the best in this profession. Get used to it."

So, why am I here?

I was here to teach, and help my kids learn. My motto, "You are here to learn and nothing will interfere with my teaching and nothing will interfere with your learning. FOCUS, FOCUS, FOCUS! That worked in the business world." Will it work in the classroom?

What can we do to help my friend and all of her colleagues achieve their mission of teaching and learning? Can it be so simple as to provide better, student-focused information? Information about their students, information about their educational histories, and information that demonstrates the uniqueness of students, what they know, and what they need to learn?

We provide this type of decision-making information every day in business settings in order to empower every employee to make better-informed decisions. It is a single view of information to support all aspects of student learning provided in real time to teachers when they ask for it. It's already a reality in business. We can make the same reality happen in schools.

Jane Lockett

Introduction

THROUGH THE LOOKING GLASS

Can anyone still remember what he or she was doing on Monday, September 10, 2001? What priorities were so important that these shaped his or her thinking and actions?

Just a few weeks earlier, Washington debated what to do with all of our projected and ongoing prosperity. Tax refund checks were in the mail. States were basking in the glow of fiscal surplus. Proponents of improving the quality and performance management of business and education enterprises were being rebuffed by the "business as usual" mind-set.

September 11 turned upside down the tidy and prosperous world Americans had come to know and had expected to continue. In a few dramatic moments, the shock of a new reality hit us right here at home. We saw with our own eyes that we were no longer insulated from global terrorism. And with this act all of our deeply entrenched priorities changed in a flash. Only now are we gradually, but deliberately, taking stock of what this all means.

Economists tell us that the fiscal impact of this terrorist act on the City of New York is somewhere between horrible and horrendous. President George W. Bush prepares us for a long and protracted campaign against global terrorism unlike any battle experienced in world history. Defense Secretary Donald Rumsfeld reminds us that the Cold War lasted fifty years; that's half a century. And Henry Kissinger tells us in unstatesman-like language that "the terrorists will learn they picked on the wrong guys this time."

The U.S. Treasury has already readied a modern version of war bonds, not seen since World War II, to help finance this expected long-term battle. The City of New York issued its first $1 billion in reconstruction bonds, which was oversubscribed. And the battle is expected to take more money, lots more money. Throughout the country, state and local governments, school districts, and all sizes of business enterprise are frantically rerunning their budget numbers desperately trying to determine how to meet their respective public obligations or stay in business profitably.

If American business and education is serious about thriving in this new environment, it needs to first recognize that this is one of those conflicts that have already begun to realign the world. Like the fifty-year Cold War, this one, while it lasts, will exert a gravitational pull on everything. It will determine who our friends are, revise our priorities, and test the elasticity of our ideals. It will influence which departments are suddenly overenrolled in colleges and who the bad guys are in our movies. It is already siphoning away charity from a hundred important but suddenly less important causes. It is turning grade school fire drills into the modern equivalent of World War II and Nuclear Age duck-and-cover exercises. It is already providing a new, opportunistic national-interest spin for lobbyists peddling everything from corporate tax cuts to medical research to farm subsidies. In the face of a new reality, it has belatedly started to reshape our lumbering military and our neglected intelligence services. In a flash, it took the missile-defense shield off of the agenda and replaced it with the need for agility, shrewdness, and daring.

The new campaign will determine which foreign leaders and which issues occupy the president's attention. For instance, a few weeks earlier President Vicente Fox campaigned for a more porous border between the United States and Mexico. Not much chance of that now. But look again. Vladimir Putin is now a soul mate in the battle against terrorism. The common fear of terrorism is beginning to drive us together, much as the fear of nuclear annihilation did. This common interest even finally got the United States to pay its long past due UN assessments.

QUALITY: AN IDEA WHOSE TIME HAS FINALLY COME

It is sometimes said that critical issues are hijacked for purposes other than originally intended. Let's see. Can the fear of terrorism really spur a resurgence of interest in the attention to quality? Consider these few examples:

- Airline passengers demand a higher degree of assurance that the plane they plan to travel in is safe. Every step in the process of airline travel will now be under constant scrutiny to help ensure the quality of air travel. Security has replaced the meal-served-aloft as the measure of quality.
- Health officials are alert for any signs of chemical or biological infestation. Local officials are taking unprecedented steps to safeguard our sources of drinking water. Designer water and safe water must meet the same rigorous standards. Only safe drinking water is quality drinking water.
- Tunnels, bridges, pipelines, and rail and bus lines are stepping up safety precautions in all stages of the process. What we took for granted yesterday is now essential to our American way of life. Every stage of the process becomes a point of quality control. It is the weakest link that must be safeguarded, and not summarily dismissed, as does the current television show that has popularized this act.

The brave New York City firefighters who gave their lives in an attempt to save others on September 11 were heroic. But we are fast learning that quality is like fire prevention, and fire protection is fast becoming as critical to our individual and collective safety as fire fighting. Preventing terrorist strikes has put America on the alert. Israel has lived with this since 1948. Great Britain has slept with one eye open for more than twenty years.

Today, and for the foreseeable future, the police, the military, and just ordinary citizens are being urged "to pay increasing attention to your surroundings." Every step in our daily process of living is being reexamined in the same way the process of quality control is practiced. Every American now feels a heightened responsibility for his own safety, his family, his neighborhood, and his workplace. Every American increasingly feels every other American is now "her customer" and someone she needs to help protect.

Economists use two measures to summarize performance management—efficiency and effectiveness.

"Efficiency" is the ratio of how much is accomplished as a proportion of the amount of effort that goes into achieving the accomplishment. It is the ratio of the useful output of the system to the total input in the system. It is how much bang we get for our buck. It is the *quality* or property of being efficient.

"Effectiveness" defines the intended or expected effect. It means producing or having the capability of producing a desired effect. It measures the extent to which the bang accomplished its intended purpose. It is the *quality* and power of being effective.

In light of the world that began on September 11, business and school leaders now must make hard choices. Leaders must increasingly look for ways to improve both their operating efficiency and organizational effectiveness or risk further erosion in performance and deteriorating results. In an America confronted with an array of emerging new priorities coupled with increasingly strained financial resources, there is no longer any middle ground.

FRAMING THE ISSUES

We're no longer grasping for something that will break the grinding cycle of substandard school performance. Nor is this about buzzwords like "standards" or "assessments" or scapegoating the schools. It's simply about writing down what our kids need to know and ensuring that they learn it in order to become successful wage earners, enlightened citizens, and informed parents.

Standards and assessments make a good start. But they're not all we need. We need two overarching commitments: (1) the agreement on an urgent need for a vastly improved teaching profession, and (2) curricula that can actually move our kids to levels of achievement that are commonplace in the rest of the developed world.

Regrettably, America's best students are just average by international standards. The grim reality is that even as our overall achievement inches up, our sons and daughters remain handicapped by an education system that expects too little and routinely rewards substandard performance against even those minimal requirements.

As a powerful example, each year when nearly three million high school seniors are ready to enter the workforce—where demands only get steeper—it's no longer any surprise that far too many of them simply cannot cut it—they cannot compete!

"Fortunately, the remedy for all of this isn't the least bit vague," says Lou Gerstner, the retired chairman of IBM. "We already know what the steps need to be. First, we need to improve our ability to test and assess student performance. Next, we need to strengthen accountability inside and outside the schools. Finally, we've got to develop, sustain and support a world-class teaching force. For those who think that short list sounds pretty ordinary—good tests, more accountability, higher-quality teachers—we agree. It's not rocket science. No. It's far, far harder!"

We really don't have much choice. Either we do something about this outrage or we're the ones standing between all of our children and a fair and equal opportunity to compete in the global economy of the twenty-first century. The answer for the public schools is not about building charter schools or diverting state or federal monies to send more kids to private school. Yet a growing chorus in the nation argues for abandoning the public schools and setting up private-sector alternatives.

Life, we have come to learn, is many things. But it's never easy. Neither is education reform. Our public schools can work. They have to! But there are no shortcuts. We have to be strong and focused. We have to try. We have to fix our schools. We also have to be smart about picking our spots and concentrating on a short list of items that will leverage high-impact change. It's about TAT: testing, accountability, and teachers.

Testing

The issue of genuine testing tied to genuine consequences was a flash point. Opponents screamed testing is "unfair, demoralizing, and discriminatory." True, bad tests, poorly administrated, are all of those things. But now we've rung the emotion out of this debate, for the most part, and finally gotten down to the business of making sure that tests do what they're supposed to do—give fair tests; that is, objective measures of progress against standards so improvement can be targeted where needed. This isn't that hard to understand.

- Schools and parents need to know what the kids are learning
- Schools and parents need to know, without mystery, what's on the tests

- We need confidence that following the curriculum ensures kids score well

Seen clearly by fair-minded people, these factors support high-stakes testing.

Accountability

It isn't about the kids. It's about the system: teachers, principals, administrators, and school board members. It's about parents, business leaders, governmental leaders, and the media. It's also about balance and fairness, and being tough—but doing it right.

Teaching

Once and for all it's time to stop whining about making teaching both a real profession and more attractive, and simply do it. We can hang our heads. We can moan about teachers' pay. We can say it's too low and call it unfair, or we can commit to fixing the problem with competitive salaries, with pay tied to performance, and with pay for expertise. Teaching is a profession and it needs to be treated like one. It means fixing the compensation issues and holding teachers accountable for results. It also means providing teachers access to the kinds of tools that are taken for granted in other professions; access to high-quality teaching materials, information tools, and professional development.

We all know there are factions in education that have vested interests in preserving the status quo. They seek to advance their own agendas behind a mask like discrimination. They hide behind the ghost of testing. And they say they speak for the kids. But listen closely! What we hear is a pathetic willingness to sacrifice an entire generation—and deny them their shot at a better chance, a better future, and a better life.

The forces that would perpetuate a legacy of mediocrity in schools are deeply entrenched. And they are not likely to back down easily. But if they are allowed to prevail, there's no doubt we'll see a further exodus out of the public school system and American public education will be reduced to what British sociologist Richard Titmuss has labeled "a poor service for poor people."

In the following pages, we document what we believe and why, and what we're prepared to do to achieve our goals. It's in our hands. There's nobody else. Let's get to work.

SOLUTIONS FOR OUR TIME

What, another book about solutions to the problems of public education? The bleak results of school performance hardly leave one optimistic about solutions.

In the television movie *The Paper Chase*, the professor warns his first-year Harvard Law School students to take a good look at the person seated on either side of them. "In three years," he growls, "only one of you will graduate." His revelation about a 66 percent dropout rate is mistakenly given to motivate, but probably only terrifies beginning students at a prestigious graduate school.

If the case can be made for such a severe selection rate at that education level, it certainly cannot be made at the start of school. Recently, we visited what was defined as one of the "better" Florida inner-city schools, where most of the students live at the official family poverty level. It can serve as the poster school for the chronic condition that ails America's public schools. Only 10 percent of these kids get their high school diploma; a 90 percent dropout rate!

The wearing away process starts very early—in kindergarten. There are no terse announcements from the kindergarten teacher to a typical classroom of thirty children on their first day of school. The teacher won't say, "Look around boys and girls. In twelve years only three of you will graduate." But the fact is that that would be an accurate forecast (see chapter 1). This math defies understanding. How can any of what we see happening in so many schools be actually happening?

Today, finding qualified workers is a major concern of business. Too many students are graduating with less-than-adequate basic skills in reading, writing, mathematics, and science. This makes their prospects for success in today's workplace—let alone tomorrow's—very bad.

A 1999 American Management Association survey found that more than 38 percent of new prospective employees tested were found to be "deficient" in these basic skill areas. Small business fared even worse; it found deficiency rates "well above average."

Public uneasiness is growing and public school systems, including those serving more affluent communities, are struggling to implement and sustain measurable change. So far, the result has been one failed education experiment after another.

WHY THIS DISMAL PICTURE?

Reasoning often starts with schools blaming the parents who are singled out as bearing the primary responsibility for the mess. According to recent studies, nearly one in three parents is seriously disconnected from his or her child's life. Nearly one-third of students report their parents have no idea of how they are doing in school, and about one-sixth of their parents don't care whether they earn good grades in school.

Too many of today's parents, critics tell us, want the public schools to take custody of their offspring, send home an unalarming report card, and otherwise not bother them. How can we properly blame schools, critics say, when parents fill schools with the unteachable?

Researchers also tell us that one of the major frauds in public education is the assumption that persons who become "certified" can teach better than those who haven't been exposed to training in our colleges of education. But numerous studies show little correlation between education courses taken and teaching success. Following two years of intense study and discussion, the National Commission on Teaching and America's Future put the assessment of the quality of teaching in public schools in a disturbing context, stating that: "It is now clear that most schools and teachers cannot produce the kind of learning the new reforms demand— not because they don't want to, but because they do not know how, and the systems they work in do not support them in doing so."[1]

Boards of education are simply historic ways for governing local schools. In most communities, board members are elected by a handful of voters (only about 12 percent of citizens on average throughout the United States) and few know what they are to do to improve student learning or how to do it. They live in the "twilight zone" by expecting teachers to be change agents, say critics. On average, boards allocate a paltry 1 percent of the total school budget for professional staff development. Too often, constituents view the school board as being there to *prevent* things from happening (e.g., don't raise the school budget or float a bond issue to build more classrooms). So there can be little surprise that there is a growing shift to state takeovers of urban public schools in Philadelphia, Chicago, Boston, Detroit, and Cleveland.

School superintendents are certified to be leaders by their state department of education. But many are not prepared to lead and learn little about performance-based management in their college of education training. Those that might lead effectively are caught in the cross fire of growing crises with their school board who holds them hostage to the status quo, the constraints of a teacher's union contract, the lack of parental support, the enormous pressures to produce test-score improvement, underfunded school budgets, and little or no job security. This has already led to a shocking rate of superintendent job turnover, a shortage of properly prepared job applicants, and the growing feeling among educator-superintendents that they are "an endangered species."

Teacher unions hold veto power over educational decisions through union contracts, tenure provisions, and statute-driven protections. Combined, these continue to be a major obstacle in improving the quality of public schools. Despite skillful advertising that teachers are in the forefront of advancing the needs of students, the basic mission of teachers remains to advance their own interests, to ensure annual pay raises, retirement benefits, and tenure benefits all with smaller classes and less accountability for results.

Add to all this state and federal mandates requiring school compliance, the latest being standards-based reform, that is, curriculum reform based on setting universal standards. To be sure, it is based on sound business-like principles. First, you decide what students should learn and then you hold teachers and administrators accountable for the results.

States have been writing tougher learning standards. Now, to make sure the schools and students are working to the standards, states are writing new tests and requiring students to pass them in order to move on to the next grade or to be awarded a diploma. Thus far, trials in some states have produced high failure rates, even in more affluent communities. This has led to the all-too-common perception that schools need to become test-preparation factories. Public outcry against state standardized testing is growing and is led by the threat of a teacher-generated public backlash.

One result of high-stakes testing has been the spread of cheating scandals. New York City is a prime example, where school investigators found dozens of teachers and two principals had given students the answers on the mandated reading and math tests.[2] Those are the high-stakes tests that help determine how schools are publicly ranked and whether students move on to the next grade level.

The cheating, studied over a five-year period, involved more students and more educators than any recent cheating case in America's public school history. In the most egregious case, the principal not only told third graders to fix wrong answers, but also gave them practice tests beforehand with questions from the actual exams.

The investigators said that the cheating occurred because "[t]heir purpose [test results] was simply to improve their reputations and further their own careers by creating the illusion that they were doing a good job." We doubt that is a good explanation. The reason for resisting change is more basic than that. Teachers and administrators, like most people, are passionate about feeling that they have some measure of control over the things that happen in their lives.

We choose to follow leaders who work for our point of view, whether that involves our unions or a political candidate. We take individual action when we want to influence events directly. According to psychologists, the feeling that we have some measure of control—personal control—is sustained in five ways: behavioral control, cognitive control, decisional control, informational control, and retrospective control.

1. "Behavioral control" is the capacity of a person to take tangible action
2. "Cognitive control" is the capability to use thought processes or strategies to modify circumstances
3. "Decisional control" is the creation of an opportunity to choose between alternatives for action
4. "Informational control" involves taking the time to collect thorough knowledge about the situation
5. "Retrospective control" pertains to beliefs the person has about what or who caused the stressful event after it has happened

When people lack personal control they feel helpless. This is the condition Martin Seligman observes and terms "learned helplessness."[3] Putting it succinctly, the National Commission on Teaching and America's Future concluded: "It is now clear that most schools and teachers cannot produce the kind of learning the new reforms demand—not because they don't want to, but because they do not know how and, the systems they work in do not support them in doing so."[4]

When it comes to meeting standards through publicly reported test results *for all students* (accountability), teachers and administrators feel they lack personal control over student success and failure. They lack the proper training and the schools they work in lack performance-management systems to support them.

Perhaps the bleakest part of this dismal picture is that we know what it takes to make substantive improvements but resist using them. What is known has been widely published in education journals and books but remains virtually ignored. Contrary to the arguments of the naysayers, most of what is known is not "rocket science." Common sense is often all that is required.

Consider the following few excerpts of the major findings of the December 2000 report from the National Center for Education Statistics:

- Teachers—"Substantial research suggests that school quality is enhanced when teachers have high academic skills, teach in the field in which they are trained, have more than a few years of experience, and participate in high-quality induction and professional development programs. Students learn more from teachers with strong academic skills and classroom teaching experience than they do from teachers with weak academic skills and less experience. Teachers are less effective in terms of student outcomes when they teach courses they were not trained to teach."[5]
- Classrooms—"To understand the effectiveness of classrooms, research suggests that it is necessary to understand the content of the curriculum, the pedagogy, materials, and equipment used."[6]
- School context—"How schools approach educational leadership and school goals, develop a professional community and establish a climate that minimizes discipline problems and encourages academic excellence clearly affects school quality and student learning."[7]

So, welcome to America's public school system as it affects a great many students' future prospects in a global, cognitive, high-achiever economy. Its problems are so profound and its organization so outdated that school management would be a challenge (with only a limited chance of success) to the most experienced business executives or political leaders.

Consider this sample from a factual litany:

- One-third of school facilities serving fourteen million students need repairs or replacement
- Antiquated teacher work rules lead to poor morale and to the inability to make changes
- Elected amateurs govern fourteen thousand local school districts, with directives from state departments of education, state rules and regulations, and federal guidelines
- Labor costs rising faster than revenues push up the costs of serving customers

An extensive assignment by the Florida Department of Education to study quality in benchmark school systems, followed by further research we did in our roles with the Florida Institute of Education, found three keys to achieving genuine solutions:

1. Using focused talk as a tool to foster solutions
2. Using data and fact-based information as tools for thinking through to solutions
3. Applying fact-based initiatives to foster quality and performance management

TALK—A SOLUTIONS TOOL

Talk is a solutions tool. Like data analysis and conclusions, talking is a tool for people exchanging observations, findings, and facts about problems with one other. It is dialogue. It can be thoughtful conversation. It is conducted in a helpful and agreeable manner. It is knowingly dominated by "problem resolution" rather than "trouble talk."

Such conversation flows from facts relayed in a tone of mutual respect. Its focus is more often on the future rather than on the past; on resources (knowledge, alternatives, practices, strategies, and leadership) rather than on feelings and failure; on sharing credit rather than fixing blame; on finding answers rather than inventing new problems.

A solution dialogue is not just a technique for fixing problems. It is a way to communicate with colleagues and others that is more likely to unearth new solutions and boost collaboration. It has been our observation that without a conscious effort at using talk as a solution tool, 99 percent of what any advisor runs into in trying to help improve education is problem talk.

Using the right talk tools and strategies for a genuine *solution dialogue* helps bring education to life. Even in situations where there seems little or no reason to hope, or where the burdens of past disappointments weigh heavy or the future looks bleak, there are always resources that have been overlooked. Problems in education often take on a life of their own by the fact that people think and talk about them obsessively until they become a kind of "fate" rather than an obstacle to be overcome.

Through using talk as a tool, the superintendent and the school board of Lancaster, Pennsylvania, helped transform their school system. Lancaster schools went from a socially disconnected institution into a family-centered, community-based organization. Lancaster demystified education practices and empowered its teachers and administrators. It did so by committing to a proven model and applying its sets of practice—what were called a "winning prescription" in *Healing Public Schools: The Winning Prescription to Cure Their Chronic Illness*.[8] These procedures respond to basic human values as well as to social needs and managerial matters.

As a solution tool, talk dramatically shifts the relationship between school and home, between school administrator and teacher, and between teacher and student. Such shifts have important consequences in the way students and educators interact with one another. Together, they team to become mature agents of change rather than acting as passive individual sufferers of their fate.

Not surprisingly, problems (e.g., conflicts, symptoms, or difficulties) are often made worse by the way participants talk about them. When problems are typically described, they become fixated in the mind; they are tightly held on to and sustained through opinions that shut out alternatives and block ways out. Finding a solution to a problem often comes about not from within the way the problem is usually framed, but through opening a back door to new ways of talking about it. This quickly leads to examining fresh solutions. By externalizing the problem, educational challenges are treated as independent of the participants and their relationships to it. Problems need to be looked at as independent rather than interconnected. They need to be viewed in a way where one problem can help lead to the solution of another.

A CASE STUDY: THE FLORIDA GOVERNOR'S COMMISSION

We engaged members of the Governor's Select Education Committee[9] in several solution conversations about the challenges in public education in Florida in 1990. We had been asked by Charles Reed, then chancellor of the state university system, to serve as a resource to the committee. The final report released in 1991 was a positive, solution-oriented document that former governor Lawton Chiles used as a set of guidelines. Its central findings:

The basic problem of public education Florida faces is that it is using the methods of the mid-twentieth century to attack the challenges of the end of that century. The schools are still organized the way they were in the 1940s. The teachers are still teaching what they taught and the way they taught at that time.

In the Information Age, the key source of wealth is human capital, men and women who can read critically, think analytically, and communicate effectively. Employers now need skills in logic, and in the mathematics formerly given only to selected "college-prep" students. Human capital development is not limited to any favored group. Simple justice demands that each student fulfill his or her potential regardless of race, ethnicity or any other assumed condition.

The most important tools we have are our schools. Our schools are still preparing students for the Industrial Age. Schools can deal with three absolute requirements:

The demand is for more skills, new skills, and more broadly shared skills. Any state that still competes based on low wages is competing primarily with the Third World. It is basing its economic welfare on its resident's ability to do repetitive work as cheaply as workers in China, Mexico, and Malaysia to list only a few. In other words, it is competing based on its ability to get poor. In today's economy, a state must compete by getting smart.

Its policy-related solutions:

Move decisions to the local level and recognize citizen needs on a continuum from birth through adulthood. Require a substantial percentage of state funds allocated for a child's education to be directly under the control of parents, teachers, and administrators at the school the child is attending. Create councils so that the "Balkanized fiefdoms" can deal with education in a comprehensive, coordinated manner. Give citizens information about the full costs and benefits of all proposed developments so they can decide for themselves whether to support them. Establish outcome measures for all programs and issue reports on their performance to the people. Use government (departments and boards) more as a catalyst and broker to engage the energies of business, non-profit organizations, and communities, than as a service provider. Put power directly into the hands of individuals whenever possible. Create a marketplace in which the people enjoy more choice, more competition, and more control as customers of public services.

A HISTORICAL PERSPECTIVE

Wealth is measured differently in different periods of history. In the sixteenth, seventeenth, and eighteenth centuries, capital was measured by the amount of *land* one owned. In the nineteenth and twentieth centuries, ownership of *physical capital*—that is, factories, equipment, and energy power—was the principal measure of wealth. The earlier period is known as the Agricultural Age, the latter the Industrial Age. In the twenty-first century, we live, learn, and work in the Knowledge and Information Age, where wealth is measured by the most advantageous use of human skill and brain power: human capital.

Understanding the importance of physical capital and human capital in each of these historic periods is significant. In an agricultural economy, land is the physical capital, and physical strength and endurance is the prime labor asset. In the industrial economy, corporations require a steady supply of relatively low-skill labor to operate their machines, factories, and the energy to run them. In a knowledge and information economy, a high-performance corporation succeeds to the extent that its workforce comprises people who can think, use information, make decisions, and take responsibility for their success and their company's success. This is the pragmatic side of human capital. Chapter 1 concentrates on the crucial role public support and a continuous flow of money play in American public education.

PUTTING THE FOCUS ON SCHOOLS

Schools are the focus of attention because there is increasing evidence that educators finally have at their disposal better tools and knowledge to do something constructive about school performance. Chapters 2 and 3 focus attention on student-centered schools and introduce the concept of using tools for improved student outcomes. Each tool is treated in turn in chapter 4, performance management; chapter 5, customer relationship management; and chapter 6, business-intelligence management.

But there are two real questions:

1. Even if given the right tools and performance-management processes that work, do educators have the passion and the will to work for continuous school improvement?
2. Are public officials and school employees willing to continue wringing their hands and putting up with high dropout rates, lower graduation rates, and depressing results from high-stakes testing?

Schools bear the focus of concern because, after the family, schools are the most important factor and potential influence in the lives of children and their future role in society and preparation for the new workplace. For this reason alone it is perfectly reasonable to place a heavier burden on the schools.

Denver's North High School, an inner-city school with the city's highest dropout rate, drives this point home with a new weapon to get kids to "think" before quitting—a "Certificate of Dropping Out." Each student must sign a disclaimer acknowledging that "I realize that I will not have the necessary skills to survive in the 21st century." Principal Joe Sandoval presented the disclaimer to the first two students who both changed their minds. "It's like a brick went down their throat" when they realized the consequences of their decisions, said the principal. North High students who want to drop out must also bring their parents to a conference.

This is powerful stuff. But the question remains: Can our schools guarantee that those students who do stay in school will have the necessary skills to survive and prosper in the twenty-first century? This remains an open question based on empirical evidence of post–high school literacy and numeracy.

CAN SCHOOLS CHANGE?

Overcoming fear of change comes through the lens of corrective action. In chapter 7, the college of engineering is linked together with the college of education, for the first time, in a twenty-first-century approach to improving teacher preparation. Today, it is understandable that administrators and teachers find themselves tightly woven into an Industrial Age mind-set. Over these past many years, schools have built a closed system that continues to insulate its members from outside pressures. Notwithstanding, it is important to keep in mind that it is at the outer boundaries where the school system "bumps up" against the pressures of the outside world of change and chaos.

A twenty-first-century information-rich global economy exerts new pressures using a totally new set of demand drivers, each powered by customer satisfaction. It is a force field that causes (or had better cause) reexamination of school management practices, processes, products, services, workforce skills, and measurable performance.

From experience, we see that an administrator or teacher can be afraid of only two things. The first, if a new idea *does not* work the educator does not want to be tagged with the blame for its failure or charged with fixing it. The second, if a new idea *does* work the educator is fearful that he or she may be left standing at the gate for not having taken part in the successful effort to promulgate the needed changes. This second reason is the motivator to attract administrators and teachers to accept performance-management processes from the outset. Student-centered efficiencies and classroom effectiveness need to be extracted from traditional efforts to change.

WHAT'S COMING?

Healthcare is a good example of what's in store for schools. Starting in 1992 and, in less than three years, the entire healthcare field witnessed hospitals and doctors' offices transformed—forced by *the paying customer*; the patient, backed by large employers and their insurance carriers, demanded lower per-unit healthcare costs, greater accountability, and measurable patient satisfaction. Today, more than half of all U.S. doctors work in an HMO–type or Medicare dependent practice.

Similarly, an impending storm, collapse, and restructure are heading toward education. From the colleges of education and universities to the secondary and elementary schools, educators around the globe are engaged in some form of change—seeking ways to deliver cost-effective user-satisfactory results (see chapter 8).

Our intention is not to change the goals of schools, but rather just to change some of the ineffective *process methods* to reach the goals (chapter 9 addresses benchmarking for world-class schools). For those educators and stakeholders who already recognize actions needed to facilitate change, we help them to focus on methods most likely to yield effective results.

In chapter 10, we conclude with the admonition that America's future as a democracy depends on a well-schooled and functionally literate citizenry. We cannot sustain many repeats of a national election as experienced in 2000 when tens of thousands of ballots were thrown out due to voter error.

Each appendix offers a model of working tools presently in use to help foster the solutions presented in this book. Appendix A, "Benchmarking the Comer School Improvement Process," is the outcome of a model developed through collaborative efforts of James Comer, with his Yale Child Study Center Staff and the New Haven Public School System. Appendix B is a copy of the State of Hawaii Act 272 entitled Student-Centered Schools. Appendix C is the Minneapolis Public Schools' School-Based Management and School Improvement Plans. Appendix D is our School Benchmark Principles. Appendix E is the New Jersey statute allowing a school district that meets the Malcolm Baldrige National Quality Program Criteria for Education to be accepted as equivalent to having met the state's standards. Appendix F is the State of Washington Quality Initiative Executive Order. Appendix G is an example of the State of Washington Balanced Scorecard application for fiscal year 2001. Appendix H is a copy of an eighth-grade final exam from 1895.

NOTES

1. "What Matter Most: Teaching for America's Future," National Commission on Teaching and America's Future Summary Report (September 1996), 5–6.

2. *New York Times*, 8 December 1999.

3. Martin Seligman, *Helplessness: On Depression, Development and Death* (San Francisco: Freeman, 1975).

4. "What Matter Most," 5–6.

5. National Center for Education Statistics, *Monitoring School Quality: An Indicators Report*, by Daniel P. Mayer, John E. Mullens, Mary T. Moore, and John Ralph (U.S. Department of Education, Office of Educational Research and Improvement. NCES 2001-030, December 2000), i-ii.

6. National Center for Education Statistics, *Monitoring School Quality*, ii.

7. National Center for Education Statistics, *Monitoring School Quality*, ii.

8. Allen Salowe and Leon Lessinger, *Healing Public Schools: The Winning Prescription to Cure Their Chronic Illness* (Lanham, Md: Scarecrow, 2001).

9. "Report of the Governor's Commission."

CHAPTER 1

Follow the Money Trail

Schools run on money. Property owners pay school taxes. States collect tax revenues. Some earmark lottery money to help pay for K–12 schools. The federal government targets dollars to specific programs aimed at realizing some larger social purpose. And all of this money, tens of millions of dollars each year, is distributed to the local school district based on a per-pupil calculation.

Even with such an impressive hierarchy of money handling, few know the real cost of educating an American student. Worse yet, schools lack an industry measure of quality to measure the true cost of education. They neither have nor use the tools currently available to manage the processes of school management.

While 99 percent of adult Americans can read in the sense that they can decode words, nearly half of adult Americans are *functionally* illiterate; they are unable to read well enough to manage daily living effectively and perform work tasks calling for reading skills beyond the basic level. Schools are charged with preparing young people to function as citizens and employees in a world in which people are bombarded twenty-four hours a day with raw data and unprocessed information. Today, the ability to synthesize facts and to give proper meaning to those facts is as much a necessary tool for citizenship as it is to hold a good job in the modern workplace.

Superintendent Hugh Balboni of the St. Johns County School District in Florida has taken the "bull by the horns" to find solutions to this chronic problem. He offers a money-back guarantee to any employer in his area if a graduate from one of his high schools lacks the requisite skills to perform his or her first job. Balboni has promised to take the student back and retrain him or her at district expense. It takes serious money to correct such shortcomings and Balboni knows that the "customer" defines quality. We are reminded of the marketing truism: Alpo dog food is not good if the dogs won't eat it.

Balboni's action is a good example of market discipline in education. In many ways, the most promising element of market discipline for schools is cost control. The true power of markets is to bring down the costs of production and the delivery of goods and services by encouraging and rewarding efficiency. Costs, rather than expenditures, are the "holy grail"—unit costs. Later, we will show how the discipline of market forces, in only three years' time, overturned some of the inefficient workings of the healthcare profession.

The annual cost of producing a proficient fourth grader in Connecticut schools ranges from $8,317 in Simsbury to $67,684 in Hartford, according to the *1998 Connecticut Public Schools Guide* published by the Hartford-based CPEC Foundation.

Troubling? That's right. It costs $67,684 to achieve *one classroom capable* Hartford fourth grader. That's more than twice the cost of sending a graduate student to Harvard, Princeton, or Massachusetts Institute of Technology. We're not picking on Hartford because its cost experience is closer to the rule rather than being an exception in today's urban school chronic poor-performance mess.

As it stands today, schools have no metric—no way of properly measuring results—that will also allow anyone to say with confidence we are spending too much, too little, or just the right amount. In a market discipline setting, schools are strongly encouraged to optimize—to do what they are good at, to learn to do better, and to set goals that are both high and realistic. To do so is the only practical way to have the schools and their staffs reap the rewards of a clearer sense of accountability.

Using performance-management tools to steer the *essential processes* of schools—that is, teaching, transportation, food service, maintenance, and so on—will help bring the entire school and classroom teaching to a higher level of efficiency and effectiveness. After all, schools may not be a business, but there should be little disagreement that schools need to be run on a business-like basis.

Measuring school performance in terms of calculating the unit cost—cost-per-prepared-student (i.e., a student meeting agreed on performance standards at a given time in the school system progress calendar)—is destined to gain rapid popularity. First, taxpayers can no longer be continually expected to shell out more money for poorer results. Already, educators are being forced to stand accountable for the costs and benefits to both students and the community. Second, the American public will not continue to accept the wasted unit cost of school dropout rates running 20 percent or more each year and one-third or more high school graduates that are ill-prepared to handle a first job that demands basic thinking skills.

Traditionally, only spending-per-student has been the dollar statistic used to show how much the community values its schools. But the spending-per-student dollar figure offers no information whatsoever about how much value the school delivers to each student in its charge or back to the community, the state, and the nation that pays the bills.

Spending-per-student is only an effective dollar measure of the resources having been invested in education, but it is still only an accounting measure. It really tells taxpayers and stakeholders nothing at all about the economic *efficiency* or the management and teaching *effectiveness* of the learning processes taking place inside the school. This situation reminds one of an old joke. A mother is asked, "What is your son studying in college?" "Oh," she replies with pride, "he's learning to be a chemist—he makes waste material out of money."

Is there any way to solve this chronically ill situation? Currently, few educators and even fewer school policymakers understand that the *processes* used to run all aspects of the school can be measured. The consequence of poor or no measurement is that when changes in test scores occur, for example, few educators are in a position to correctly diagnose the causes. More often than not, the result is a misdiagnosis or no diagnosis at all of cause and effect. It is increasingly common to tag the so-called quality of the students (i.e., the raw material of the process) as the reason test scores (the end-result) are either falling or remain static. This is precisely like blaming the defects in a new car solely on the parts (materials) that are assembled, rather than looking to the assembly process (as the predictor of the end-result) of the finished product.

Such a typical educator diagnosis is not a feature of car manufacturing, in that enterprise leaders do not jump to finger-pointing the workers, but rather shift the focus to examining the processes that govern the worker. In schooling, to misdiagnose is much more serious than in car making. In schools, it is harmful and defeatist and it generates the fear of accountability on the part of school leadership and teachers.

"When the organizations fail to measure what they have achieved, we lose influence over them," writes Leon Lessinger in *School Reform News*. Lessinger calls for the introduction to education of the industrial concept of cost-per-operable-unit because "[w]hen we measure organizations in terms of what they achieve for society for our investment of resources, we control them."

It is embarrassing, wasteful, and disgraceful that one in four college freshmen in 1995 required at least one remedial reading, writing, or mathematics course. Schools simply must turn to using the right tools to efficiently manage school processes and to effectively measure the outcome of these processes. Only in this way can schools sharply increase the number of prepared students—students that meet agreed on performance standards. Schools' continual failure to cure this illness can only result in more and more U.S. high schools graduating young men and women with Third World skills and relegating them to a lifetime of potentially earning only Third World wages.

Of course, this sounds harsh. But the fact is that the school systems have been permitted to go along without including the full cost of their economic causal "scrap"—that is, those students who cannot function in today's interconnected global economy society—as part of its full unit cost of educating each student. If one out of three new cars coming off the assembly line process was unable to properly function—would not start when needed, or did not meet quality and performance standards—how long would that car factory remain in business? "Scrap" in human terms is a lack of proficiency to compete for livable wages. It is wasted cost.

Working independently, the CPEC Foundation has included in its latest guide to Connecticut schools the statistic spending-per-proficient-student. Research analyst Susan W. Beckman calculates the new metric by dividing each school's spending per student by the percentage of students in that school who meet or exceeded state goals on the Connecticut Mastery Test for fourth-grade mathematics, reading, and writing.

Although spending per Connecticut fourth-grade student varies by less than a factor of two, from $5,874 in Union to $10,909 in Greenwich, spending-per-proficient-student varies by a factor of over seven, from $8,317 in Simsbury to the outrageous sum of $67,684 in Hartford. Even when comparing towns or districts with similar wealth and family education background in the same region, large differences in cost-per-proficient-student are often noted: for example, $8,767 in Union, $11,958 in Coventry, and $20,673 in Scotland. "Capable," "skilled," and "expert" are a few of the synonyms used for describing proficiency.

Forty states now require school-level report cards, but none has yet gone far enough! To warranty sure solution possibility, states must begin to calculate and publish the extensive comparative information provided by the CPEC Foundation's *1998 Connecticut Public Schools Guide*. There, municipalities are grouped into six regions to make it more efficient for educators and stakeholders to benchmark comparisons with neighboring communities. It also provides information on demographics, school enrollments, and average teacher salaries.

As newspapers and commercial publishers become increasingly aware of such wasteful unit costs as discovered in Connecticut schools and the effective solution-prone power of calculating and comparing school districts by the cost-per-proficient-student metric, the public can expect these sources to rapidly start to fill the information void. This focus on measurable school results will only further ratchet up the pressure on schools for greater accountability, especially in the face of the economic drain on public school finance and more school choice.

THE ILLUSION OF A MONOPOLY

K–12 public schools no longer enjoy a monopoly. But once they came close to having one. It's true that state laws do require school attendance up to a designated age. To that extent, schools may be viewed as a monopoly. Now, there is intense competition for each student's mind—television, peers, and family pressures to name only a few "competitors." After all is said and done, isn't this what the schools are competing for—the student's attention and mind? To merely have his or her body sitting in a classroom is not enough.

Currently, a warm student body, registered in school, is all that it takes for the school to secure from various sources the dollars for per-student funding. Even the truant officer, now renamed the attendance officer, pays his or her own way by helping keep kids in school, but for what rationale?

Schools, like other nonprofit organizations, need money, and lots of it, to lubricate the wheels of its array of services. It may be that school policymakers and leaders have become desensitized to the amounts of money needed, where the money comes from (and how hard it is for people to come by it), and the educational purposes for which educational funding has been put in their trust.

Here is one example to help sensitize school policymakers and leaders. According to the U.S. Department of Education, in 1999 there were at least 850,000 students learning at home, almost double the 345,000 in 1994.[1] Some educators feel the number may actually be closer to double the study results. Given such estimates as 4 percent of the entire K–12 student population means more kids are learning at home than currently enrolled in all the public schools of ten states combined—Alaska, Delaware, Hawaii, Montana, New Hampshire, North Dakota, Rhode Island, South Dakota, Vermont, and Wyoming. This home schooling number exceeds the half million kids enrolled in such highly publicized efforts as charter schools and the sixty-five thousand receiving vouchers.

This home schooling trend, which is expected to continue its 11 percent per year growth trajectory, means the school districts that are intended to serve these students will continue to "dollar-hemorrhage" badly; millions of dollars in per-pupil funding will continue to be bled away. Two examples drive home this point:

- Maricopa County, Arizona, lost $35 million in per-student funding in 1999 as seven thousand students (1.4 percent of school-age kids) switched to home schooling.
- Florida had 41,128 children (1.7 percent) learning at home in 1999; up from just 10,039 in 1991–1992, representing a loss of nearly $130 million to local school budgets.[2]

As former U.S. senator Everett Dirksen is remembered for saying, "A million here a million there; before you know it we're talking about real money." These are serious dollars. Almost three-fourths of home schooling families say they do so because they are worried about the *quality* of their children's education according to U.S. Department of

Education study findings. Allen Salowe and Leon Lessinger devote their entire book *Healing Public Schools: The Winning Prescription to Cure Their Chronic Illness* to applying quality improvement processes to chronically ill K–12 school classrooms and to head off such a financial catastrophe.[3] In Florida, a 2001 report shows well over a quarter of home schooling families do so for religious reasons. The 1999 U.S. Department of Education study found 38.4 percent do so for religious reasons; 25.6 percent because they feel school is a poor learning environment; and 48.9 percent feel they can give their child a better education at home.

No less than Bill Bennett, a former U.S. secretary of education, talks of the home schooling trend as "the revolution of common sense." Bennett is traveling the country promoting *K12*, his for-profit online home schooling Web-based service. It is as though Colin Powell, the former chairman of the Joint Chiefs of Staff, promoted the abandonment of the U.S. Army and the assembly of local militia units in its place. In California and Texas, school districts are forming strategic alliances with home schooling families by allowing their home schooled kids to sign up for science lab classes or sports.

The critical issue is simply this. These trends are as much about the serious erosion of public support as the glacial meltdown of monetary resources for schools. But this loss of public support can only lead to the further loss of financial support. In a way, school taxes and accountability for cost-per-proficient-student holds the potential explosiveness of a twenty-first-century Boston Tea Party.

Every day, and in so many ways, K–12 schools are driving concerned parents into looking for learning alternatives for their kids. Parents face the fears of school violence, the inability of teachers to maintain classroom civility, stagnant results from years of schools trying improvement programs that haven't stuck, and increasing employer demand for better-prepared workers.

This erosion of students and public support is a slippery slope. Who will put up the money to fill the gaps to sustain locally based schools given the chronic problems that go unattended? Why would parents and grandparents willingly support new bond issues to build school facilities that are unable to deliver quality schooling? Which of us is willing to allow ourselves to be taxed and pay more to support an eroding public institution?

FINDING NEW APPROACHES TO FINANCING SCHOOLS

The issue of school finance is really centered on performance management of school processes. First, money fuels the essential schooling processes. The following studies help shed new light on financing schools. But educators need to keep in the forefront of their thinking that the efficient and effective management of school processes is what delivers proficient students.

Two recently released publications look at school-funding issues from different perspectives. *Making Money Matter: Financing America's Schools* from the National Academy of Science's (NAS) Committee on Education Finance advocates a new approach called "funding adequacy." A policy briefing by Allan Odden, *Creating School Finance Policies That Facilitate New Goals*, sums up three publications by researchers at the Office of Education Research and Improvement and the Center for Policy Research in Education (CPRE). It looks at school financing from this new perspective.

NAS reminds us that since *Brown v. Board of Education* equity in funding still remains the primary focus of policymakers and lawmakers. A number of innovative ways have been devised to try equalizing the amount of funds going to children in different school districts. Few would disagree that glaring inequities exist in the dollars spent on children from affluent areas versus children from poverty areas. This issue of most concern focuses on urban schools where some of the largest and most persistent pockets of poverty exist.

Brown v. Board of Education spawned the nationwide effort to erase the separate but equal doctrine. And at last count, some 440,000 school buses take 24 million children to and from school every day, traveling more than 4 billion miles each year. Those rides cost nearly $10 billion every year reports the National School Transportation Association, a trade organization for school bus contractors. Of course, not all bus transportation is intended to foster school integration but how much of that $10 billion has been examined as a cost-benefit trade-off to potentially improve student-centered learning?

Because of the intractability of equalizing funding, attention has finally shifted to studying how to *equalize the effective educational experience* for all children. NAS argues for the more effective use of education dollars in the emerging concept of funding adequacy. This is an outcome-oriented view of funding. It forces schools to focus on educational achievement and how much money is needed to reach a defined academic goal such as the agreed on performance standards reflected in the mandatory testing programs. It is a cost-benefit formula.

Funding adequacy is such a new idea that implementing it represents a potentially radical departure and different experience in different school locations because of many unknowns. First, there is presently no standard definition of "adequate education" for education policymakers to build a financial system around. Second, there is no clear idea what amount of funding is necessary to reach a goal once it has been defined. To top it off, other problems include how much additional funding is necessary for disadvantaged children and children with disabilities.

Researchers believe the process of reaching funding adequacy involves three things: (1) investing in the capacity of the education system, (2) promoting performance by ensuring the incentive system to recognize achievement, and (3) bringing schools and parents into the process by empowering them to help make funding decisions.

The NAS report is gaining notice because it calls for more research into charter schools and voucher systems, rather than interdistrict and intradistrict choice programs, to improve poor-performing schools. Because existing voucher efforts are small scale and cannot provide adequate data on the results of the program, it calls for a "large and ambitious" research program that includes the participation of private schools. To aid in these and other reform efforts, better and more focused education research is identified as being needed and three areas of needed research are listed: (1) capacity building, including developing and retaining well-prepared teachers, (2) incentives designed to motivate higher teacher performance, and (3) the voucher program. The study also calls for more integration of special education because the previous distinctions have "compromised educational effectiveness." It also refers to a "perceived" crisis in urban education. It is startling and says much about a head-in-the-sand view of school improvement when a prestigious group meets in Washington, D.C., with that urban school system right under its nose, and still refers to the urban education crisis as "perceived."

The CPRE policy brief is based on three studies: "Improving State School Finance Systems: New Realities Create Need to Re-Engineer School Finance Structures,"[4] "School Finance Systems: Aging Structures in Need of Renovation,"[5] and "School-Based Financing in North America."[6] The composite study advocates statewide policy initiatives because states provide between 30 percent and 100 percent of school funding. The new financial structure would be based on adequate funding linked to educational standards. Four elements would be involved:

1. A base spending level considered adequate for the average child to reach high standards
2. Since the base spending level is targeted to the average student, consideration must be given to those groups of students who require additional resources to achieve standards
3. An adjustment for area economic factors
4. Yearly inflation rates to be factored into annual allotments

HOW DOES THE SCHOOL DISTRICT FOLLOW THE MONEY?

Under these reforms, the role of the school district would change. First, individual schools would require more control of their funds to make necessary changes in order to meet educational standards. It was suggested schools receive their funds in a lump sum so they can reallocate funding more easily.

This leads directly to using performance-management tools and accounting practices needing to be configured to a school-site level. With well over 50 percent of all education dollars going to teachers' salaries, incentives need to be evaluated and structured to support the new achievement goals.

Next, rigorous evaluations of teachers' knowledge and teaching skills would be needed with compensation for those teachers who meet expectations. Incentives would also be linked to school performance. Both teacher expectations and school performance would need to be measurable.

Up to now, these incentive programs have been controversial because of their poor design, but incentives supported by performance management tools and effective logistics (this will be discussed later) can help focus and motivate school personnel to produce student achievement. Putting it another way, all school processes must be geared and measured to achieving student-centered results. There would also be a change in the federal role in education, as federal resources would be targeted to states, particularly in the South and West, that would have trouble providing adequate funding by themselves.

One way or the other, it all comes down to the reality that the local school district needs the tools to self-evaluate, to implement, and to measure school improvement programs *and* the tools to effectively measure the results of their efforts.

PUTTING SCHOOL RESULTS ON THE LINE

In a bid to prove itself more accountable to the public, the school district of Jefferson County, Colorado, which contains part of the Denver metropolitan area and Columbine High School, proposed a new tax levy linking higher tax revenues to improvements in student test scores.[7] Jefferson County is the largest U.S. school district to become ISO 9000–quality certified. ISO 9000 is the quality designation being pursued by school systems around the globe, but thus far only a few U.S. schools have achieved it. ISO 9000 around the globe is discussed in chapter 8.

In the fall of 1999, voters in Jefferson County were asked to approve a tax plan to raise an extra $25 million annually for the local schools. But the plan also provides for up to $20 million more in revenue, depending on school officials' success in increasing the number of students scoring at grade level.

"I think it's absolutely revolutionary," says board president Jon De Stefano. "For a long time, there's been a misconception that public schools are not accountable for what they do. We feel that we're doing something that is accountable to the public."[8]

Fiscal accountability has been an issue in Jefferson County since officials disclosed that district spending on computers drained millions of dollars from cash reserves and that $27 million in loans must be repaid. Recently, the school board agreed to set up a volunteer citizens committee to oversee school finances in the future.

Despite questions surrounding the spending snafu, there's strong community support for a new tax levy, officials say. A citizen's task force, formed to support a tax increase, collected more than eighteen thousand signatures on a petition asking the school board to put the proposal on the ballot.

This public support reflects growing recognition that Jefferson County's $455 million school budget isn't adequate, says district spokesperson Marilyn Saltzman. "If we do not get additional revenue, we'll have to make significant budget cuts," she warns, noting the district faces possible layoffs and larger class sizes.

County voters rejected a $37 million tax increase in 1998, however, and both school board members and leaders of the citizen's task force have said publicly that any new tax plan must include some kind of performance guarantee.

"This fiscal responsibility piece is important," task force member Ann Kirwin told the *Denver Post*. "People need to know the district will be good stewards of our money."

The performance guarantee proposed by the school board would link additional funds to the percentage increase in students classified as "proficient" or "advanced" under the Colorado Student Assessment Program tests. Starting with the 2001–2002 school year, the higher the percentage increase of students achieving grade level compared to the 1999–2000 tests, the higher the tax revenues awarded to the district.

As much as $20 million more can be earned annually if the school district can increase student proficiency on state tests by 25 percent. "That's a figure that'll challenge the district," Saltzman acknowledges.

In the 1998–1999 school year, for example, 71 percent of third graders scored at grade level. Using that figure, a 25 percent increase would require 88.75 percent of future third graders to score at the proficient level or higher.

De Stefano believes the school district will be better off if the public has a benchmark to watch. "Sometimes in education, it seems it doesn't matter what you do," he says. "Everyone thinks their children's schools are doing great, but ask them about the school district, and they think the rest of the schools are doing lousy. This [performance guarantee] will allow the public to draw a more realistic view of what's happening."

FROM THE DESK OF THE PRINCIPAL

We asked Rick L. Utz, a high school principal, this question by e-mail: What do you consider the most serious obstacles and the most promising opportunities for moving ISO 9000 Education Standards, Malcolm Baldrige National Quality Program Criteria for Education, or other quality processes ahead into schools on a wider scale? His response:

> The future of the Quality movement in schools will be based on the success of those of us who have already taken the first step. The benefits of a quality program are as follows:
>
> 1. Most schools do their job well, but if you ask them what they do they can't tell you. In this age of accountability, it is very important that we as educators can show in concrete terms what we say we do and to have evidence that we do what we say.
> 2. The quality program also allows us to better monitor our cash flow as to why we spend money on certain programs. Through the quality planning process we have to justify what we do. This is a new concept in education.
> 3. Educators are the best starters of projects known to the world, but we are not great at bringing them to a conclusion. The quality planning gives us more direction than we have ever had before.
> 4. Finally, we [educators] have always added new programs to the schools but have never had a method of doing away with the old programs. ISO 9000 gives us that vehicle.[9]

TOWARD ACTIONS

Utz summed up these matters in uncomplicated terms. Accountability means knowing and measuring where you're headed and demonstrating results for all to see. After all, if you don't know where you're trying to go, any place you arrive is good enough. Better cash management tools mean knowing and measuring the costs and benefits of each program. Quality standards are the tools to help bring objectivity to the *why* question. Like Congress, schools start lots of new programs but they need the tools to measure when to bring them to conclusion. Metrics help promote professional objectivity. And schools need to use the right tools to measure program results against other options (cost-benefit analysis) to decide which programs are no longer effective and need to be pruned as dead wood.

NOTES

1. U.S. Department of Education, *Home Schooling in the United States: 1999* (Washington, D.C.: U.S. Department of Education, 2000).

2. *Time*, 27 August 2001.

3. Allen Salowe and Leon Lessinger, *Healing Public Schools: The Winning Prescription to Cure Their Chronic Illness* (Lanham, Md: Scarecrow, 2001).

4. Allan Odden, "Creating School Finance Policies That Facilitate New Goals" (paper prepared for the Consortium for Policy Research in Education, University of Wisconsin–Madison, Wisconsin Center for Education Research, 1998).

5. Allan Odden and William Clune, "School Finance Systems: Aging Structures in Need of Renovation," *Educational Evaluation and Policy Analysis* 20, no. 3 (1998).

6. Allan Odden, "Case Study 3: North America. School-Based Financing in North America," in *Needs-Based Resource Allocation in Schools via Formula-Based Funding*, ed. Kenneth Ross and Rosalind Levacic (Paris: International Institute for Education Planning, UNESCO, 1998).

7. *School Board News*, 28 September 1999.

8. *School Board News*, 28 September 1999.

9. Rick L. Utz, e-mail to authors, 14 August 2001.

CHAPTER 2

Student-Centered School Management and Technology

Technology has changed everything from the way we live and do business to the way we communicate with each other. Technology also affects the way we teach and learn.

According to the National Council for Accreditation of Teacher Education (NCATE), the skills needed in today's workplace are also the catalyst to spur technology use in the classroom. By now it is clear that the world of work demands that schools prepare students who are skilled at working in teams, who can effectively solve problems, who are able to process and apply information, and who can use technology effectively in order to maximize their own productivity. This is today's global workplace.

Schools need to focus on creating learning situations that integrate technology with problem solving as a way to foster the needed skills to empower students. This educational goal separates the outmoded teacher-centered classroom and tools of the last century from the new student-centered learning environment of this century. This is the challenge to school leaders.

In the traditional teacher-centered classrooms of the nineteenth and twentieth centuries, teachers were expected to be subject matter experts. And in most cases this still exists. Teachers present the information from textbooks and when students ask questions, the teacher's job is to guide the students to think in such a way that students arrive independently at the "correct" answers. Students are expected to learn fact-based knowledge and formal assessment is often based on the information students derive from their rote skills. But in the twenty-first-century student-centered classroom, the teacher's role is to *facilitate* learning by means of coordinating learning resources and helping students to learn to ask the right questions. Teachers must guide students toward the vast information available and help them to develop their critical thinking, problem-solving, and decision-making abilities.

Student-centered teaching encourages student participation in the discovery of learning. Assessment is increasingly based on group as well as individual project portfolios. With technology in the classroom and the drastic change in the role of the teacher, the learning environments also need major reform. To this end, the National Educational Technology Standard provided by the International Society for Technology in Education (ISTE) for student-centered teaching environments recommends the following:

Traditional classroom	*Student-centered classroom*
Teacher-centered instruction	Student-centered instruction
Single-sense stimulation	Multisensory stimulation
Single path	Multipath progression
Single media	Multimedia
Isolated work	Collaborative work
Information delivered	Information exchange
Passive learning	Active/exploratory/inquiry-based learning
Factual, knowledge based	Critical thinking, informed decision making
Reactive response	Proactive/planned action

However, the ISTE model of the student-centered classroom environment could not materialize without teachers' understanding and appreciating what technology can do to enhance *their* teaching, and thus, promoting student learning. Technology used in and to support the twenty-first-century classroom, when implemented correctly, can enrich the learning environment by using it as a medium of instruction and as an information tool to enhance teaching resources for student learning.

TEACHER EDUCATION FOR K–12 STUDENT-CENTERED CLASSROOMS

According to Kent L. Norman, the proper design for education technology supports the teacher–student relationship by enabling teachers to create student-centered learning environments.[1] Computer technology offers attributes that allow a shift toward problem-based learning and a chance for students to learn in ways they learn best. Teachers can propose more ambitious challenges, tailor guidance to individual student and team needs, and give more detailed evaluation. By integrating classroom tools into the problem-solving assignment, it helps support creative, collaborative work among students and teachers. However, the way teachers choose to use technology is ultimately based on their knowledge, skill, and comfort level in technology. This raises the significance of teacher training.

PROBLEM-BASED LEARNING

If asked, most educators would agree that one essential goal of education is the development of students who are effective problem solvers for the Information Age. By now we know that most reports, such as the national Survey of Necessary and Comprehensive Skills and Goals 2000 documents, recommended such instruction. Most school goal statements pay homage to the need for critical thinking and problem-solving skills. Too often, problem-solving instruction takes the approach of using teaching models on students by having them conform to neat case studies rather than tackling the messy problems of the real world.

Research indicates that critical thinking and problem-solving skills are not typically addressed in the classroom. A number of studies indicate that in the typical classroom, 85 percent of teacher questions are at the recall or simple comprehension level. Questions that elicit synthesis and evaluative skills of thinking are rarely asked.

In problem-based learning (PBL), students act as professionals and confront problems as they occur—complete with fuzzy edges, insufficient information, and a need to determine the best solution by a given deadline. This is the manner in which engineers, doctors, attorneys, and, yes, even teachers, approach problem solving. It is unlike the many classrooms where teachers are the "sage on the stage" and steer students to neat solutions to contrived problems.

WHAT IS PROBLEM-BASED LEARNING?

PBL is a curriculum development and delivery system that recognizes the need to develop problem-solving skills as well as the necessity of helping students to acquire necessary knowledge and skills. Indeed, the first application of PBL was in medical schools, which rigorously test the knowledge base of graduates. PBL utilizes real-world problems, not hypothetical case studies with neat, convergent outcomes. It is in the *process* of struggling with actual problems that students learn both content and critical thinking skills.

PBL has several distinct characteristics that may be identified and utilized in designing such a curriculum. They are:

1. Reliance on problems to drive the curriculum—the problems do not test skills, they simply assist in development of the skills themselves
2. The problems are intentionally ill structured—there is not meant to be one solution, and as new information is gathered in a reiterative process, perception of the problem, and thus the solution, changes
3. Students solve the problems—teachers are coaches and facilitators
4. Students are only given guidelines for how to approach problems—there is no one formula for student approaches to the problem
5. Authentic, performance-based assessment—this is a seamless part and end of the instruction

PBL assists students to solve problems by the process of continually encountering the type of ill-structured problems confronted by adults or practicing professionals. As with information literacy, PBL develops students who can:

- Clearly define a problem
- Develop alternative hypotheses
- Access, evaluate, and utilize data from a variety of sources
- Alter hypotheses given new information

- Develop clearly stated solutions that fit the problem and its inherent conditions, based on information and clearly explicated reasoning

Students with such ingrained skills are well prepared for new occupations, which rarely have a supervisor who has the time, the inclination, or the knowledge to tell the worker what to do. They are also well prepared for the explosion of knowledge that gluts the world today.

PBL also fosters cultural change in three main ways:

- Students at first may feel shaky. Students trained in the more traditional model of teaching featuring the teacher as "sage on the stage" and disseminator of knowledge may experience culture shock of a sort. Students wish to know expectations for receiving a high grade. Though constructing a rubric with a teacher may allay fears, there is initial suspicion of the new approach.
- Students may feel uncertain learning to work as part of a group. As with real-life tasks, one person cannot conduct all research and make the entire presentation of the problem solution. Complaints about "hitchhikers" (those in the group who do not pull their own weight) will be heard from hardworking students and their parents.
- Teachers may also experience major adjustments. More preliminary work must be done to design the problem and to ensure that there are enough materials available (in print, online, and through human resources) for this resource-ravenous approach. They must learn to construct problems that assist students to learn appropriate skills and knowledge. They must learn to facilitate, rather than direct, student learning.

THE PAYOFFS?

Though change from a teacher-centered to a student-centered problem and project-based environment causes some early discomfort, those teachers that have made the transition speak of new energy and enthusiasm for their classes. And the students praise PBL for the challenging tasks that prepare them for learning and earning.

A number of years back, we observed just such a PBL method in use in an eleventh-grade laboratory class at the Melbourne High School

Aerospace Academy, a public school in Florida. The teacher divided her class into four-student, one-computer teams, with the computer designated as the fifth team member. Each team comprised one "advanced" student, two "average" students, and one "slower" student. This student mix reflected a composite of the class average. The teams were given "practical" problems to solve, such as building a working model rocket, a motor boat, and so on. When a team ran into a math problem it couldn't handle that was connected with the assignment, a math mentor was there to help it work through the problem. If a team ran into a project-related reading or writing difficulty, an English mentor was there to help break the logjam. Most interestingly, the facilitating teacher told us that quite often it was the "slow student" that actually came out of his or her shell and made the breakthrough recommendations.

WHERE DOES TECHNOLOGY FIT IN STUDENT-CENTERED SCHOOLS?

Many educators, parents, and students came to believe that integrating technology into education seemed to be the perfect answer to school restructuring to improve educational outcomes. They mistakenly compared a high-tech classroom environment to high-quality education. According to the Quality Educational Data's "1997 Educational Technology Trends" report, billions of dollars are spent in computer hardware and software in the nation's K–12 classrooms.[2]

While many barriers to technology use still exist, the national survey conducted by the Milken Exchange on Education Technology found the major barrier to schools effectively using technology are the teachers' lack of understanding and skill in using technology and the lack of quality and informed technology planning by educators. The report further indicated that teacher and administrator inability to employ technology effectively to promote student learning can only result in the waste of billions of dollars invested in educational technology.[3] As such, it is important to better educate school administrators about the importance of empowering teachers to provide the best education experience for every student by training teachers to use technology effectively to promote student learning.[4]

In light of the changes in the classroom due to the impact of technology, many in-service teachers feel that they have not had adequate training to help them use technology effectively. According to L. K. Bradshaw, teachers' concerns about technology vary broadly.[5] Many teachers admit they know very little about computers and are not interested in learning. While others may try to seek new uses for technology in the classroom, they do not have sufficient technical and logistical support. Many teachers see the value of technology but feel frustrated because they are not trained to use these resources in the classroom setting.[6] For the enthusiastic teachers who want to learn, staff development in technological skills as well as alternative classroom management skills and sufficient technical and administrative support are essential to the effective use of technology in the classroom.

For the retiring teachers needing to be replaced by more than two million new teachers, integrating technology into the teacher education programs is vital to the success of the envisioned twenty-first-century classroom.[7] According to the Office of Technology Assessment, the obvious place to train teachers in more effective uses of technology and to promote the student-centered learning environment is in the nation's teacher education programs (chapter 7 speaks to such opportunities by linking the colleges of engineering and education). This is the most direct and cost-effective way to bring new teachers up to par with technology use.

According to the NCATE, when resource funding is available, most funds are allocated to hardware and software, not to training. College of education faculties lack the knowledge and skill to include technology in their own teaching programs. They fail to model instructional technology use in their professional education courses because they themselves are ill equipped to do so. Students of today's teacher education programs, therefore, lack the skills to use databased information for decision making and the necessary skills to lead the twenty-first-century classroom.

Finding a willingness to change the current education system is the key if teacher preparation programs are to serve the needs of K–12 schools. Colleges and universities need to improve access to technology for faculty and students alike. More funds need to be allocated toward the much needed technology training for professors as well as to increase technical support to faculty members seeking to blend technology into their courses. In addition, faculty need the support and recognition from their department administrators and to be allowed the time and necessary resources to redesign the course curriculum in order to incorporate technology.[8]

The keys to the success of technology in the classroom, both improved teacher database decision making and the student-centered learning environment, equally depend on one major factor: the level of teacher training. Technology itself is merely a tool to support development of programs and to provide data, information, and the programs that teachers are expected to develop. Teachers must be trained and given sufficient logistical support to implement technology in their classroom. It takes the combination of learning and experiencing the concept in the student-centered learning environment.

Technology needs to be integrated into the training of in-service K–12 teachers as well as faculty in higher education. Then preservice teachers will have the necessary knowledge and skills to integrate technology and data management into the twenty-first-century classroom. Well-trained preservice teachers have the potential to be leaders in the technological revolution that is unfolding in the traditional classroom. We live in a technology-driven world and the need for instructional technology must not be ignored.

In order to accomplish the vision of implementing technology in the classrooms, colleges of education must commit sustained funding to comprehensive instructional technology and to update teacher education programs. If the goal of education is intended to truly improve student learning, this investment must be made.

LOGISTICAL SUPPORT FOR THE TEACHING AND LEARNING PROCESS

Tools, both physical and "mental," tool making and tool using, are the lifeblood of all occupations and professions. Technology is a tool to help teachers and students do their respective jobs of teaching and learning. Data, when properly managed, offers administrators and teachers powerful tools for better decision making (see chapter 6). Studying an occupation's tools and materials, their use and misuse, their availability or absence, and their supply, repair, replacement, and training for use make up the field of learning called "logistics."

Though widely taught in the college and university business and engineering curricula, education lacks an adequate field of logistics. Worse yet, education is unaware of the dimensions of such a field and its value in supporting a teacher's classroom duties. Can we really expect technology in the classroom to blossom into student-centered learning without giving teachers logistical support?

The contrast between logistical support of teaching duties and tasks and that of other occupations in carrying out their duties and tasks explains why there are such poor results in education. Construction carpentry provides a good example. A carpenter has to accomplish a range of tasks in different settings. He (or she) successfully carries out his job description (or the foreman's assignment) with the support of logistical support that is routinely available.

A good carpenter has many tools and materials available that are tailored to the job demands and he knows how to use them properly. He has hammers, saws, rulers, squares, drills, chisels, and so forth—some hand driven and some power driven—to help him do his job. Every year, there seem to be newer, more versatile and easier-to-use tools, processes, and materials developed and made available. A good carpenter uses his tools to perform their intended function. A saw cuts wood, not the hammer; the hammer drives nails, not cut boards. A poor carpenter is one who doesn't have the necessary tools, or has the necessary tools but doesn't know how to use them or for whatever reason chooses not to use them properly.

These dimensions of carpentry directly relate to classroom teaching: having the right tools and materials available when needed, knowing how to use them properly, and using them as intended.

Since the 1880s, the standing school practice is to furnish teachers with a chalkboard (or an equivalent marker) and a single textbook for each student in a particular subject. There may be a teacher's guide for the course and a curriculum guide, but often it is either unavailable or out of date. Occasionally there is a course syllabus. The teacher may have access to supplemental materials and tools like workbooks, audiovisual equipment, a computer, and/or a copier.

But most often such tools are rarely available at the moment of need, and teachers cannot anticipate the moment of need in learning. Teachers are expected to order tools, such as equipment, well in advance of need, and then they may not be available in the time amount required to serve all students adequately; there is no provision for getting these tools to the teacher in a timely manner; or the teacher cannot be sure that the tools are always in working order and repaired or replaced if not previously working. Teachers often have to buy the tools and materials they need out of their own pockets, even those prescribed in the official curriculum guide, because they are not supplied. Many of the tools and materials have not been tailored for the particular program and to the unique needs of the learners, including the ubiquitous textbook.

Technology can best be understood as providing a major part of the logistical support for the teaching and learning process. The personal computer is the quintessential example. With the computer as the teacher's "assistant," teacher support is given at the point of need: to score tests, to list learning objectives mastered, to make individualized assignments including those needed for quality control, to assign and locate resources required to accomplish an assignment, to provide target completion times and rates of progress, to select and assign alternative lesson approaches, to flag students with entry deficiencies and proficiencies, to provide reports on individual student performance and attendance, to furnish student data profiles for use in student counseling, and to provide feedback for corrective action to the teacher on his or her instructional effectiveness.

By applying such examples of educational logistics, teaching can become a partnership between teacher and student in a very practical way. The most important reform of education can come closer to reality: the focus of the classroom can shift dramatically from teaching to learning! Also, with adequate logistical support, it is possible for teachers to move nearer to providing a student-centered learning environment. Given a competent, confident, and caring teacher, with logistical support he or she can meet the needs of individual students.

Consider for a moment the amount of logistical support needed and provided to professionally run a modern hospital or medical clinic. Logistics in education is the induction, training, procurement, distribution, maintenance, and replacement of technology, equipment, apparatus, and supplies in support of teaching. If done well, it handles—and removes an awesome burden—important job details required by professional teachers in their duties and tasks to provide the tools, activities, materials, and guidance necessary to meet the needs of all the pupils in a typical school classroom.

All too often efforts at school improvement fail to take into account the value of giving the teacher the proper tools, materials, and activities to meet student learning and psychological differences at the time of need. Tools are needed in the right amounts, in working order, and without burden for teachers having the know-how to use them properly. This neglect helps explain why school reform is not possible without taking logistics into account. We expect that when schools benchmark efficient and effective organizations (see chapter 9) they will discover the most neglected aspect of classroom teaching is the lack of logistical support of the teaching and learning process.

The lack of logistical support in education goes a long way toward explaining what is wrong with the conventional process. Each teacher has little choice except to use the dominant process tools found in most classrooms: lecture, textbook, homework assignment, and student recitation. And the results of this "stuck in the rut" process are predictable:

1. Students whose reading levels are above or below that of the textbook are neglected and are therefore not served well
2. Teachers are short of time to give the array of explanations needed to meet the different needs of the students, therefore some students grasp what is taught, some do not get it, and some are bored stiff because they already know the topic
3. The generally passive nature of the learning experience makes it impossible to have each student interact and less likely that students fully understand and retain the material taught

Teachers that heavily rely on homework assignments worsen the efficiency and effectiveness of the conventional classroom teaching. There is likely to be little help with homework for those students who most need it. The teacher is likely unaware of the time needed by different students to do their homework. In the departmentalized grade levels, generally from grade 6 on, each student has several teachers, with each making assignments with consequent worsening of the problems already identified. Many students have no adequate place or opportunity to study at home and frequently lack study skills and approaches, since such skills are rarely formally taught.

DATA DRIVES SCHOOL IMPROVEMENT

"Accountability" is a nice-sounding term. It conjures up the image of strong leadership and tough management. It has a parental and authoritative ring to it. It makes a president sound profound, an educator seem on the ball, and a politician look involved. But there's more to school accountability than rhetorical pronouncements. In May 1998, the Annenberg Institute for School Reform held a colloquium on the use of data to help achieve school improvement. The conference report highlighted the following five lessons learned from schools around the nation:

1. Two factors are essential to effective accountability:
   - A belief that principals, teachers, and community stakeholders can help improve teaching and learning
   - Effective use of data to support that effort to improve

   Said the report, "Effective accountability efforts are accomplished by people who *believe* that they can improve teaching and learning" (emphasis added). "Determined educators are resourceful in finding ways to change their schools into places where *all* students learn to high standards" (emphasis added). "The belief that they can make a difference is bolstered by their effective use of data."

2. A clearly stated purpose and well-planned data collection and analysis are the cornerstones of an effective accountability effort.
   - How do you make sense of all the data?

   "Having a purpose helps people narrow their focus and leads to greater involvement and commitment." "When faculty, parents, community and students hold a common purpose, teachers and principals say it is easier to buy into the process." "Purpose helps people refine questions and integrate multiple sources of data in search of answers to important concerns."

3. Assessment tools need to be carefully chosen, suitable to the task at hand, and aligned with purpose.
   - Tools such as standardized tests are common
   - Teacher Journals are common but not thought of as tools
   - "Home-grown tools, developed by local schools meet their own specific documentation needs"

"No one tool works for all assessment needs. It is important to have, gather, and invent a variety of assessment tools for the assessment 'toolbox.'"

4. Accountability is difficult for schools to accomplish alone. Schools need to be creative in finding resources to help with planning, coordination, collection, interpretation, and reporting of data.
   - Working with someone knowledgeable about accountability from the outset saves time and other valuable resources
   - Such support is available from consultants, state departments of education, and educational support groups

"There needs to be recognition that the school is the unit of change and that teachers are the most important players. But the school being in the center of change shouldn't be translated to mean that the school should be responsible for doing it all." "Outside support is very helpful when schools are taking on new data-collection approaches. Organization and interpretation of data is another area where schools have used outside expertise."

There are some questions that are simply better than other questions. Questions that ask "which?" are better than questions that ask "how many?"

5. Effective accountability recognizes the need to engage the larger school community—district and school administrators, teachers, students, parents, and community.
   - Increasingly, community members are becoming active school leaders and are accepting more responsibility for effective teaching and learning at the school

"By developing partnerships with parents, a reciprocal sense of accountability starts to take shape, with schools responsible to their communities and communities responsible to their schools." "Another important ingredient in successful accountability efforts is teachers making on-going connections with parents about their children's progress."

THE STAGE IS SET

There are four purposes in setting the stage for the tools presented in this book that address a variety of topics: student-centered schools, quality processes for school improvement, the balanced scorecard, customer relationship management, data warehousing, linking the colleges of engineering and colleges of education, global quality and school improvement initiatives, and benchmarking for world-class schools. These purposes are:

1. To develop a deeper understanding of the role of data in student-centered school improvement
2. To share with education stakeholders promising practices for collecting, analyzing, and using data at the school level
3. To provide practicing educators with methods and tools that are usable for student-centering your school
4. To give education stakeholders—parents, teachers, administrators, and community members—the courage to tackle student-centered school improvement, one step at a time

NOTES

1. Kent L. Norman, "Teaching in the Switched on Classroom: An Introduction to Electronic Education and Hyper-Courseware" (1997), <http://www.lap.umd.edu/SOC/sochome.html> [last accessed: September 28, 1999].

2. O. E. Dyrli, "Stats Making News," *Technology and Learning* 18, no. 8 (1998): 82.

3. K. Fulton, "Technology Fluency," *Milken Exchange* (1998),<http://www.milkenexchange.org> [last accessed: June 19, 1999].

4. M. N. Malone, "Make Them Believers," *Technology and Learning* 18, no. 7 (1998): 44–45.

5. L. K. Bradshaw, "Technology-Supported Change: A Staff Development Opportunity," *NASSP Bulletin* 81, no. 593 (1997): 86–92.

6. C. L. Faison, "Modeling Instructional Technology Use in Teacher Preparation: Why Can't We Wait," *Educational Technology* 36, no. 5 (1996): 57–59.

7. National Council for Accreditation of Teacher Education, "Technology and the New Professional Teacher: Preparing for the 21st Century Classroom Report" (1997), <http://www.ncate.prg/projects/tech/TECH.HTM> [last accessed: May 26, 1999].

8. R. B. Hill and J. A. Somers, "A Process for Initiating Change: Developing Technology Goals for a College of Education," *Journal of Teacher Education* 47, no. 4 (1996): 300–306.

CHAPTER 3

Why Student-Center the School?

The shift in emphasis from inputs (books in library, teacher salaries, and so on) to student outcomes (performance test scores—*accountability for results*) is now preserved in state and federal regulations and will inevitably lead to a qualitative change in public schools. It is a change that most schools are likely to find to be culture shock.

- "Culture shock" is an ailing that causes problems to most of us at some time in our lives. It is a malady for many of us who at one time or another have been transplanted abroad into another culture in some part of the world. To promote a mind-set for better managing student results in school organizations is almost perceived as just such a cultural upheaval.
- Culture shock runs on personal anxiety that comes from losing all familiar signs and symbols. These signs are the thousand and one ways in which we get used to the situations of daily life. It is captured in the timeworn phrase "that's the way we do things around here." When an individual enters a strange culture, all or most of the familiar cues are removed and he or she is like a fish out of water. No matter how open minded or full of good will this individual may be, familiar props have been removed and a feeling of frustration and anxiety follows.
- Most people react to these frustrations in much the same way: they first reject the environment that causes the discomfort. For example, when Americans in a strange land get together to commiserate about the host country and its people or lack of amenities we can be sure they are suffering from culture shock.

FOCUS ON SCHOOL ACCOUNTABILITY

The answers to school improvement currently mandated by each state and reported to the public by the media are very generalized and leave too much to interpretation and political debate. When we talk about "accountability," we are really talking about measuring student-centered school outcomes. This process begins with knowing *what* we need to measure and *why* we measure it.

- "Accountability" in education can best be defined as a results mind-set—holding the school management and teachers answerable for student outcomes in terms of their learning, rather than solely in the school's use of input resources—that is, money, manpower, and physical plant. With the passage of the 2001 federal education act and the previous actions of most states, there is no longer any doubt that accountability for student learning results is the most important measure of each state's education programs in terms of need, opportunity, and cost.
- State governors have long set out specific goals for their noneducational state agencies over a period of one to ten years. Examples include reducing the incidence of violent crime, getting welfare recipients off the rolls and into jobs, and lowering deaths and injuries due to auto accidents per passenger mile. Given accountability as the new watchword for a "results mind-set" in education, governors may cringe more than a little when they review the typical objectives for education and find that all of the previous goals are *inputs*, such as completing the installation of full-day state-supported kindergartens, lowering class sizes in grades K–3, adding a specified number of computers per student, and raising teachers' salaries. Now, they will also want to list as goals for education such measures as reducing high school dropouts by a certain percent, ensuring that every child entering the fourth grade can read and understand the subject matter of that grade, and reducing to less than a very small percent the number of minority students who do not earn their high school diploma (see appendices B, F, and G).
- Educators and stakeholders traditionally think of school improvement in terms of improving the inputs, such as starting new

programs, getting more dollars for materials, raising teacher salaries, and the like. There are files and wastebaskets full of statistics about education, such as how many schools, how many teachers, how many strikes, and how many campus crimes. In principle, the American educational commitment has been that every child should have an adequate education. This commitment has been stated solely in terms of resources expended, such as numbers of teachers, books, space, and equipment. In fact, most of the outmoded accreditation techniques for elementary and secondary education still use measures of input as their prime criteria for performance quality.

When a child fails to learn, school personnel have all too often labeled the child "slow," "unmotivated," "retarded," or "coming from a dysfunctional home." To be truly accountable, our schools must now take up the professional dedication (like that of the physician whose desire it is to cure disease individual by individual) that every child shall learn. Such an obligation must include the willingness to carefully study their systems of schooling, training, and management; to change the processes that do not work or to find one that does; to seek causes of performance failure in the schooling processes; and to understand how the school personnel do their work in the system instead of focusing entirely on the students, parents, or conditions external to the school.

TO ACHIEVE SYSTEM IMPROVEMENT

Every school system has a purpose. The purposes may be extravagant and general as is often found in education textbooks. Components of the school system must be carefully managed to accomplish its purposes. Today, through the state and federal mandates for accountability, the purpose of the school system is more clearly spelled out—it is student-centered results. Through the application of systems thinking, educators are guided to better understand and measure the components that must be more smoothly integrated in order to accomplish the purposes of the school system.

Most of us now recognize that a system comprises a group of components that are intended to run smoothly to accomplish a purpose. The general idea is illustrated in the human body, through its circulatory or digestive system, or in transportation, such as the interstate highway system or the air controller systems operating at each of the nation's airports as well as integrated for domestic and international flights.

The power of systems thinking springs from two main ideas: the idea of purpose and the idea of coordination of the parts to achieve the system's purpose. Systems have purposes and once they are clearly stated and focused, the individual components that comprise the system must be carefully aimed toward accomplishing its purposes.

For application of the systems concept to classroom teaching, contrast these two situations. As a superintendent, Leon Lessinger visited two schools to benchmark the use of television as a classroom instructional medium for the Spanish program. In the first school visited, an excellent system was in place and ready for use. Both television and classroom teachers had clear goals for the teaching. Both groups met regularly to work out problems that arose from time to time. There were teachers' manuals and student workbooks by which the classroom could support television instruction with extra practice. The principal had a list of formative evaluation criteria to ensure that the quality was built in before the instruction began.

To benchmark best practice, Lessinger visited another school. The second school teaching the same language experience through television functioned bit by bit; it was a typical nonsystem. A summative evaluation showed that most of the students not only failed to learn successfully, but also they actually learned to hate the subject of Spanish. Classroom teaching worked like this: For three successive years in the project, and for three times a week, the teacher turned on the television set and kept the class quiet for thirty minutes. The students watched the program that was all in Spanish, and which only a few who had that background could understand. At the end of the television program, the set was turned off and the teacher proceeded to teach something else. Spanish was perceived as a dull program that few students could understand. This eventually translated into "I hate Spanish."

To put the systems concept to practical use in a classroom teaching:

1. A set of valid and clearly stated objectives is prepared to directly reflect the purpose of the classroom teaching

2. A criterion test to measure the achievement of the objectives is obtained
3. The content required to make possible the students' mastery of the objectives is set in appropriate media (textbook passages, computer programs, photographs, and so on), with the teacher applying the appropriate principles of learning and student management
4. The approach is studied through a review of the test results and corrective actions are put in place
5. On the basis of such actions, all teachers pursuing the same purposes are given the benefit of what has been learned

TO GAUGE RELIABILITY

A student-centered school must operate *reliably* or it is left to operate under a tyranny of chance. Chance stands in the way of any accountability for results. Reliability needs to be measured and then subjected to corrective action.

An unreliable system is one that has faulty components or errors in its coordination. Error or failure rates can be measured and related directly to system performance and component goals and objectives. Reliability is what can be depended on each and every time. The opposite of reliability is trial and error and uncertainty. Causes of unreliability need to be uncovered by metrics geared to measuring progress toward specific system improvement goals.

Every parent of a school-age child can relate to the following experience. At the opening of the new school each year the parents worry about the teacher their child will get *this* time. From personal experience, they know that what that teacher can do for their child in that classroom is the most important factor in their child's success. And when clear-eyed, they *know* that it is strictly a matter of chance, a roll of the dice, whether the teacher their child gets this time will be a good one.

Parents have always sensed that it really does matter which teachers their children get. That is why savvy parents with the time and skills work so hard to make sure that, by hook or crook, *their* kids get the best teachers. This is also one reason why the children of less "school-savvy" parents often end up with the most ineffective teachers.

What's missing most in teaching at the basic skills levels of reading and math is an understanding of what constitutes *reliability* in the quality of classroom instruction. Reliability is what we count on getting *every time*. A car is reliable if it starts every time, not some of the time. Airplane maintenance is reliable if the systems are taken care of on schedule. A bank is reliable if it keeps your accounts up to date and accurate. Words like "dependable" and "durable" are synonyms for reliable. Parents and citizens should expect each student to get a good teacher who is competent in the basic subjects every time and not, as at present, by chance. This is especially true for the skills all children need in school and in their life after school.

WHY ARE WE SO SURE CLASSROOM TEACHING IS OFTEN UNRELIABLE?

Teacher-made tests cover topics differently than the textbooks they use. This often leads to different student achievement results even in classes using the same book. The curriculum that the teacher offers varies even when teachers use the same textbook.

For decades, teacher personal *habits and decisions* have been the most important factors in classroom teaching. They often use intuition, guesswork, and folklore rather than tested practices. Some teachers use solid approaches for instruction. They use lessons, books, and other resources in ways consistent with sound teaching strategies. They believe passionately that their students can learn and that they have the responsibility to help make it happen. They have measurable objectives that their teaching approach aims to achieve. Their lessons are well thought out and structured and advance step by step. Teachers regularly check to determine how well *each* student is doing, whether some need more work, and the like.

In contrast, too many teachers lack a consistent teaching strategy. They use their resources in scattered and badly chosen ways. They operate with only vague objectives. Their lessons are neither well thought out nor organized. Classroom work is poorly paced. Teachers fail to regularly check to see how each student is doing. If they do check, they do not help the student correct what may be wrong.

GENERAL MEASUREMENT CONSIDERATIONS

It is a truism for *all* enterprises: When performance is measured, performance can improve; if it is not measured, only chance rules. When performance is measured *and* reported back, the rate of performance speeds up and the motivation to improve the performance of the system multiplies.

Measurement and feedback of results to staff and learners are the twin forces to be encouraged by school performance management. When a spouse returns from a hair stylist and asks how you like his or her haircut, he or she is seeking feedback. Is there a child who after completing something worthwhile says "look at me" and waits for a response? Without knowledge of results (feedback) there can be no improvement. Without timely knowledge of results, learning is seriously impaired.

PERFORMANCE MEASUREMENT

Measuring human achievement has a long history. Our earliest records show that it was reached through performance assessment. We still evaluate achievement through performance. Tests are used in music recitals, marksmanship, driver's license exams, written examinations for civil service jobs, and licensures in insurance and real estate.

Before standardized tests, with their true–false questions, paper and pencil multiple-choice items used as regular testing devices, and machine scoring, teachers relied on direct approaches to assessment of results. Students wrote essays, were asked to spell words, answered questions, solved problems at the blackboard, and made things work. Also, school board members went into classrooms selecting students at random to perform academic tasks. Testing was direct and observable; it was not inferred from a proxy like the so-called objective multiple-choice test.

THE NATURE OF MEASUREMENT

Measurement is focused. Measurements have meaning in terms of their designed use. The results are a direct function of the methods and measurements used. To repeat, things that are not measured are left to chance.

Some examples. Land is surveyed to tax and convey it. Carpets and curtains are measured for cutting to fit floors and windows. Stock shares owned and their market values are measured to pay interest and dividends or to calculate return on investment. Distance is measured to aim weapons, charge for airplane tickets, and to conduct the Olympic trials and games. Time is measured to schedule work, to study, to play, to serve a prison term, and to mark the start of enforced retirement.

Measurement is a means of direction and agreement. Measurement is always deliberate, not disengaged; it is shaped by societal structure and not independent; it is slanted by intellectual conventions and never un-biased. By not measuring the reliability of teaching, administrators, school boards, and citizens forfeit their influence over achieving results and turn over that control solely to those who are supposedly responsi-ble for doing that job.

The absence of measures of output in classroom teaching stands in stark contrast to the obsessive measurement of inputs. Schools know to the penny the cost of busing students and the cost of paper and chalk. In business, budgets are measurements intended to control costs, set prices, and yield a margin of profit. In a nonprofit organization, like schools, budgets are simply "permission" to incur costs without measuring re-sponsibility for results. The school mind-set is *funding costs* not *measur-ing benefits and returns*. The school budgeting process follows an almost exact law: organizational needs expand to consume available funds. Old activities (and new ones) continue as long as funding continues. Budget-ing in schools is ongoing, and new development is opportunistic—new activities are added principally by new funding. Improved school per-formance cannot come about as a consequence of budget measurement.

It should come as no surprise that in schools and colleges measure-ment controls results. College professors who are rated by the number of their publications devote more time to research and less to teaching, more time to writing and less to student conferences. If the measure-ment of a school or teacher is student performance on a statewide ex-amination, contents of courses tend to be defined by test areas and methods of teaching tend to include drill in prior years' examinations, in anticipated questions for the current year, and even in actual ques-tions for the current year if these become known in advance. Measure-ment and values are part of the same system, each being the reciprocal of the other—cause and effect. Looked at another way, these are part of a never-ending circle of plan-do-act-revise. Together, they cast the present and forecast the future. When schools classify non-English-speaking children as retarded because of low test scores in English, the test measurements are seen as being used to comply with social values and expectations. Unhappily, our conventional measurements often create what conventional values demand—essentially winners and losers, successes and failures. If we perceive the creation of losers and failures as counterproductive, we must find measurements to express and implement our perceptions and values. Measuring the reliability of classroom teaching to achieve success for all children of the basic skills is a direct start at making winners.

WHY WE FIND UNRELIABLE CLASSROOM
TEACHING DISTRESSING

Students, whose families and communities have many economic, social, and cultural advantages, arrive in class with plentiful educational assets. On average, they do relatively well on various measures of academic achievement. But students from families and communities with fewer economic, social, and cultural advantages come with fewer educational assets. These students find it difficult to automatically make good use of what schools offer unless the school is prepared to invest time and effort with them. They generally do poorly on tests and other measures of academic achievement.

Studies show that students from less advantaged circumstances are as bright and curious as those in the advantaged groups. However, they may not have learned to read or to write at home as is common in more advantaged circumstances. They often receive less help at home with schoolwork. They may lack breakfast or a quiet space in which to read or do homework. But these are factors that can be overcome. The facts are that a prime reason for poor school performance is that schools lack know-how to deal with such situations.

When students from disadvantaged homes come to school poorly prepared to take advantage of conventional teaching, most schools and teachers are woefully *ill prepared* to help these students. And it is precisely *here* that the lack of reliability in classroom teaching is so destructive. The students do not know how to deal with adults and conventional schoolwork. The teachers do not know how to organize books, lessons, and conventional school resources to take advantage of the curiosity and intelligence that the student first brings to school. This mutual incapacity is crippling for many students. It eventually defeats many teachers.

STUDENT-CENTERED SCHOOLS WHERE UNRELIABILITY IS NOT A PROBLEM

There is a growing body of evidence that some important characteristics greatly influence teaching results and lead to genuine accountability. In student-centered schools, faculty and students share a vision of the purposes of teaching and the commitment to success. Teachers pledge to help all students succeed. In such schools there is teamwork. They use what works as a standard operating procedure (SOP) to help students master standards, have lots of contact between teachers and students in class and outside, and develop high morale. They have administrators who operate to support the teaching under board-adopted quality system policies.

In student-centered schools:

1. Students, teachers, and parents know the required standards
2. Teacher-made exams are put in line with the standards
3. Curriculum is aligned to the standards
4. Students receive expert instruction
5. Schools offer as much time and teaching as students need to learn
6. "Stakes" in student and teacher success are high, thereby holding the system accountable

The most significant characteristic of all is *expert instruction*.

CAN "EXPERT INSTRUCTION" BE CLEARLY DEFINED?

It certainly can. Here is just one example. In early April 2000, the National Reading Panel released a long awaited report. The panel consisted of leading reading research scientists, representatives of colleges of education, reading teachers, educational administrators, and parents. The panel, mandated by Congress in 1997, was formed to give public schools conclusive guidance on teaching beginning reading.

The panel examined approximately one hundred thousand reading research studies published since 1966 and another fifteen thousand having been published before 1966. "For the first time, we now have guidance based on evidence from sound scientific research on how best to teach children to read," the director of the panel said.[1]

The panel found that the research conducted to date strongly supports the concept that explicitly and systematically teaching children to manipulate phonemes significantly improves children's reading and spelling abilities. The evidence for this is so clear-cut that they said in unambiguous language that this method should be an important component of all classroom reading instruction.

A similar case for expert instruction can be made for math, speaking, listening, and study skills.

STAKEHOLDERS KNOW RELIABLE CLASSROOM TEACHING WHEN THEY SEE IT

Parents and the public visiting reliable quality classes where teachers use a business-like student-centered approach to learning are visibly impressed and enthusiastic. They see well-trained teachers conducting lessons in an orderly environment. They see students mastering the basics. They watch, often in amazement, even prekindergarten and kindergarten children who are often termed "at risk" reading at quality levels much like affluent youngsters in the first and second grades.

They know reliable classroom teaching when they see:

- Time is allocated for individual and team teacher lesson planning
- Students and parents know what the teacher expects in avoiding wasted time and hopeless confusion
- Teachers align teaching to curriculum standards so that both subject matter and standards are likely to be met
- Teachers follow their union contracts that strictly specify the *minutes of teacher time* using those minutes as a precious commodity for classroom learning

- Teachers avoid labeling students as "slow," "bright," or "lazy" and treat each student as an individual
- Discipline problems are more rare because the teacher masters the "take charge of the workplace" process so that students have less time to misbehave
- Student performance improves because teachers motivate students and measure results with real-time feedback and corrective action
- Teachers use a consistent strategy for instruction and resources selected to avoid vague objectives
- Lessons are planned, thought out, well organized, and well paced
- Teachers follow as SOP what solid research says really works to achieve reliable quality classroom teaching

Is it too harsh to use the term "tyranny" to describe the effects of chance caused by unreliable classroom teaching quality?

When *reliable* quality teaching methods are encouraged and used by the school system, students succeed in the foundation subjects. If these processes are ignored, students fail. It's as simple as that. We know a great deal about what it takes to create and manage a school system to produce reliable classroom teaching. Although there are many well-researched and effective teaching methods and management systems available, there are still far too many useless—even damaging—techniques actually in use. And shamefully, many reliable quality-teaching methods are ignored.

In an earlier book, *Healing Public Schools: The Winning Prescription to Cure Their Chronic Illness*, we show how ISO 9000 Education Standards and the Baldrige National Quality Program Criteria for Education, by working together, forge a winning prescription to heal the chronic suffering of all public schools: unreliable classroom teaching.[2]

TO STRENGTHEN EDUCATIONAL SYSTEMS

All school subsystems interact. Each requires data and information to effectively perform its assigned responsibilities. Each subsystem needs to link with other subsystems to achieve optimal efficiency. Each subsystem is accountable to the other parts of the system as well as to the school customer. Performance management means keeping these subsystems from clashing with one another and to assist each in achieving its purpose to the student.

TO REINFORCE INSTRUCTIONAL SYSTEMS

The heart of the school is instruction. It can best be viewed as an integrated set of media, equipment, methods, and personnel performing the functions required to achieve the subject matter and human development objectives of teaching.

There are several key points in the concept of this heart of the school system:

1. The classroom teaching system must be designed to accomplish objectives that mirror the performance standards set out by the district. The definition and derivation of these objectives so that they are "measurable" is a critical aspect of the engineering mindset for education.
2. There are several functions that each teacher must carry out skillfully. These functions include an optimal presentation of the knowledge, the practice of the performance objectives for mastery, the practice of the knowledge that underlies the performance standards, the management of the classroom performance of the students, and quality control (feedback and corrective action).
3. The systems concept is very neutral about the nature of the teaching itself. The answer to the question about whether or not to use human beings or technology or some combination is a function of experience. With an engineering mind-set, the educator asks that the required classroom teaching functions be carried out effectively and economically.

TO REMOVE SYSTEM CONSTRAINTS

Present-day school systems remain the target of criticism. Leading citizens claim that the public has gradually gained confidence in the ability of the schools to educate the future citizens of a more ethnically diverse United States. Others maintain that the school system focuses more on the cream of its students, while leaving too many others to be rejected, allowed to drop out, and eventually repaired by society at large. One recent prominent study revealed that early indicators of reading deficiencies are a marker for later bouts with the law.

The system is also the *context* in which a person works. The context determines how we behave. We whisper in hospitals and become anxious in doctors' offices. We are sad in cemeteries and cheerful at parties. Contexts control our mind-sets and therefore determine how we interpret each circumstance. Systems are made up of processes and results. The processes determine the results. Systems thinking therefore favors a process orientation, the basic requirement for reliability in classroom teaching.

We know a lot about processes and systems. These ideas, so vital in improving classroom teaching, are no longer a mystery. Think about any team sport you have played or observed. With just a little reflection, you find that you know quite a bit about processes and systems, and projected forward, what is required to support reliable quality in classroom teaching.

The sport matters less than what is described as universal.

- There are players and names for the positions each one holds
- Each person in the game is a process (shooting a basket, guarding a goal, catching a pass, pitching a baseball)
- When the processes are joined, there is a system (a group of parts to be coordinated to get something done); this is a team
- The job of running the system—the coaches and assistants use plans and playbooks—that guides each process so that the system as a whole will function at its top potential (the team will play to or even beyond its supposed ability)

It is obvious that no team player or process is complete in itself. To win you have to look at the system as a whole. In the world of education, the system includes not only your processes (employees and leaders), but also your suppliers and customers. Your customers' likes and dislikes, wishes and desires, have to be pored over and fed back into the system so that the system can continually improve, always delighting your customers with results that exceed their expectations.

What is critical to the success of any system, be it a sports team or a school classroom, is how you coach, lead, or manage that system.[3] You cannot get the best from any system unless every process in the system cooperates as well as does its best individually. An orchestra is a great example to demonstrate the likely consequence of failing at such an approach. It's not hard to imagine the jarring sounds that would result if each member of an orchestra tried to show off his or her individual musical ability rather than to play together to demonstrate the orchestra's ability. The goal must be a harmonious mutual benefit.

To fully understand the central ideas in systems thinking, it is instructive to watch children given a new game or toy that they need to understand. They naturally start a three-step process. First they take it apart. Second, they try to understand the conduct of each part separately. Third, they try to gather together an understanding of the parts into an understanding of the whole. That is a good description of analysis.

Analysis has been the leading method of Western thinking for more than four hundred years. Coaches, leaders, and managers have used analysis to organize sports, businesses, and schools. Regrettably, you cannot explain the performance of a system solely by analysis. You must use synthesis. Instead of only taking things apart and looking at each part separately, you must put them all together and look at them as an integrated and coordinated team trying to achieve some purpose. Indeed, you must also see that system in terms of a larger one to which it belongs. You must expand your thinking and consider those elements that are outside what you control but that influences what the system can do.

Russell L. Ackoff gives us this example of the influence of a larger system to which a system belongs. He likes to point out that auto mechanics can take as many English and American cars apart for as long as they like and they will never discover why the English steering wheel is on the right and the American on the left. The reason for the placement of the steering wheels is not in how the cars are assembled; the reason is in the two different societies, the expanded systems in which those cars are used.

Analysis deals with how each part works; synthesis deals with how the parts work together, not from a mechanical point of view, but from a design and function viewpoint. If you had automotive experts pick the world's best auto parts separately and you assembled those best parts, the car wouldn't work except by chance. The parts were not intended to fit together. Once you understand that the object must be to manage the system as a whole to achieve the best *interaction* of the parts, it is easier to see why so much of what we have tried in recent years to improve the quality of our public schools could not possibly work in the long run. To improve the education system, we must have communication, coordination, and cooperation among the processes. Even the best fiddling with the parts won't do.

TO CLEAR UP PERPLEXING SYSTEMS

One of the most surprising aspects of managing complex systems is to discover just how highly interrelated their subsystems are. By this, it is meant that an intuitive change in an input does not automatically or necessarily result in a concomitant change in the output. Nor does a change in the characteristics of one of the components of a subsystem necessarily result in a corresponding result in the output. The behavior of complex systems is the most telling example we have of the law of unintended consequences. For example, the evidence is clear that the amount of money spent per pupil in the various schools seems to have little relationship to the scores of students on achievement tests.

The key to clearing up perplexing systems—ones with disturbing results—is to invoke the mantra: process before outcome! Surprisingly, a fixation with results may hamper getting them to reliably work together because, in fact, *every* outcome is literally caused by a process. Like the egg and the chicken, the outcome is inborn in the process that is its cause.

All achievements can be broken down into a series of steps that lead to the results. A practical effect of this kind of thinking is that people can imagine themselves taking steps while often not being able to imagine some great achievement as being possible.

A process orientation not only sharpens our judgment, but it also makes us feel better about ourselves. A purely outcome orientation can take the joy out of life. Playing sports demonstrates this wisdom clearly. During a game, we clearly see the process at work, with the individual performance and player cooperation within the system as being the two main things that matter. It is the same in school improvement. From kindergarten on, the focus of schooling is usually on goals rather than on the processes by which they are achieved. This single-minded pursuit of one objective or another, from tying shoelaces to getting into a college, makes it difficult to have a wise attitude about what makes getting results reliable.

When children start a new activity with a single focus on results, questions such as "can I do it?" or "what if I can't do it?" are very likely to dominate, thereby creating an anxious worry with success or failure rather than drawing on the child's natural, exuberant desire to explore. Instead of enjoying the color of the crayons, the designs on the paper, and a variety of possible shapes along the way, the child sets about writing "correct" alphabet letters while not paying attention to mastering the processes that will ensure making the correct ones.

FOSTERING STUDENT-CENTERED IMPROVEMENT

For a school system to become fully accountable, the operational and teaching methods used to achieve student-centered purposes must work reliably. This approach represents a fundamental breakthrough in educational thinking because it suggests dismissing long held practices and beliefs in favor of accepting authoritative measurable research in "what works."

Using what works as SOP with management logistical and psychological support leads a school into the status of a high-reliability organization (HRO). We know the chief characteristics of the HRO whether they are in the private sector (nuclear energy facilities), in government (airport security), or in schools (thus far, only a few are even at the starting gate). They have a clear mission and achievable goals and communicate these to staff and stakeholders and then passionately focus on seeing that they are actually achieved. And if they are not achieved, corrective action is immediately taken.

In a high-reliability school, all classroom teaching is student-centered and a given subject is given the same clear "teaching treatments" known to be effective in getting student accomplishment. Student-centered schools show a strong sense of mission in helping all students achieve the educational standards reflected by the objectives. They communicate, honor, and vigorously pursue the achievement of the standards set out for them in their subject fields. They don't add on too many other less important objectives.

High-reliability schools obsess over the quality of their processes and insist on taking steps to continuously improve them because they know that processes literally make up the heart of the school and the school system.

High-reliability student-centered classroom teaching is built on the use of good practice as SOP. The lack of attention to SOPs in classroom teaching is the hallmark of the tyranny of chance and the reason luck is the chief operating factor.

There is an erroneously held notion that SOPs do not apply to classroom teaching, that teaching is always some kind of a uniquely mysterious personal act, and that the desirable end of all teaching is creativity. Nothing could be farther from the truth.

NOTES

1. National Institute of Child Health and Human Development, "Teaching Children to Read: An Evidence-Based Assessment of the Scientific Research Literature on Reading and Its Implications for Reading Instruction," report of the National Reading Panel, NIH Publication No. 00-4769 (Washington, D.C.: U.S. Government Printing Office, 2000).

2. Allen Salowe and Leon Lessinger, *Healing Public Schools: The Winning Prescription to Cure Their Chronic Illness* (Lanham, Md: Scarecrow, 2001).

3. Leon Lessinger and Allen Salowe, *Game Time: The Educator's Playbook for the New Global Economy* (Lancaster, Penn.: Technomic, 1997).

CHAPTER 4

Performance Management

THE BACKDROP TO CHANGE

What it takes to improve schools is becoming clearer. Schools have changed in some ways, and yet have changed little in other respects. A century ago, student desks and chairs were bolted to the floor and faced to the front. Discipline was just as tight, with students needing individual permission for a bathroom trip. Students and teachers addressed each other according to rule and teachers dressed formally. In the twentieth century, classrooms gradually grew less organized, a trend that really picked up steam in the 1960s and 1970s.

Today, teachers are probably more considerate of student feelings than they were ten decades ago and discipline is greatly relaxed. The tone of the classroom is less formal, the furniture can be moved around, and many elementary students sit in small "cooperative learning" groups facing each other. Teachers dress casually and students are granted more self-rule by moving around more freely to do their work. Most seem able to hit the "John" when they wish.

Students also enter and leave the classroom at their own initiative to attend special classes or other activities. Even teachers who describe themselves as disciplinarians tolerate noise, side conversations, and mischief that would have been quickly stomped out only a generation or two ago. These changes now sound trivial in the twenty-first century.

Classroom talk has also changed a great deal. Only a few decades ago, students and teachers worked within a fairly rigid format. Teachers put questions to the individual student who was expected to answer on the spot. Premium was placed on speed and precision. The teaching-learning exercise took place at a brisk clip. There was little or no room for students to develop a point, let alone to ask questions or discuss the matter. Students usually stood when called on to speak. They were also graded on posture and behavior. Today, student presentation is an extinct animal of the school landscape. When these activities do take place, if at all, they are quite informal.

Today, students manage more of their own instruction. The materials used have also changed. Now there are more texts, supplementary works, and trade books for students than in previous years. The materials are also diverse in style, format, content, and intended audience. They are designed better and presented more attractively than anything available even a few decades ago, let alone in 1900. Topping it off, there is new instructional media—television, radio, audiotape, videotape, and computers—making their way into wider classroom use, with many showing astounding instructional possibilities.

If these changes show promise for school reformers, other instructional features refuse to give way. The egg-crate, age-graded organization of school life is inherited from the nineteenth century and still remains intact. So too is the snapshot approach to topic definition and content coverage. Concepts of knowledge seem to have changed little.

While education reformers have successfully changed the behavior, culture, and social organization of the classroom and improved learning materials, they have not come close to touching the core process features of classroom instruction. The spread of cultural and organizational breakdown has brought with it the spread of unreliable teaching practices for such basics as reading and math. And these unreliable practices remain dominant today.

PARENTS ARE RUNNING OUT OF PATIENCE

Competency-type malpractice suits are the newest tort area of education and once this door opens wider, an avalanche of litigation can be expected to follow. If every student who is failing to master the survival skills of an information-based workplace society should decide to bring suit against his or her school district and its teachers for educational malpractice, the country's courtrooms would be overwhelmed.

The San Francisco Case

The first of the major competency malpractice cases was *Peter W. v. San Francisco Unified School District*.[1] Peter W. graduated from the San Francisco schools with a high school diploma. California statutes require that high school graduates read at a level above the eighth grade. Allegedly, Peter W. could not survive in the workplace society because he lacked reading or writing ability, so he sued the San Francisco Public Schools on five counts:

1. "Negligence and carelessly" failed to apprehend his reading disabilities
2. "Negligently and carelessly" assigned him to classes in which he could not read "the books and other materials"
3. "Negligently and carelessly" allowed him "to pass and advance from a course or grade level" with knowledge that he had not achieved either its completion or the skills necessary for him to succeed or benefit from subsequent courses
4. "Negligently and carelessly" assigned him to classes in which the instructors were unqualified or which were not "geared" to his reading level
5. "Negligently and carelessly" permitted him to graduate from high school although he was "unable to read above the eighth-grade level, as required by Education Code 8573 . . . thereby depriving him of additional instruction in reading and other academic skills"

Peter W. was seeking two sets of damages. First, he sought general damages because of his "permanent disability and inability to gain meaningful employment." In parallel, he sought specific damages to compensate him for the cost of tutoring to correct the injury that the San Francisco schools had inflicted on him.

The California Court of Appeals affirmed the superior court's dismissal of the suit against the school district.

The New York Case

Less than two years later, the second important competency malpractice case was decided three thousand miles away from California.

The New York Supreme Court, Appellate Division, also ruled against a pupil alleging educational malpractice in *Donohue v. Copiague Union Free School District*.[2] In this case, Edward Donohue sought $5,000,000 in damages based on two allegations. First, his attorneys claimed that the public schools failed to "[t]each the several and varied subjects to plaintiff, ascertain his learning capacity and ability, and correctly and properly test him for such capacity in order to evaluate his ability to comprehend the subject matters of the various courses and have sufficient understanding and comprehension of subject matters in said courses as to be able to achieve sufficient passing grade in said subject matters, and therefore, qualify for a Certificate of Graduation."[3]

Since Donohue did not have basic skills in reading and writing, the suit claimed that the school system breached its "duty of care" because it

Gave to the plaintiff passing grades and/or minimal or failing grades in various subjects; failed to evaluate the plaintiff's mental ability and capacity to comprehend the subjects being taught to him at said school; failed to take proper means and precautions that they reasonably should have taken under the circumstances; failed to interview, discuss, evaluate and/or psychologically test the plaintiff in order to ascertain his ability to comprehend and understand such subject matter; failed to provide adequate school facilities, teachers, administrators, psychologists, and other personnel trained to take the necessary steps in testing and evaluation processes insofar as the plaintiff is concerned in order to ascertain the learning capacity, intelligence, and intellectual absorption on the part of the plaintiff; failed to hire proper personnel . . . ; failed to teach the plaintiff in such a manner so that he could reasonably understand what was necessary under the circumstances so that he could cope with the various subject . . . ; failed to properly supervise the plaintiff; [and] failed to advise his parents of the difficulty and necessity to call in psychiatric help.

The New York court, using the Peter W. case as precedent, also claimed that public policy does not allow the judiciary to become embroiled in education affairs.

The Illinois Case

A teacher dismissal case with implications for the competency malpractice area can be found in *Gilliland v. Board of Education*.[4] An Illinois school board dismissed a tenured elementary teacher because she: "Ruined the students' attitudes toward school, had not established effective student/teacher rapport, constantly harassed students, habitually left her students unattended and gave unreasonable and irregular homework assignments."

With more and more states implementing minimal competency tests as prerequisites for receiving a diploma, there is only one thing certain in the future. Pupil suits to recover damages as a result of educational malpractice have laid the groundwork for more attempts.

The Texas Case

A January 7, 2000, decision by a federal district judge in Texas is decisive in this litigation area.[5] The following excerpt from a recent publication presents the case: "Who should issue driver's licenses to teenagers? Should it be the driving instructors who are responsible for teaching teens to drive? Or should it be an impartial examiner who tests each teen to see if he or she has the skills and knowledge needed to drive?"[6]

Most people agree that using an examiner is the better way of making sure that driver's licenses aren't given to teens who can't read traffic signs and don't know the rules of the road.

Judge Edward C. Prado of the U.S. District Court, in an important and closely watched Texas case, handed down a similarly commonsense decision in January 2000. The case asked: Who should be responsible for issuing high school diplomas? A student's teachers, who may give the student passing grades in all classes? Or the Texas Education Agency (TEA), which may flunk the same student for not possessing a minimum set of academic skills?

Judge Prado gave the nod to the state, and not to the teachers in upholding the right of TEA to make the award of the high school diploma conditional on passing a competency test. "In spite of projected disparities in passing rates [of different ethnic groups], the TEA determined that objective measures of mastery should be imposed in order to eliminate what it perceived to be inconsistent and possibly subjective teacher evaluations of students," wrote Prado, noting the state agency presented evidence of subjective teacher evaluations. The problem with subjective teacher evaluations, Prado noted, is that they "can work to disadvantage minority students by allowing inflated grades to mask gaps in learning."[7]

"Texans want a high school diploma to mean something," explains Texas Education Commissioner Jim Nelson.[8]

Education officials in several states had anxiously awaited the outcome of this case. Many already have or are developing similar high-stakes graduation tests. Nineteen states have tests required for graduation. Currently, another eight have plans to put them into place. The court ruling preserves the Texas school accountability system, where the state holds educators accountable for student learning, attendance, and drop out.

The use of the Texas Assessment of Academic Skills (TAAS) test to deny high school diplomas was challenged by the Mexican American Legal Defense and Education Fund (MALDEF). It argued that the test was discriminatory simply because the failure rate for African Americans and Hispanics was higher than for whites. MALDEF claimed the test had "an impermissible adverse impact on minority students in Texas" and violated their right to due process.[9]

A case was brought on behalf of nine students who did not pass the TAAS exit-level examination prior to their scheduled graduation dates. They requested that their respective school districts issue their diplomas. The court denied their request.

MALDEF presented an argument frequently made by apologists for the poor performance of urban public schools—that the state could not hold students accountable for acquiring any knowledge unless it guarantees that all students are given an equal opportunity to learn. According to MALDEF, it is unfair to penalize minority students by denying them a high school diploma when their school district has not provided them with the same opportunity to learn what white students have. Teacher assessments, not TAAS test results, should be the main criteria for awarding diplomas, argued MALDEF.

Judge Prado *rejected* this argument. He recognized that minorities were underrepresented in advanced placement courses and in gifted and talented programs, and that noncertified teachers disproportionately taught minority students. He went on to find: "The Plaintiffs presented insufficient evidence to support a finding that minority students do not have a reasonable opportunity to learn the material covered in the TAAS examination, whether because of unequal education in the past or the current residual effects of an unequal system."[10]

Prado further went on to say the TAAS test accomplishes exactly what it sets out to accomplish, which is "to provide an objective assessment of whether students have mastered a discrete set of skills and knowledge." Since the state has linked the test to the state curriculum, "the Court finds that all Texas students have an equal opportunity to learn the items presented on the TAAS test, which is the issue before the Court."[11]

While acknowledging that "[t]he TAAS test does adversely affect minority students in significant numbers," Prado ruled there was an "educational necessity" for the test. The plaintiffs, he determined, had failed to identify equally effective alternatives. He also concluded there had been no violation of due process rights, since TEA provided adequate notice of the consequences of the exam and ensured that the exam is strongly correlated to material actually taught in the classroom. "The system is not perfect, but the Court cannot say that it is unconstitutional," wrote Prado.[12]

THE LIKELY FUTURE SCENARIO

The prospect of more malpractice suits for educational incompetence is needless but likely. Very simply, recognizing a cause of action in negligence to recover for "educational malpractice" would eventually require the courts to oversee the administration of a state's public school system. Thus far, courts have held that state public policy recognizes no cause of action for educational malpractice.

However, the New York court also felt that the process of education is a two-step process. *First, there must be teaching. Second, there must be learning.* The court was not willing to conclude that when a pupil does not learn it is automatically the fault of the teacher. The New York court put it this way: "The failure to learn does not bespeak a failure to teach. It is not alleged that the plaintiff's classmates, who were exposed to the identical classroom instruction, also failed to learn."

The court placed a certain amount of the burden of fault on the student himself and on the parents as well: "The grades on the plaintiff's periodic report cards gave notice both to his parents and himself that he had failed in two or more subjects, thus meeting the definition of an 'underachiever' provided in the regulations of the Commissioner of Education (8 NYCRR 203.1/2). Having this knowledge, the plaintiff could properly have demanded the special testing and evaluation directed by the statute."

But since neither the student nor the parents requested special help, the court felt that they could not blame the failure to learn on the school system or its teachers.

The one vital difference between the *Peter W.* and *Donohue* decisions is this: The New York Supreme Court, Appellate Division, *did not completely rule out* future education malpractice suits. The court suggested that if more than a single individual suffers injury as a result of educational malpractice, a negligence suit might be successful. The court wrote:

> This determination does not mean that educators are not ethically and legally responsible for providing a meaningful public education for the youth of our State. Quite the contrary, all teachers and other officials of our schools bear an important public trust and may be held to answer for the failure to faithfully perform their duties. It doesn't mean, however, that they may not be sued for damages by an individual student for an alleged failure to reach certain educational objectives.[13]

GOOD PRACTICE, POOR PRACTICE, AND MALPRACTICE IN EDUCATION

"Good practice" is the professional way, the SOPs of doing things in the instructional process. Using good practice *will* reliably produce the intended student-learning outcome. Good practice is the legacy of experience as well as the product of competent research and development.

"Poor practice" is a way of doing things that yield unpredictable or chance results. For example, none of us *would* care to ride in an airplane that is piloted by a crew that has irregular results, because the results we demand include safety and reliability.

"Malpractice" reflects ways of doing things that generally produce a *harmful* result or are *illegal*. When we choose a surgeon, we expect that the doctor will do no harm. We should expect no less in schools or

teaching. We demand that the doctor's activities be legal and we anticipate helpful results. Consider these other examples:

- Good practice in medicine is to sterilize a wound. In law, to exercise due process. In engineering, to build safety factors into a
structure.
- In medicine, it is poor practice to routinely use antibiotics. In law,
to release privileged information about a pending trial. In engineering, to place a part that will require servicing in an inaccessi-
ble place.
- In medicine, it is malpractice to leave a surgical instrument or
other harmful materials inside a patient. In law, to force a client to
perjure him- or herself. In engineering, to knowingly use materials
that do not meet specification.

Regrettably, in education there is only the barest understanding of the
notion of good practice, poor practice, or malpractice in the instructional
process. In fact, when the classroom door closes almost any instructional process the teacher uses is protected and free from correction.

Susan Markle highlights the outrageous failure to achieve a good
teaching practice this way: "The idea of a major industrial concern
turning out, on a standardized production line, 10 per cent superior
products, 20 per cent good products, and 50 per cent average products,
with the remainder classed as disposable is so ludicrous in this age of
modern technology that it would hardly bear mentioning were it not for
the obvious parallel between this outlandish image and the present situation in education."[14]

We must face the reality that any profession that is unable to distinguish among good practice, poor practice, and malpractice is doomed to
remain in a primitive state. All persons working in such a field will have
difficulty proving their professional credibility. The major obstacle to
improving school effectiveness and educator status is based on two factors: educators unable to adopt known good practice as SOP in the classroom and educators needing to adopt a performance-management system to ensure reliable classroom teaching.

In *Healing Public Schools: The Winning Prescription to Cure Their
Chronic Illness*, we ask for the answer to two key questions: How is

school improvement to be achieved? How is what is to be achieved to be measured and evaluated?[15]

USING THE RIGHT TOOLS TO DO THE RIGHT JOB

Computers and data systems might help create more knowledgeable parents who become active participants in their children's education. This would not render the teacher or school unnecessary. Sometimes, the information itself will do the work of the teacher. The major error of twentieth-century education is the belief that learning only involves the application of facts to an objective problem that can be separated from the student.

In schools, it is *how* to solve the problem that counts. To do so, one needs to use the right tools to help uncover the underlying reasons for the problem. It wouldn't make much sense to put together a team of sharp educators and then neglect to give them the right tools to do their jobs.

A businessperson would no more communicate today with a colleague halfway around the globe using a first-class letter when e-mail or fax could be used. Similarly, none of us would care to be treated in a healthcare facility without the proper diagnostic tools. A school organization with good practices uses the right tools to do the job.

The fact is, good tools make us smarter and we witness evidence of this almost everyday. There is only so much we can learn and remember. But we have powerful tools to extend our memories. We invent things that make us smart.

But things that make us smart may unintentionally make us dumber because they may entrap us with their seductive powers. Television captures us with thousands of hours of commercials each year. And twenty-four-hour news is capsulated into easy-to-swallow dosages. But do we really know any more about what is going on in the world? Tools must fit the task and if we need to learn we need to use the right tools.

The power in using the right tools is that they do not ask the user to become someone else. Tools help create an extension of oneself. With a little time and skill, using the right tool helps us become more than what we are.

Marshall McLuhan told us in *Understanding Media* that tools are a medium for self-expression.[16] An appreciation of good tools offers us a way to influence the world. We learn to listen differently, to see differently, and to view with a different sense of proportion. So also, the doctor and teacher see the world differently when using the right tools. Good tools expand our perceptual boundaries.

To look at technology and tools as a way to either reduce costs or speed up output is too limiting. This may lead to the narrow view that the only tools worth having are those that create and enhance value. *Technology is a medium for creating productive management and work environments*. Education leaders must face this organizational reality — the school workplace is where teachers and administrators interact to create value. And the tools educators use and the ones their school organizations choose reflect the sort of value they wish to create.

THE MEANING OF TOOLS

Accurate measurement underlies all of science. Without reliable measurements, science would be denied the use of its most powerful tools. By this, we include precise measurement, repeatable experiments under controlled conditions, and mathematical analyses. The problem is that when it comes to measuring human capabilities we feel somewhat limited.

People are complex creatures. Our actions result from multiple interactions, from a lifetime of experiences, from knowledge, and from subtle personal interrelationships. Scientific measurement tools help us strip away the complexities by studying a single variable at a time. But much of what is of value to a person results from the interaction of the parts: when we measure simple, single variables, we miss the bigger point in systems thinking that we are "dealing with the elephant" as a very large complex creature.

We choose tools to enrich our personal lives. Tools help us create the values that we judge important and these same choices need to be available to make our professional lives meaningful and productive.

TOOLS FOR TEAMWORK

Tools force us to choose between two schools of thought: experiential thought and reflective thought. Tools for experiential thought provide us with a wide range of sensory stimulation and with enough information to minimize the need for logical deduction. The telephone extends our voice as well as lets us hear spoken words from hundreds or even thousands of miles away. Tools for reflective thought support the exploration of ideas. They make it easier for us to compare and evaluate, to explore alternatives.

Both the Baldrige National Quality Program Criteria for Education and the ISO 9000 Education Standards give us similar guidance. In each case the tools are invisible; they do not get in the way.

The school principal's office has lots of tools. Behind the desk is a chair as well as a visitor's chair. On the desktop stand the ubiquitous tools of this trade—the phone, the calendar, in and out baskets, pencils and pens, paper clips, rubber bands, a stapler, a letter opener, and the personal computer with a collection of software packages. Nearby stands the family photo as a morale booster and the file cabinet overflowing with reams of paper. The principal may have ready access to a secretary and schedules a conference room when needed.

Individuals need such tools to support their work, but there is nothing in the typical school to support *collaboration*. Synchronization and cooperation do not call for much brainpower. Ants, for example, cooperate in an impressive variety of tasks and not through any conscious desire to work together. Similarly, birds fly in a *V* formation and schools of fish dart this way and that, not as a result of any knowledge, but in response to the situation. Still, it shows how hardwired behaviors lead to sophisticated behavior.

Cooperative behavior calls for sharing knowledge as well as the conscious desire to work together. Unfortunately, organizations are not intuitively structured for collaboration. As a result, efforts that result in breakthroughs in science, the arts, and technology come about infrequently.

Tools play a major role in shaping the way work gets done. So it is also reasonable to expect that using the proper tools that have been designed for collaborative work can help motivate teachers and administrators.

Language is a collaborative tool. In fact, language is at the core of virtually all the tools in a typical office—the phone, copier, dictating machine, and word processor. Without language, these tools are mute.

Most people can speak a language fluently. But it takes care, crafts-manship, and sincerity to speak in a way that consistently evokes un-derstanding and commitment. Most people also aspire to a high level of expression, so they need tools to help them achieve their goal. Under these circumstances, language is the main tool for teamwork because it boosts *collaborative* relationships.

Good tools do not ask you to become someone else. They invite you to create an extension of yourself. With a little time and skill, tools let you be more than what you are. Tools are a medium for self-expression.

Tools to support collaboration are qualitatively unique. Applying the collaborative tools explored in *Healing Public Schools*—total quality management (TQM), Baldrige, and ISO 9000—set the stage for using the tools treated in this and later chapters. And there's also the balanced scorecard (BSC), customer relationship management (CRM), and the data warehouse (DW). Each tool is vastly different from the array of antiquated tools provided to support administrators and teachers in to-day's school building. And well they should be!

STARTING WITH THE BALANCED SCORECARD

In the early 1990s, Robert Kaplan (Harvard Business School) and David Norton (Balanced Scorecard Collaborative) recognized some of the weaknesses and vagaries of long-standing management approaches. The BSC provides a clear prescription as to what the organization needs to measure in order to "balance" the financial and operating per-spectives (e.g., purchasing teacher consumables, operating a bus ser-vice, costs and returns in running the cafeteria, and productive class-room teaching time).

Like quality prescriptions dispensed in *Healing Public Schools*, the BSC is a management system (not just a measurement system) that en-ables the school organization to clarify its vision and strategy and to translate these into measurable action. For schools, the BSC provides feedback around both the internal business operating processes and ex-ternal educational outcomes in order to continuously measure and take decisions to improve strategic performance and results. When fully de-ployed, the BSC transforms the district's strategic planning from an ac-ademic exercise into the nerve center of the organization.

Kaplan and Norton describe the innovation of BSC as follows:

The balanced scorecard retains traditional financial measures. But financial measures tell the story of past events, an adequate story for industrial age companies for which investments in long-term capabilities and
customer relationships were not critical for success. These financial measures are inadequate, however, for guiding and evaluating the journey
that information age companies must make to create future value through
investment in customers, suppliers, employees, processes, technology,
and innovation.

The BSC asks that we observe the school organization from four
viewpoints and to develop metrics, collect data, and analyze it relative
to each of these angles:

- Learning viewpoint
- Business processes viewpoint
- Customer-centric viewpoint
- Financial viewpoint

MEASUREMENT-BASED PERFORMANCE MANAGEMENT

The BSC builds on key concepts of TQM, ISO 9000, and Baldrige, including customer-defined quality, continuous improvement, employee
empowerment, and, most importantly, measurement-based management and continuous feedback.

As discussed in *Healing Public Schools* and prior to ISO 9000 and
Baldrige, traditional industrial activity viewed "quality control" and
"zero defects" as watchwords. In order to protect the customer from
getting poor-quality products, efforts were aggressively focused on
end-of-the-production-line inspection and testing. The problem with
this approach—as repeatedly stressed by W. Edwards Deming—is that
actual *causes* of defects could never be identified, and inefficiencies
would remain high due to the rejection of defects. What Deming spot-
ted was that *variation* is created at *every step* in a production or service-
delivery process. The *causes* of variation need to be identified and
fixed. If this can be done *as it happens* (continuously), then we have

found the way to indefinitely reduce defects and improve product and service quality. To establish such a reliable process, Deming emphasized that all operational processes should be viewed as part of a system with feedback loops. The feedback data should be constantly examined by managers to determine the causes of variation and where the processes with significant problems are, and then focus attention on fixing that subset of processes.

Here's an example from everyday life. Jerry Seinfeld goes into the coffee shop and orders his favorite lunch—a tuna sandwich on rye bread with lettuce and tomato, no mayo. In a few minutes Seinfeld's waitress delivers the sandwich. He immediately notes the following: The lettuce is brown at the edges, the tomato is green at the center, the tuna looks slightly dried out, and the bread is as stiff as toast. Where in the process is the best place to catch and correct such quality variations? Is it Seinfeld's job to be the quality-control person? Is it his waitress at the point of delivery? Is it the sandwich maker in the back who assembles the ingredients for Jerry's sandwich? Is it the kitchen or coffee shop manager who sets out the daily ingredients? Or is it all of these persons who are in business to satisfy Seinfeld, the customer? Or should Seinfeld just stay silent and take the sandwich home to Cosmo Kramer?

The BSC includes feedback around internal operational process *outputs* (results), as in ISO 9000 and Baldrige, but also adds a feedback loop around the *outcomes* (results) of operational strategies. This creates the "double-loop feedback" process in the BSC.

OUTCOME METRICS

Straightaway you cannot improve what you cannot measure. Metrics need to be developed based on the priorities of the strategic plan to provide the key organizational drivers and criteria for metrics managers to track. Processes are to be designed to collect information relevant to these metrics and to reduce it to numerical form for storage, display, and analysis. Decision makers examine the results of various measured processes and strategies and track these results to guide the organization and provide feedback.

The value of metrics lies in its ability to provide a factual basis for defining:

- Strategic feedback to display for decision makers the present status of the organization from many viewpoints
- Diagnostic feedback into various processes to guide improvement actions on a real-time (continuous) basis
- Performance trends over time as the metrics are tracked
- Quantitative inputs to forecast methods for decision support systems

MANAGEMENT BY FACT

The goal of taking measurements is to allow administrators and teachers to see their school and classrooms more clearly—and from many viewpoints—to make better informed decisions. The Baldrige Education Criteria (2002) booklet and ISO 9000–2000 both stress fact-based management.

The BSC is not project management. It is also not another "flavor of the month" project. School administrators, reared on project management as the way, commonly think this way about achieving their mission. There is a long-established tradition of on-the-job training for young people to learn and be mentored by experienced project managers. Many guidebooks, manuals, software programs, and other means have been devised to aid the project manager. Project management has been in the management culture for several decades, and corporations have thousands of project managers who routinely track and run complex events. In fact, many project managers may have never seen or considered any other way to get things done.

The BSC management system is not project management. It is fundamentally different in several respects. To illustrate the radical nature of this difference, a clock diagram of the BSC performance measurement process would have the do-plan-check-act steps at its 12-3-6-9 time positions when installed in an organization.

This topology, the BSC management process, flows directly from Deming's TQM and it is a *continuous* cyclical *process*. It has neither a beginning nor an end. Its task is not directly concerned about the mission of the school organization, but rather with *internal processes* (diagnostic measures) and *external results* (strategic measures). The system's control is based on performance metrics that are continuously tracked over time to look for trends, to look for best and worst practices, and to identify areas for improvement. It delivers information to administrators and teachers for guiding their everyday decision making. But these are self-assessments, not stakeholder requirements or compliance data.

Persons trained only in project management may have difficulty at first in figuring out how to accomplish the BSC, simply because it is such a different kind of management paradigm. One of the practical difficulties is to figure out how to get the process started in the first place. If this is not a project, where does one begin? What kind of plan is appropriate for deployment of the BSC system?

The lesson is simply this: If we want to ride a rotating merry-go-round, we had better not attempt to just hop on. We will probably get hurt—so we won't get on. The situation is similar with the BSC. To get on the BSC plan-do-act-revise merry-go-round, we need to run alongside in the same direction for awhile, then hop on when our speed equals that of the circular floor. In other words, there needs to be a ramping-up phase, where everyone "comes up to speed." This includes training or retraining administrators and teachers, and probably focused deployment of pilot efforts before attempting to cover an entire large school district. Sustained, patient leadership is needed before the real payoffs are attained.

In the school, the first question asks school leadership and teachers to think through and then write down their approach to each process step. With this question, administrators and staff seek to unravel the complex processes used for meeting or improving each standard of the selected quality improvement process. This method asks the school to start from scratch and to evaluate each of its methods, tools, and different techniques. The second question begins to trigger the feedback of results and corrective action. Both steps are essential to the improvement of the school's quality control.

Deming is the expert whose quality processes helped to reshape postwar Japan. He gives us the following well-respected standard of continuous improvement: "Constantly improve design of product and service. This obligation never ceases . . . everyone, everyday must ask himself what he has done to advance his learning and skill on the job."

By now, it should be clear that achieving quality improvement is a step-by-step process. The quality school avoids "reinventing the wheel" each time a problem or situation crops up. The quality school strives to keep that proverbial wheel turning constantly. In this way, continuous improvement becomes ingrained into the school's daily practices. The quality school uses two rules of quality thinking: develop a plan for corrective actions and look for measurable feedback from quality actions.

PROCESSES LEAD THE WAY

The BSC and *Healing Public Schools* prescription demands that the school wrestle with the value of process improvement. At the outset, the major stumbling block may be the difficulty in grasping the consequences of processes. However, only in this way can school leaders, administrators, and teachers expect to achieve dependable teaching time in every classroom. And that is precisely what we are looking for.

Most people are in the habit of thinking solely in terms of *things*. We ordinarily think of products and specific elements. Most folks do not think much about the processes or underlying ways in which things— and services—are created and delivered.

Look at it this way: A process is merely a repeated activity that changes something. Grasping and improving the processes that underpin the BSC and *Healing Public Schools*'s six elements is central to school success. Putting it another way, the first step toward quality success is acceptance of what Baldrige and ISO 9000 are trying to get the school to do: to say what you're going to do, to write it down, to do it, to measure it, and to take corrective action. Evaluating and steadily improving all school processes is the challenge for approaching, organizing, and continually improving the reliability of classroom teaching time.

Resolving parent complaints is just as much a process as is recruiting, orientating, training, and staff development. Every repeatable school activity throughout the school district can be—no, in fact, needs to be—viewed as a process of events. In schools, the processes *are* the system. So the next time one of your neighbors declares that the #@$% school system has a problem, you can correct that angry statement. The problem needing attention is located in one of the processes that comprise the system (chapter 5 discusses CRM to help build more cooperative bridges with all school stakeholders).

One process step badly in need of continuous improvement is determining the readiness of the class when students start a new class. Teachers need to be notified of previous student performance in order to build this vital link into instruction (chapter 6 deals with using such data links when it discusses application of the DW to informed decision making).

THE MEASUREMENT PROCESSES

Two sets of more-or-less continuous data flows—downward and upward—comprise the double loop and help drive quality process decision making. Once the metrics and data collection procedures are defined, an information infrastructure helps manage the data flows. A database-backed Web intranet, a powerful CRM tool, is recommended both for data collection and data reporting. This can be developed at relatively low cost using available components. Web technology can support survey data collection and data reporting fairly easily.

Deploying public school quality process improvements is neither easy nor straightforward. Beyond the challenges of change management there are several other issues that confront implementers of quality process improvements. Among the most notable are who should best define mission-oriented metrics, the cost of collecting data, the need to balance staff fears with genuine incentives, and maintaining objectivity by avoiding micromanagement.

The concepts and data management efforts that are involved in quality process deployment are now well understood. It is clear that information technology (IT) systems can help support this work. However, the big implementation problems remain people problems: change of administrator and school staff perceptions, fear in the employee culture, and the limited incentives available within most school systems to counterbalance that fear. This is where we are now and these are the same issues to be continually confronted.

RESPONSES TO OBJECTIONS FOR DEPLOYING THE BSC AND QUALITY PROCESSES

1. The costs outweigh the benefits. What will we find that we didn't already know?
   • What is the cost of not proving your value?

- Today, stakeholders expect schools to show evidence of progress.
- Web sites can enable and automate much of this work—a new method that is easy and inexpensive to implement, relative to the tools available just a few years ago.
- Performance measurement has been demonstrated to be a "best practice" in terms of improving the student outcomes.

2. But some tasks will be labor intensive: metrics definition, software development, and data collection.
   - It's true that defining metrics is time-consuming and has to be done by administrators in their respective areas. But once they are defined, they won't change very often and some of the metrics are generic across all units, such as productive classroom time, customer satisfaction, staff attitudes, and so on. Software tools are commonly available to assist in this task.
   - Software development efforts should be kept to a minimum. There are now companies that specialize in this kind of software product, but most districts can probably leverage the existing DW to support this system.
   - Data collection can be supported using Web-based forms. Manual work such as collecting customer data, telephone interviews, and so on can be supported by broadening the work of the existing noninstructional personnel.

3. We have only limited control over results. Why should we be held accountable for things we can't control?
   - A school district's strategic initiative of customer service demands that it take responsibility for mission effectiveness and to improve customer relationships.
   - There is no alternative. School customers will understand its limitations if they are in a close partnership with the school.

4. The results will be used against us.
   - The results can also be used for us. What has been hurting schools more is not having any results to show.
   - What better way to gain resources from the sponsor than to clearly show them the consequences of the present situation.
   - We can't see our own blind spots. We need someone else to point them out to us. The measurements add visibility, even if it is painful.

- If the school excels, it is no longer generally true that a successful organization loses its budget.

5. Management will misuse or misinterpret the results. The process will be gamed.
   - That's why quality process improvement calls for several measures. Inspections such as the Baldrige assessments are done by a variety of dedicated people across the organization. They want to do a good, honest job.
   - The measurements will be validated by an independent team or third party.
   - The main purpose of quality process improvement is not individual performance, but collective organizational performance (another separate system is used for individual performance evaluations).
   - Results at the staff levels can be aggregated in such a way that individual employee performance is not reported out. This helps eliminate a source of fear that leads to gaming or failure to produce data.

6. They will score us by inappropriate or unfair standards.
   - Quality process allows each school to define its own metrics, at least the ones that are pertinent to each mission. That's the only way for the school to define its mission effectiveness.
   - Other metrics, like time and customer satisfaction, are generic across all organizations.

7. Too much complexity: There are numerous systems and quality assessment criteria, how will we combine them all (ISO 9000, Baldrige, TQM, and strategic initiatives)?
   - It is unnecessary to make a complex system. What's needed is a minimum basic set of measurements across various business perspectives and aligned to the strategic plan, as quality process improvement prescribes. We do need to develop ISO 9000 certifications when appropriate, but the metrics for them could be simple.
   - The purpose of system improvements is to clarify staff situations for senior administrators, not to make the system more complex.

8. It's too big, ambitious, and expensive to deploy a quality performance measurement system in an entire school district. We can't afford such large-scale efforts.

- Agreed. That's why we do not propose deployment across an entire school organization all at once.
- Rather, we propose to start small, in a school unit, and to develop incrementally.
- Experience will be gained before districtwide deployment is considered. This reduces cost, risk, and disruption.
9. How will you get everyone to do this?
   - We won't!
   - We know that one-third of administrators and teachers will welcome quality changes with open arms, one-third will sit on the fence to see what will happen, and the remaining one-third will fight it from the outset.
   - This is where administrative leadership earns its salary. It concentrates on bringing along the middle one-third while dispersing the resistant one-third to other assignments or early retirement.

DEALING WITH COMMON MISTAKES

A common mistake is to think that problems belong to an individual or to some special event. Today, we know that most problems are not isolated situations or special causes. They are not disconnected events. Those problems are built into the system. They are often chronic problems that persist over time. They are the consequence of some cause and effect that is buried deep in the unstudied processes of the complex linked system. Such flaws, if allowed to persist within the system, eventually reveal themselves in unexpected ways to block the school's desired end result.

Deming's lifetime of experience gives us insight into the character of processes deeply entrenched within the system that results in a startling statistic. Deming's experience is often quoted: "Fully 94 percent of the troubles an organization has can be attributed to the system. Only 5 percent are due to special causes."[17] Special causes are the occasional glitches that follow Murphy's Law. The bottom line to quality experts, parents, and educators is simply this: Concentrate on the processes and the end result will take care of itself.

A SHORT STORY WORTH REPEATING

The image of Ignaz Semmelweiss haunts America's schools and class-rooms. At the turn of the nineteenth century, Semmelweiss was an important and well-respected physician in Vienna. As a solid science professional of his day, he studied the reported birth and death statistics. He took special note of the higher incidence of death among women in childbirth that were attended by physicians than among those women attended only by a midwife.

Being intrigued, astonished, and curious, the doctor decided to study the reasons why this might be happening. He found that the physicians did not use as common practice the thorough washing of their hands or the washing of their equipment when they treated more than one woman.

When the data he collected became sufficiently large to allow him to make valid predictions, he went to his medical society to share his findings. He alerted his fellow doctors to the dangers of their lack of hand washing practices.

Understandably, his fellow physicians and former friends were, at first, very skeptical. When he continued to insist that they adopt as standard practice rigorous hand washing, they voted almost unanimously to remove him from the medical society. Furthermore, they discredited him publicly and ruined his reputation as a physician. He died a pauper in disgrace.

Today, a statue stands in his honor in the Vienna medical society headquarters. Medical doctors in Vienna, as well as all other doctors, now routinely use as an SOP the good practice of washing their hands and instruments thoroughly before working with a patient.

A patient going to a doctor in Vienna, Austria, or Vienna, Virginia, does not need to wonder or even be concerned about the reliability of his or her doctor using as an SOP in the office or hospital what the profession now accepts as good practice. Practitioners teach proper hand washing during orientation to all new healthcare employees and daily whenever the need arises. Hand washing is considered serious business and proper practice is enforced. We now know hand washing is important in the home, in schools, and in the workplace, as well as in hospitals. It is the number one prevention against the spread of infection.

With respect to accepting what the best that research has to offer, school teaching is a carbon copy of the doctor's mind-set in the Vienna Medical Society when Semmelweiss made his presentations. Tested, scientifically based teaching and management practices compete regularly in schools with untested, unscientifically based teaching and management practices. Worse yet, even when teaching or management practices in use are proven to be useless or even harmful for learning, they continue to be used. Customers—the students and the parents, as well as other stakeholders of this day—cannot assume that any particular teacher or school knows about or uses good practice in administration, teaching, and learning as its SOP.

Currently, school administration and teaching are unreliable professions. No parent sending his or her child to any school in any state can honestly be ensured by school administrators that his or her child's teacher will know his or her subject, know how best to teach it, or know how best to lead and manage the classroom so all children get maximum benefit.

It is the ghost of Semmelweiss that haunts America's schools and classrooms today. When it comes to receiving reliable quality classroom teaching, parents, students, and those who care deeply about the quality of schools need to substitute reliable performance management for the current tyranny of chance. Then someday we will be able to put Semmelweiss's ghost to rest from his job of haunting American education.

Given what we currently understand about using quality processes, the BSC, and other tools to improve the practice of school performance, it is a disgrace to continue to accept poor results.

SUMMING UP THE BSC

Ask any school board member, administrator, or teacher "What is your school district's most valuable asset?" and the answer is predictable: "Our people."

Every school organization has at least some good people. But if good people are everywhere and that's all it takes, they can't be a competitive advantage.

The correct answer is *good measurements*.

"A good metric," says Robert Kaplan, the author of the BSC, "is like a laser pen. It fits into the palm of your hand. You can take it with you wherever you go. Inside it is photons, and the photons keep the beam in phase and coherent. That's what good measurements do for you— they keep you in phase and coherent. They do not break up over distances. They keep telling the truth no matter how far out you go."[18]

These are Kaplan's four ground rules for the BSC:

1. When is a measurement good? When it measures what needs to be measured.
2. When is a measurement great? When it, like the BSC, is a powerful tool not just for diagnosis of the recent past (how're we doing?) but beyond that into the future for strategic implementation (where are we going?).
3. Diagnostic measures are vital signs. They tell you your current status.
4. Strategic measures go beyond that. They describe outcomes (results) and drivers (causes) of long-term value creation.

Healing Public Schools shows us the prescriptions and a good BSC tells everyone in the school organization, in a single page, the story of its entire district strategy:

• Every measure is part of a chain of cause-and-effect linkages
• All measures eventually link to organizational outcomes
• A balance exists between outcome measures (financial and student) and performance drivers (values, internal processes, learning, and growth)

The key to strategy is efficient implementation. Estimates are that fewer than 10 percent of all strategies that were effectively formulated are later effectively executed.

NOTES

1. *Peter W. v. San Francisco Unified School District* (60 C.A. 3d 814, 131 Cal. Rptr. 854, 1976).

2. *Donohue v. Copiague Union Free School District* (407 N.Y.S. 874 2d 64 A.D. 2d 29, 1978).

3. Eugene T. Connors, *Education Tort Liability and Malpractice* (Bloomington, Ind.: Phi Delta Kappa, 1981), 151.

4. *Gilliland v. Board of Education* (365 N.E. 2d 322, 1977).

5. George A. Clowes, "Texas Academic Standards Upheld," *School Reform News* 4, no. 3 (March 2000).

6. Clowes, "Texas Academic Standards Upheld," 1.

7. Clowes, "Texas Academic Standards Upheld," 1.

8. Clowes, "Texas Academic Standards Upheld," 2.

9. Clowes, "Texas Academic Standards Upheld," 2.

10. Clowes, "Texas Academic Standards Upheld," 2.

11. Clowes, "Texas Academic Standards Upheld," 2.

12. Clowes, "Texas Academic Standards Upheld," 3.

13. Connors, *Education Tort Liability*, 152.

14. National Society for the Study of Education, "Programmed Instruction," in *The Sixty-Sixth Yearbook*, pt. 2 (Chicago: National Society for the Study of Education, 1967), 261.

15. Allen Salowe and Leon Lessinger, *Healing Public Schools: The Winning Prescription to Cure Their Chronic Illness* (Lanham, Md: Scarecrow, 2001).

16. Marshall McLuhan, *Understanding Media* (Cambridge, Mass: MIT Press, 1968).

17. W. Edwards Deming, *Out of the Crisis* (Cambridge, Mass: MIT Center for Advanced Engineering Study, 1986), 315.

18. Robert Kaplan, The Masters Forum, University of Minnesota, Minneapolis, Minnesota, July 13, 1999.

CHAPTER 5

Customer Relationship Management in Education

Quality is never an accident. It is always the result of intelligent effort. It is the will to produce a superior thing.

—John Ruskin[1]

WHO IS THE SCHOOL CUSTOMER?

This question nags administrators and teachers when they start to think about the process of school change. By following a customer relationship management (CRM) path, the school leader can better define the school customer. Start by checking the following list for ideas on who fits the "C" in the school CRM. In education, customers may be:

- Students and prospective students
- Parents and guardians
- Alumni
- Faculty, administrative staff, and other employees
- Citizens
- Stakeholders in education
- Media contacts
- Businesses that are potential school partners
- Businesses that are future employers of the school's students
- Suppliers
- Government agencies
- Other educational institutions

Words like "competition," "efficiency," and "customer-trust" don't usually conjure up the image of school buildings, yellow buses, teachers, and students. But the same forces that have sparked large-scale changes in the world of business—the Internet, globalization, and the New Economy—have also left their mark on education. Chapter 1 briefly explored the enormous competitive impact of home schooling. Combined with the number of students in charter schools, the impact on conventional schooling is indeed considerable and growing. For the first time, the business world and the education sector face the same challenges and are increasingly being held to the same standards. As a result, schools need to turn to the same strategies as businesses—CRM—to accomplish the same types of objectives.

BREAKING DOWN BARRIERS AND BUILDING RELATIONSHIPS

Faced with heavily burdened taxpayers demanding more "bang for their school tax buck," education organizations have spent more time and effort to improve back-office operational processes, such as payroll, purchasing, and budget management. Now, the time has come for school organizations to break down departmental barriers and concentrate on building working relationships. To do so, they need to change "front-office" practices—that is, the way they provide services, market and present them, and collaborate with others.

This is where CRM comes in. CRM is part technology solution and part process redefinition; it connects the front and back office using analytical capabilities to help school organizations effectively manage all of their relationships. Automation figures significantly in this strategy, as does distribution of intelligent knowledge (data) and integration of schoolwide technology.

The result is collaboration, not compartmentalization. Service, support, and communication models are always proactive, never merely responsive. The payoff? Efficiency rises, which in turn drives costs down and quality of service up. Customer services are more directed and insightful, and partnerships become more productive. The customer's experience of interacting with such an education organization is more satisfying. This increases trust among the school's internal and external customer base.

NEW CHALLENGES NEED A PROVEN APPROACH

Such benefits make a world of difference whether you make widgets, teach math or English, or govern a nation. The ability to reduce costs, improve service, and increase trust is crucial for the education organization—especially now.

Educators may mistakenly assume that competition exists exclusively in the business world, but it's a factor for schools as well. Schools compete for faculty and students. Witness the turnover and shortage of teachers and the earlier discussion on competitive factors. Local and state governments aggressively compete for families and businesses that judge the quality of schools when considering relocation to an area. And everyone competes for skilled employees—and for scarce funding.

Such increased competitive pressures demand that a school organization differentiate itself. CRM helps them do so by concentrating the entire staff on improving service delivery and targeting customer satisfaction.

Budget accountability also defines the new customer age for schools. Sharp customers know the cost of schooling and they know that they are the ones paying the bill. Customers expect the school to operate efficiently not only because it will relieve their frustration, but also because it controls costs.

CRM helps provide answers. Processes are redefined and standardized, time-consuming tasks are automated, and knowledge is centralized. As a result, school employees are more productive—and increasingly cost effective. CRM Internet applications can help reduce expenses while building greater collaboration and trust.

The Institute for Electronic Government (an IBM affiliate) estimates that governments could save nearly 70 percent by providing services online rather than via traditional, over-the-counter methods. Today, it is increasingly common to access blank forms online and return them completed via the Internet. Add to this the time-and-cost savings the customer receives and the return on investment is even more compelling.

RELYING ON THE EXPERTS

Solution suppliers such as IBM are at the forefront of the CRM revolution in education. By leveraging their expertise, they offer educational institutions a solution that improves relationships with customers, employers, suppliers, and partners while reducing operational costs.

- The approach focuses on collaboration—technologies working together so that people can work together
- Schools can leverage CRM to target students, then orient them with personalized communications, upcoming courses, and campus activities
- CRM makes it easier for students to select and register for courses, review history, and receive online technical support
- Integrating human resources with financial management puts information at the fingertips of teachers and administrators serving customers

WHAT IS NOT CRM?

Without a clear definition of customer relationship, a school can hardly be expected to develop CRM tools to build and enhance its customer relationships. And since CRM is a fairly new concept, few people can give it a clear and workable definition. So it might be useful to look at what is not CRM. Rose Palmer, who pioneered the computer application of CRM, of PeopleSoft, a software developer and vendor, has done much work in this field.

CRM Is Not One-to-One Services

So far, CRM does not fit conventional marketing theory, so CRM application developers have had to find some new theory to promote their products. One-to-one marketing fell in place as the first logical choice. At the same time, one-to-one marketing needed to find more marketing applications to prove it. So to each it seemed ideal. This definition seems like the story in *Fiddler on the Roof* when the matchmaker wants to make a match between an unattractive girl and a man who can hardly see. It's a perfect match!

Such a match may cause people to immediately think CRM is one-to-one marketing. But this thinking is misleading to the future use of

CRM. Of course, one-to-one marketing is about customer relationship, but it is only about *one* possible relationship. It is one-to-one customer relationship. More importantly, this one-to-one relationship with customers is incorrect.

First, it is harmful as an operational philosophy. Perhaps the most important difference between people and other animals is that human beings can think in the aggregate. When we see a tree, we see it as a tree in a forest. When we see a student, we see him or her as *one* of the students. When we know the needs of a student, we are able to aggregate such information to conclude if other students have the same needs and if we should meet such needs (i.e., if such needs are not individual). There are many statistical techniques to help aggregate such information. However, one-to-one services would try to treat each student separately. They force teachers and administrators to think and treat students individually even though they are from the same segment. So in a one-to-one school enterprise, teachers would be trained to isolate students individually and to treat each student differently. This we know by definition and in practical terms does not apply.

CRM Is Not Personalization

Strictly speaking, personalization is also not one-to-one marketing although people use these two concepts interchangeably. Here's an example: The Amazon.com personal book recommendations illustrate that most personalization applications are actually market segment targeting. If I bought a book on Dante's *Divine Comedy*, I belong to one segment and all others belong to other segments.

Personalization sounds hot because it is about being personal. To personalize or not to personalize? Before such a decision is made, we need to know the danger in front of us.

CRM Is Not Database Applications

Did we manage to manage customer relationships before we had the computer? The database applications used in CRM are only a *tool* to help the school administrator and the teacher manage student and customer relationships more effectively. But they are not CRM itself.

Can CRM Really Help Build Customer Relations?

Most people worry about the detriment of its customer relationship after implementing CRM tools. They're rightly concerned about the infringement of customer privacy by CRM tools.

How could it be possible that a CRM application will be damaging to customer relationship?

When education leaders define the most important relationships among the internal school customers (teacher to teacher, support persons to educators, and so on) and between the school and its external customer (choose from the previous list), school leaders will be off to a strong CRM start.

LESSONS LEARNED IN CRM

Let's say the goal is to increase utilization of one of the school district's highly technical course programs. Presumably, there are technical experts within the staff and customer base that are internal champions for these programs. First, if we can get those experts to get more education about those programs, they are likely to become more enamored with the programs, and thus become a more supportive staff or customer.

Then, if we use a bit of fancy footwork to integrate the training registration information with the staff and customer records, we can track the correlation between more training and higher utilization rates. That's step one of CRM, and an easy win.

Step two is to begin harvesting the information we have about a staff member or customer and the resources he (or she) owns to suggest additional training, or additional services, that will be useful for him and his company. We might even get input on what a customer specifically needs or wants in the way of product training and develop courses to suit that customer. If a customer feels more in control of his professional development, he is likely to be more loyal to the vendor helping him to develop. Increased loyalty leads to increased utilization.

While these "discoveries" may not seem earth shattering, the school district is excited to learn how easy it will be to link some apparently disparate databases to be able to associate and harvest potential customer information. It seems reasonable that the school district could have some quick wins from CRM, while seeing results in less than two months at relatively low costs. Though the data itself won't score the district any big returns on investment, the users can turn the data into action plans that directly address customers' needs and interests, and that will yield the district a nice return on investment.

If district leadership wants to get its professional staff thinking more in terms of what CRM can do for their customers with the tools and information they have available today, there are numerous CRM consultants available. This approach might just open a few pairs of eyes to a whole new way of serving the district's staff and customer base.

CRM CASE STUDIES

Decision Making—New Hampshire Department of Education

The New Hampshire Department of Education (DOE) is an executive branch of the state government and is responsible for providing regulatory, oversight, and management services to New Hampshire schools and nearly eight thousand vocational rehabilitation clients.

The Challenge

New applications were needed to support the strategic decision-making processes for three different bureaus:

- Bureau of Information Services, which manages education statistical data
- Bureau of Credentialing, which regulates educator credentialing and standards
- Bureau of Career Development, which manages a variety of vocational, technical, and apprenticeship programs for the state

All three of these bureaus had been working with antiquated systems that no longer adequately supported their data collection, analysis, and reporting needs. Three new systems were required.

Solutions

Initially, Sierra Systems was asked to assist the DOE in ensuring that all new systems would be developed around a common core of well-defined data. Completed in 1996, the project provided Sierra Systems with a comprehensive understanding of all data collection and reporting requirements.

In a later project, Sierra Systems applied this knowledge to produce detailed Functional Requirements for the Education Statistics and Educator Information system projects using standard systems development and business process reengineering methods.

In 1998, Sierra Systems designed and developed a new Education Statistics System application. In this case, it employed object-oriented principles to design a multitier, Web-based data collection and reporting application to replace the then current, paper-based data collection process.

In the new Web-based application, users were able to enter information directly into online forms or through file transfer. In addition to facilitating the data collection process, the new database design provided DOE staff access to a variety of analytical reports, previously unavailable or difficult to produce.

The supplier's long-term view of the DOE–client relationships and the understanding of how to integrate new technologies into existing paper systems was the winning combination to provide the New Hampshire DOE with increased customer satisfaction.

Procurement Case Study—Chicago Public Schools

The Chicago Public School System has more than 600 schools and annually enrolls approximately 430,000 students. It employs 46,000, of which 26,000 are teachers and 580 principals.

In fiscal year 1998, the Chicago school system spent over $400 million on its major product and service categories: textbooks, office supplies, printing services, food, equipment, and education programs. The scope of the purchasing organization was limited, so volume discounts and opportunities for competitive pricing negotiations were not being realized. There were no processes in place to prevent maverick buying or to ensure the quality of products and services, so savings went unrealized.

The entire purchasing function went into a Strategic Sourcing Program model to be analyzed to help the school system align purchasing practices with its budget. Using an initial set of commodities, it began by:

- Providing analysis of existing purchasing expenditures, policies, processes, and organizational constraints
- Advising on appropriate best practices and cost-efficient and responsive purchasing strategies

The Solution

The focus fell in two key areas: past purchasing performance and supporting infrastructure. School system leadership and process owners gathered information, reviewed purchasing data, and mapped out purchasing processes. They then developed a detailed analysis of the existing purchasing organization, human resources, and IT infrastructure. From such reviews, short- and long-term improvement initiatives included:

- Prioritizing vendors and supplier relationships into high-, medium-, and low-value categories
- Evaluating opportunities to consolidate purchases of similar goods and services to leverage cost-saving benefits
- Analyzing purchasing patterns of key product groups to identify price negotiation opportunities

The Benefits

The strategic sourcing diagnostic effort provided a comprehensive review of personnel, processes, technologies, and the existing purchasing organization. Specifically found:

- Lopsided amounts of time and resources were spent on low-value transactions and suppliers accounting for a small percentage of total expenditures

- Significant opportunities to consolidate vendors in four out of six product categories

As a result, the Chicago school system realized a 35 percent savings on office supplies, office equipment, and printing services for a total savings of $26 million in its first year's annual budget. The supplier/vendor review and analysis also helped the district meet a federally mandated goal of awarding 30 percent of its business to Chicago-based minority-owned firms.[2]

Data Sourcing Case Study—California Department of Education

There's no substitute for hard facts when it comes to influencing decisions about funding education. There's certainly no shortage of information since departments of education across the United States amass a wealth of data on their school districts. But the fact that computers store data doesn't mean that people can easily get at it.

The Sacramento-based California Department of Education (CDE) began giving policymakers, education professionals, and the general public access to data on the school system from the convenience of its Web browsers. This is part of an overall effort by the CDE, in conjunction with the Alameda County Office of Education and other public agencies—collectively called the Education Data Partnership—to provide easy access to consistent, reliable, and objective information about the public school system.

Ways to Perform Complex Queries

The Web site, which can be accessed from the Education Data Partnership home page, provides fiscal data on all of California's one thousand elementary, unified, and high school districts.[3] Users can see how federal, state, and local funds allocated to their district compare with those allocated to other districts and to the state as a whole. They can select and search variables and the range of each variable, and they can output a variety of reports. Using the query tool, education professionals can locate districts that are similar to their own in particular respects. These districts can then serve as references when the educators argue their case for additional funding. The site uses pull-down menus as a means of drilling down to whatever information is needed.

Lower Unit Costs and Better Decision Making

The CDE expects the primary users of the site will be education professionals who deal with fiscal information. The districts are required by the CDE to submit the information, but the state has not done a good job of managing the data and putting it in a place where these professionals can get at it.

Prior to making the data available to the school districts, many had to join various associations and pay membership fees. The associations would come to the CDE to get the data, which, as public information, would be provided for a nominal fee. Then the association would develop the data and charge the districts for the reports, which were based originally on data that districts themselves had submitted. Essentially, districts spent money to get their own data back. Currently, the CDE is giving the districts direct access to the data, thereby helping them cut costs and providing information to more people, which leads to better decisions and to a higher quality of education.

Easier Access and Reporting

With the Internet and its own Web site, the CDE is better prepared to handle queries from education professionals and calls from the news media about the status of various education programs. University students and research groups ask us for data for their analyses. Businesses who sell to the education market are also interested in this data so they can follow trends in education programs and better position their product or service offerings. Even construction companies take advantage of data on funding for new schools to pinpoint upcoming building opportunities.

Soon, the CDE expects to provide school-level data that parents can use at school board meetings. There is also a wealth of data on teachers' education, pay levels, and benefits. Both the teachers' unions and the schools districts need this data to make intelligent decisions.[4]

In the private sector, enterprise-wide systems integrate data networks to better deliver services and products to their customers. These enterprise-wide systems are often referred to as "customer-centric" because they can provide information "responsively" to customers from synchronized databases. When a customer makes an inquiry, the vendor can respond with real-time information unique to that customer. This type of delivery system is CRM. It not only improves the customer-centric functionality of the company's networks, but it also enhances the services, manages the relationship, allows for meaningful segmentation, and provides unique treatment of each customer.

In the public sector, and especially in school systems, it is possible to mirror this same type of functionality within your IT structure. New tools tailored to school districts, cities, and counties are being developed and implemented. Such systems may come to be called *citizen* relationship management because citizens are also on our list of customers, and they have come to expect twenty-four-hour service and interactive delivery systems. All government entities, including schools, will need to respond to this heightened expectation.

USING TECHNOLOGY

School districts and city, county, and state governments are also being affected by the one-to-one trend. The possibility of treating each citizen differently is now here. There are many tools available to help. Some are designed specifically for the public sector to provide improved information services to citizens, making it easier for citizens to fill out forms, get answers to questions, and be informed on controversial public projects.

Technology can help enhance communication with citizens. The first step may be the use of a database for building a mailing list with intelligence. Starting with a current mailing list, the database would have various segments depicted based on interest, such as agriculture, traffic, utilities, technology, cultural arts, and development. Unique outreach messages can be sent to segments as various topics need to be addressed. Additional interests could be added as necessary. Sorting by category, geographic areas, level of interests, and alphabetically is now possible. Such a database can also note preferences on how *each* individual prefers to receive information, either by mail, e-mail, fax, or phone. Studies have shown an increase in response to messages sent through a person's preferred channel of communicating.

In addition, a project database allows recording a history of the individual's interaction with the process by noting such events as meetings, documents sent, and telephone and e-mail records. Anyone who has done business in the public sector immediately understands the value of ensuring that the right people receive the right information from the agency and that there is a record of it.

The next step is a Web site dedicated to current issues or projects and its processes. Picture for a moment a change in student dress code policy that previously was sent home with a mimeographed notice. Designed as a link to the existing home page, a series of Web pages dedicated to clarifying the purpose and implementation of the issue or project can clearly state the purpose, note a schedule of events and important public meetings, and further make available key reports and studies. The site can also be a place allowing dialogue to take place. Stakeholders can talk directly to the right persons or department or have a forum where questions can be asked as the process unfolds. In addition, if there are maps involved, various mapping concepts could be posted and made readily available to everybody involved in the process.

Combined, the database and the Web site will help reinforce traditional forms of outreach, such as notification mailings, feedback reports, surveying, important documents in draft and final stages, and any legally required notices.

Examples

In Santa Rosa, California, the city's Geyser Pipeline Project Data Instincts is responsible for public information and notification to areas potentially impacted by this unique public project that will pump millions of gallons of treated reclaimed water to geothermal wells forty-two miles away. Through its Web site and custom databases, detailed information is made available to those potentially affected.

In the Monterey County, California, General Plan Update, Data Instincts is responsible for public information and notification to areas potentially affected by the project.

The St. Johns County (Florida) School District Strategic Plan, two years in preparation, involved a significant cross section of the school stakeholder community. Plans are under way to evaluate CRM tools to extend the scope of citizen contact.

These projects use unique databases configured especially for them. The databases contain information on those who have an interest or are potentially impacted by such important projects, noting what meetings to attend, what documents are sent, and important e-mail and telephone communications.

A MONOPOLY AGENCY RESTORES THE TRUST

Even more so than the public schools, the Social Security Administration (SSA) is a full-fledged monopoly. And dealing with an SSA field office was once like dealing with the registry of motor vehicles. But now it's virtually painless. One after the other, satisfied customers stream out the door of an agency that provides a safety net for disabled workers, retirees, and survivors—and whose customers-for-life include every working citizen of the United States. People don't go into details. They just say good, good, good.

And that's what the SSA wants to hear. Faced with an uncertain future, the agency focused on using IT to better serve and educate its customers, both current beneficiaries and the public at large. And we need to constantly keep in mind that the SSA has less competition than public schools.

Through automation, SSA hopes its employees can better serve a growing number of beneficiaries, customers can better serve themselves, and the agency can gain greater public support. "One way people come to trust us is when they do business with us and we do a good job," says Antonia Lenane, senior adviser to the SSA commissioner on customer service integration in a *Washington Post* interview. "And getting the American public's trust is everything."

Motivation

Social Security has been a publicly charged issue since the 1930s, when politicians were divided over whether or not the government should provide such benefits. Today, advocating the elimination of such a popular program would be political suicide; debate focuses instead on how to solve the agency's long-term financial challenges and reform the system.

Andy Landis, the author of *Social Security: The Inside Story*, puts his finger on the implicit promise the agency makes to American workers with every paycheck deduction. "*Social* meaning we all go into it together, and *security* meaning it's secure. It's a safety net, not high-flying benefits."[5]

Some fear that this safety net is torn and can't be mended. They have reason to worry. Early in 2001, the General Accounting Office (GAO) reported to Congress that today's longer life expectancy, lower birthrates, and the coming retirement of baby boomers means that by 2030 there will be only 2.1 workers for every beneficiary, compared with 3.4 today and 5.1 in 1960. Once the SSA trust funds are depleted in 2037, annual current revenue will cover only 72 percent of annual promised payments. While politicians and pundits wrangle over whether to mend the net, reweave it, or throw it out, the SSA seeks to serve a growing pool of beneficiaries with a minimum increase in administrative costs. Customer service has always been woven into the agency's culture. But there are new incentives to providing good service to people who *have* to be customers.

Self-Help

Vice President Al Gore's National Partnership for Reinventing Government—created from the National Performance Review (NPR) in 1993 with the aim of making government work better and cost less—sparked Social Security to redouble its customer service efforts. And by many accounts, the efforts have paid off: in 2000, twenty-six million customers visited its thirteen hundred field offices, seventy million called its toll-free number, and ten million visited its Web site.

In the University of Michigan 1999 American Customer Satisfaction Index Survey, SSA courtesy and professionalism ratings were comparable to the *best* private companies. In the 1999 Government Performance Project conducted by Syracuse University and *Government Executive Magazine*, the agency received the only *A* awarded to a federal government agency for its use of technology to improve transactions. In the mid-1990s, Boston-based financial services research firm Dalbar ranked the SSA call center the *best* in the nation for courteous and efficient service.

In the late 1980s, the agency established one of the government's first toll-free, nationwide call centers. Social Security led the charge for showing that you can create customer service solutions using new technology.

Social Security online is already a big part of the agency's strategy for disseminating information.[6] Visitors can go to a "Top Ten" section that reflects what most people do at the site. They can download over two dozen forms, sign up for an electronic newsletter, find the hours and location of the nearest field office, and calculate estimated retirement benefits. Ultimately, SSA executives want customers to be able to conduct all Social Security–related business online, with full authentication and privacy guarantees. They also want to use the Internet to exchange wage data with employers. Meanwhile, they are installing more sophisticated routing software for the call center, getting field office employees the same automated onscreen answers that call center agents have, and making sure that information is available in several languages, with files coded so that notices are sent in the appropriate language.

The agency is constantly trying to automate whatever it can. Not only does automation speed things up, but employees have good tools at their disposal that make it easier for them to be courteous.

Outreach

Fifty million Americans receive Supplemental Security Income and Old Age, Survivors, and Disability Insurance payments each month. But the SSA now considers the entire taxpaying public its customers, too, and is reaching out to it in the form of earnings information and benefit estimates sent each year to workers aged twenty-five and older. Commissioner Kenneth Apfel states, "If we can touch each person on a yearly basis, we can help them not only think about what else they need to do to prepare for retirement but also when to retire."

In truth, retirement is the least of SSA concerns. Benefits are straightforward — a set amount based on lifetime earnings and retirement age — so those systems have been pretty easy to automate, administrators say. Disability, however, is another "beast," one that the GAO makes clear is hurting the agency. Although most payments go to retirees, a disproportionate amount of administration is spent on disability. Situations are harder to evaluate, medical conditions change, and sometimes beneficiaries are dishonest. Claims can spend many months backlogged, tied up in paperwork, or under appeal. The agency is working on software that will streamline the process of determining who qualifies for how much disability and making sure that every single check SSA writes is the right amount for the right person.

Independent organizations are involved in the program. Private companies focus on selling, marketing, and improving the customer interface and collecting the bills. The agency tries to make sure that customers are in the situation they say they are. They don't classically think of that as customer service, but think of it as broader service to taxpayers.

At any government office, serving customers is more complicated than just doing what makes them happy. The staff feel they are the stewards of the taxpayers' money. Whenever they look at an initiative to improve customer service, they have to ask whether there are risks: To avoid bad publicity like the uproar when benefits information was put online, they have to figure out how to make it happen with the resources they have.

Stones Unturned

Even a model government agency with a stack of customer service awards has a long way to go. Younger people especially mistrust the agency—fueled by opponents of government-sponsored social services and by investment houses that stand to make a profit if the system is privatized. In their early years, young people think it's just a rip-off. As they near retirement, they begin to think it's a valuable benefit and they take interest in seeing it preserved. Every generation has thought "it probably won't be there for me," and it turns out to be there. Social Security could run dry, but only if it doesn't make the necessary changes. In its 2000 annual report, the Social Security Advisory Board noted that although the agency's difficulties will grow in the next decade, it has a number of service delivery problems that need attention now.

Never mind getting worse—things are bad enough already, the report seems to say, citing problems with telephone hold times, crowded field offices, and heavy employee workloads. A February 2000 testimony from the GAO stressed the extent and seriousness of SSA's challenges, reporting that the agency had "mixed success" in implementing IT initiatives, such as a failed seven-year effort to automate disability claims.

At headquarters in Baltimore, administrators are undaunted. They were happy but not satisfied with the results. The SSA will keep finding new ways to listen to customers and to serve them more efficiently. It already has a searchable database on its Intranet, where employees can read the results of surveys, focus groups, and interviews with customers. The SSA is also developing a uniform, automated system for tracking the resolution of both individual complaints and larger, systemic problems.

Commissioner Apfel says the answers to the SSA's service challenges must come from IT. "The Internet has to be our way to provide service to millions and millions in the future," he says. "I think the Social Security Administration will always be part of the fabric of this country, but we could be hurt if we don't stay up with the technology."[7]

SERVING THE PUBLIC CAN ONLY GET TOUGHER

Serving the public has never been more challenging for schools. And as economic and social conditions change, this calls for school administrations to rethink their responsibilities as well as their methods for delivering services, managing costs, and communicating with professional staff, stakeholders, and customers. By integrating CRM process flows, higher-quality data can help teachers and other employees create more service-oriented administrative processes and more accurate cost-management initiatives. Such application can also help users gather, analyze, and distribute the information needed for better planning and decision making.

The benefits and efficiencies of CRM lie in the seamless integration of process flows—accounting, budgeting, funds management, procurement, and personnel management—to deliver fast, productive, and tightly organized management processes. School-specific capabilities include the following:

- Stakeholders can use Internet portals to gain role-based, personalized access to public information, services, and functions. Such platforms offer access to central directories of school services and information, as well as collaborative procurement opportunities for the agency. CRM can also support online services and payments through Web-based interfaces and provide other customer service management functions. Electronic records management helps control document storage and provides proper documentation of business transactions.

- CRM can help deliver transparent, organization-wide control of budgets and financial planning with financial accounting functions. Other tools can handle grant allocation, planning, and management, as well as reporting requirements. In addition to providing personnel and payroll procedures, the CRM solution facilitates human capital planning and management.

- CRM tools can seamlessly integrate data from various sources to help school organizations better understand the alignment of tactical activities with strategic goals. Administrations can link strategic goals with operational considerations, execute budgetary simulations, and monitor demographic shifts in the district. CRM can also create knowledge libraries to handle structured and unstructured information in a wide variety of formats and support e-learning scenarios.

- Users can also integrate business processes for all essential tasks arising from processing and managing facilities and equipment maintenance and property administration.

In summary, CRM can help guide the school organization toward meeting the changing and demanding needs of its stakeholders through readily available information and workable tools. CRM provides a consistent view of each customer (internal and external), and the organization can customize information and services to meet the needs of specific groups. Stakeholders can access public information over the Internet, at a contact center, or face to face. CRM helps schools to measure their performance, to keep up with changing citizen needs, and to determine how and when to alter services. E-functions of CRM enable the school organization to provide valuable public information in a timely manner. At the end of the day, CRM helps schools build public and staff support.

NOTES

1. Karen Leland and Keith Bailey, *Customer Service for Dummies*, 2nd ed. (Foster City, Calif.: IDG, 1999).

2. KPMG Consulting Services, August 3, 2001, <http://www.kpmgconsulting.com/library> [last accessed: January 7, 2002].

3. See <http://www.ed-data.k12.ca.us> [last accessed: January 7, 2002].

4. IBM Business Intelligence Web site, August 2, 2001, <http://www.ibm.com> [last accessed: January 7, 2002].

5. Andy Landis, *Social Security: The Inside Story* (Menlo Park, Calif.: Crisp Publications, 1997), 25.

6. See <http://www.ssa.gov> [last accessed: January 7, 2002].

7. Sarah Scalet, "Repairing the Trust," *CIO Magazine*, 15 August 2000, <http://www.cio.com/archive> [last accessed: January 7, 2002].

CHAPTER 6

The Right Data Guides Student-Centered Decision Making

To this point, our story has focused on *why* there is the need for student-centered performance management and *how* to use currently available tools to reach this goal. We have explored the extensive benefits of applying customer relationship management across the board to serve a broad array of school customers. Together, serving each customer group helps bring the school organization to peak performance.

The tool that helps administrators, teachers, and staff keep the gears of school processes moving smoothly and professionally is *useful* information. And such information is drawn from *useable* data. The collection of computer-based information that is critical to the successful execution of school enterprise-wide initiatives is called a data warehouse.[1]

DATA WAREHOUSING FOR SCHOOL IMPROVEMENT

In school improvement, we are constantly looking for a shared commitment to outstanding student outcomes and continuous improvement of those results. We also know that teachers, building administrators, parents, district administrators, support staff, and so on may differ in their commitment to such improvement. When we move into the world of designing and building data tools to foster school improvement, we are treading into areas not normally ventured into by educators.

RAISE THE CEILING NOT LOWER THE FLOOR—DATA EXPECTATIONS FOR STUDENTS

Administrators, teachers, and staff must believe that they can make a real difference in the life of each student. That's a tall order, but in the most successful higher income schools, expectations for children are at the excellent level rather than the satisfactory level.

In less successful schools, there are belief statements that all students can learn. While teachers may say this and some may even believe it, the lack of a uniformly challenging curriculum that is repeatedly and reliably measured for results casts doubt as to whether there is a genuine belief that all students can really learn at high levels. As much as teachers may try to distance themselves from the self-fulfilling prophecy that students cannot perform at levels established by their state departments of education, there are pained explanations that reflect teacher and staff lack of conviction that they can make a difference in the learning lives of their students.

CLEAR AND EXPLICIT GOALS

Data strongly influences the development of agreed on goals. While all schools now have written goals and mission statements, they differ with respect to the real focus and measurements on meeting the stated intentions. Better schools put more attention on academic achievement; other schools focus on attendance and attitude as priority. But in the most successful schools, goals for high-level results are clear, explicit, and measurable.

In too many schools, there is more attention to short-term goals in the school improvement plan and these are not clearly linked to the underlying needs of the school to align with state assessments, even though student improvement on assessment tests is spelled out as a goal. In too many cases, teachers are unable to articulate what the mission or goals are for their school. A concern that many teachers express is a lack of standards and sticking by them.

WHAT IS DATA WAREHOUSE AND WHAT ARE ITS INTENTIONS?

A data warehouse (DW), or more accurately an "information warehouse," is a subject-oriented database designed with enterprise-wide access in mind. The enterprise can be defined as a school, a district, a county, or a state. DW provides tools to satisfy the information needs of managers at all organizational levels—not just for complex data queries, but also as a *general facility* for getting quick, accurate, and often insightful information. A DW is designed and intended so its users can easily recognize the information they want and then access that information for use in making better decisions using simple tools.

A DW blends technologies, including relational and multidimensional databases, graphical user interfaces, and more. The data in the DW differs from operational systems data in that this data is read-only, meaning that it cannot be modified. Operational systems create, update, and delete production data that "feed" into the DW. The principal reason for developing a DW is *to integrate operational data from various sources into a single and consistent warehouse that can support analysis and proper decision making within the defined school enterprise.*

For those school enterprises that believe information is a valuable resource, a DW is analogous to a physical warehouse. Operational systems create data "parts" that are loaded into and stored in the warehouse. Some of those parts are summarized into information "components" and stored in the warehouse. DW users make requests and are delivered "products" that are created from the components and parts stored in the warehouse.

DW has become one of the most popular and stable industry trends—for good reason. A well-defined and thought out DW, properly implemented, can be a valuable performance management tool.

SUMMARY OF DW BENEFITS

- More cost-effective decision making. A DW allows for simplification. It eliminates staff and computer resources ordinarily required to support data queries and reports against operational and production databases. This typically offers significant savings by eliminating the resource drain on district IT systems when executing long-running complex queries and reports.

- Better enterprise intelligence. Increased quality and flexibility of school analysis results from the multitiered data structures of a DW that support data ranging from detailed performance level to high-level summaries. Guaranteed data accuracy and reliability result from ensuring that a DW contains only "trusted" data.
- Improved customer service. The school enterprise can maintain better relationships with all classes of customers by linking customer data via a single DW.
- Process reengineering. Allows unlimited analysis of school information often by providing fresh insights into school processes that may yield breakthrough ideas for reengineering such processes. The act of defining the requirements for a DW almost always results in better school goals and measures.
- Information system reengineering. A DW based on districtwide data requirements provides a cost-effective means of establishing both data standardization and school system interoperability.

DW COMPONENTS

The following primer describes each of the components of a DW based on the work of W. H. Inmon, the father of the DW concept.[2]

Current Detail

The heart of a DW is its current detail. It is the place where the bulk of data resides. Current detail comes directly from operational systems—district consolidation of individual schools—and may be stored as raw data or as an aggregation of raw data. Current detail, organized by subject area, represents the *entire* school enterprise, rather than a given application.

Current detail is the lowest level of data granularity (ranging from coarse to fine grain) in the DW. Every data entry in current detail is a snapshot, a moment in time, representing the instance when the data are accurate. Current detail is typically two to five years old and is refreshed as often as necessary to support district requirements.

System of Record

A system of record is the source of the best or "most correct" data that feed the DW. The "most correct" data are those that are most timely, complete, accurate, and conform best to the DW. The "most correct" data usually come from closest to the source of information—teachers, principals, and so on. In other cases, a system of record may be one containing previously summarized data.

Integration and Transformation Programs

Even the "most correct" operational data cannot usually be copied, as is, into a DW. Raw operational data are virtually unintelligible to most end users. Additionally, operational data seldom conform to the logical, subject-oriented structure of a DW. Furthermore, different operational systems represent data differently, use different codes for the same thing, squeeze multiple pieces of information into one field, and more. Operational data can also come from many different physical sources: old centralized computer files, nonrelational databases, indexed flat files, and even proprietary tape and card-based systems. Thus, operational data must be cleaned up, edited, and reformatted before being loaded into a DW.

As operational data items pass from their original systems of record to a DW, integration and transformation programs convert them from application-specific data into enterprise-wide data. These integration and transformation programs perform functions such as:

- Reformatting, recalculating, or modifying key structures
- Adding time elements
- Identifying default values
- Supplying logic to choose between multiple data sources
- Summarizing, tallying, and merging data from multiple sources

When either operational or DW environments change, integration and transformation programs are modified to reflect that change.

Summarized Data

Lightly summarized data are the hallmark of a DW. All school enterprise elements (department, school, district, specialized function, and so on) have different information requirements, so effective DW design provides for customized, lightly summarized data for every enterprise element. A districtwide element may have access to both detailed and summarized data, but there will be much less than the total stored in current detail.

Highly summarized data are primarily for districtwide administrators. Highly summarized data can come from either the lightly summarized data used by districtwide elements or from current detail. Data volume at this level is much less than at other levels and represents an eclectic collection supporting a wide variety of data needs and interests. In addition to access to highly summarized data, generally administrators have the ability to access increasing levels of detail through what is commonly called a "drill down" process. As the term implies, the user digs deeper for the desired information.

Archives

DW archives contain old data (normally over two years old) of significant, continuing interest, and value to the school district. There is usually a massive amount of data stored in the DW archives that has a low incidence of access. Archive data are most often used for forecasting and trend analysis, such as student registrations and geographical distributions. Although archive data may be stored with the same level of detail as current data, it is more likely that archive data are aggregated as they are archived. Archives include both old data (in raw or summarized form) and metadata that describes the old data's characteristics.

Metadata

One of the most important parts of a DW is its metadata—or data about data. Also called DW architecture, metadata is integral to all levels of the DW, but exists and functions in a different dimension from other warehouse data. Metadata that is used by DW developers to manage and control DW creation and maintenance resides outside the DW. Metadata for DW users is part of the DW itself and is available to control access and analysis of the DW. To a DW user, metadata is like a "card catalog" to the subjects contained in the DW.

DW Structure

A DW may have any of several structures:

- Physical DW—a physical database in which all the data for the DW are stored, along with metadata and processing logic for scrubbing, organizing, packaging, and processing the detail data.
- Logical DW—also contains metadata including districtwide rules and processing logic for scrubbing, organizing, packaging, and processing the data, but does not contain actual data. Instead, it contains the information necessary to access the data wherever it resides.
- Data mart—a subset of a districtwide DW. Typically, it supports an enterprise element (department, school, specialty function, and so on). As part of an iterative DW development process, an enterprise builds a *series* of physical data marts over time and *links* them via an enterprise-wide logical DW or feeds them from a single physical warehouse.

DW Development

There are three popular "approaches" for DW, two of which are bad.

1. "Data dump"—all enterprise data is replicated or made available with no attempt made to "scrub" or even categorize the data. Its like *dumping* all the contents in a physical warehouse in the middle of the floor and asking people to pick out what they need.
2. "Magic window"—access to the data wherever it exists throughout the enterprise, again without ensuring data quality. It's like a big sack in which there are rubies, emeralds, gold nuggets, broken glass, rat droppings, and poisonous snakes. At some point, you quit putting your hand in the bag.

3. "Strategic DW"—is enterprise-wide data based on the organization's requirements.

Computer-based tools provide the flexibility and capability to easily develop an enterprise-wide, strategic DW.

THE ENTERPRISE-WIDE STRATEGIC DATA APPROACH

The key to DW development success is using an iterative approach that includes active participation of the potential users—administrators, teachers, and other staff.

Like any large information systems project, DW development can get bogged down if the scope is too broad and the number of people involved is too large. A *clear purpose* and *scope* is necessary to manage the application of information systems resources as well as manage the expectations of the potential DW users. The enterprise-wide approach limits the scope by building a DW, one data mart at a time. Each data mart supports a single organizational element, enterprise function, or object (i.e., customer, service subject, curricula, and so on), and the scope of development is limited by the data mart requirements. To start with, the initial data mart usually provides the DW *proof-of-concept*; the scope is sufficient enough to provide real, immediate, and high-profile benefits. After the first data mart is developed and implemented, additional data marts are developed and integrated over time as enterprise needs dictate and as resources are available.

Designing and developing a DW using this approach involves four very different activities: (1) identifying enterprise-wide needs, (2) designing DW architecture, (3) applying appropriate technology, and (4) implementing the DW.

Identifying Enterprise-Wide Needs

Identifying enterprise-wide needs is a major component in the life cycle for any information system, and it is crucial when building a DW. When developing operational systems, there is often one single enterprise administrative sponsor or one group of users with a clear view of what he or she needs, what the system should look like, and how he or she sees using it. Conversely, when developing a DW, there are normally multiple potential users, each with a different idea of what a DW is and what it will provide, and all requesting or demanding action. Because of this lack of focused direction, *identifying precise enterprise needs* is critical to the success of a DW project.

DW needs must be expressed in terms of both enterprise-wide measures and critical success factors. What is it the school user is going to measure and what is it intended to prove. A school district's strategic plans typically provide the basis for defining preliminary enterprise needs. The best technique for refining these preliminary enterprise-wide needs (or defining them if no strategic plan is in place) is to conduct a series of facilitated focus group sessions. Participants in these sessions are the potential DW users (customers) for whom the information in the DW is important. Because the DW is important to them, these individual customers are willing to invest the time needed to describe their information needs.

Planning takes great pains to resolve all data conflicts in the DW model before continuing with the next phase of the development cycle.

Designing DW Architecture

Clearly defining the enterprise DW architecture involves identifying the correct source of raw operational data to populate the DW. This effort also addresses possible integration and transformation logic. Identifying the systems of record for DW data entities is one means of validating enterprise measures.

Measurement Intervals

To completely define the enterprise-wide measures includes describing the intervals or time periods to be used for measurement. How often is it useful to capture and measure student or teacher performance? How much historical data will be needed? This varies greatly by administrator and school district. The U.S. Federal Reserve Bank measures in monthly, quarterly, and annual increments and uses years of historical data to determine trends in the economy. A telephone sales operation, however, uses hourly measures and may only keep a few weeks of information.

Applying Appropriate Technology

The enterprise documents the measures (outcomes) and critical success factors (results) as planning statements and documents the supporting data entities in a corresponding data model. DW data entities are those whose values at any point in time are necessary to tell DW users how well the enterprise is performing. Providing a clear and unambiguous definition of every key data entity, describing the way each is used, as well as defining derivation formulas, aggregation categories, and time periods, are activities critical to capturing a clear understanding of a school's measures. The resulting enterprise model links enterprise needs with DW data entities and enterprise rules. Together, these become required documentation and a source for communicating the contents of the DW to its customers.

Implementing the DW

After identifying and defining enterprise-wide needs, structuring the architecture, and applying proper technology, it needs to be communicated throughout the school enterprise. The best justification for pursuing a DW project is the synergy the school organization realizes through the *process* of defining and then communicating the critical departmental success factors and measures. Everyone in the school organization becomes aware of precisely what defines success and how it is measured. In addition, the measures undergo a "reality check" by people who were *not* involved in their development. This feedback is used for refining the measures.

Resolving Data Conflicts

A well-defined DW model cannot contain homonyms, synonyms, and other data definition conflicts. The reason such data conflicts may exist is because most enterprises have one or more major terms that are used by everyone in the organization but mean different things in different organizational settings. One of the most commonly misused terms is "customer."

To the finance department, "customer" could mean the school organization (or the individual) who initiates a purchase order. "Customer" could also mean the student (the individual receiving service) or the board (whose policies the school employees serve). To the public information department, "customer" could mean the community, business entities, political structure, the media, school employees, as well as parents and guardians. Providing any one of these interpretations as the enterprise definition of customer would not meet the needs of the school enterprise and would doom its DW effort to failure due to "bad data."

USER NEEDS

Naturally, the amount and specificity of data aggregation categories in a DW depends directly on the types of individuals who participate in the design sessions.

- Strategic thinkers tend to be looking for the *big picture* answers and therefore need very few aggregation categories. The "roll-ups" for each strategic aggregation of data, however, can be quite complex.
- Operational thinkers have a tendency to want to dissect and review *every measure* by every category used in their part of the enterprise. This will tend to require large numbers of less complex aggregation categories.

CONCERNS FOR SECURITY

A DW is a read-only source of enterprise information; thus, administrators and teachers need not be concerned with controlling create, update, and delete capabilities. But developers do need to consider trade-offs between protecting a valuable education asset against unauthorized access and making the data accessible to anyone within the school organization who can put it to good use. The best solution found thus far is to allow everyone in the school organization to have access to the enterprise-wide measure definitions and derivations, but limit access to the underlying detailed data on an approved, need-to-know basis.

USER INTERFACES

DW users get useful information through a user interface. It is such user interfaces that have the most impact on how effective and useful the DW is perceived by users. Two criteria for selecting an effective user interface are ease of use and performance. For ease of use, most enterprises turn to graphical user interfaces that Windows or Mac users are familiar with. For performance, developers need to ensure that the hardware/software platform fully supports and is optimized for every chosen user interface.

The key selection criteria for user interface are the *information needs* and the level of *computer literacy* of potential users who will retrieve the needed information from the DW. Since there is no right or wrong type of DW user, the following categories may help define the interface based on levels of literacy and information needs in the future.

- Information-systems challenged—DW users who are hopelessly lost when it comes to information systems. In management roles, they rely on their secretaries or assistants to retrieve information for them. These users need an extremely easy-to-use and highly graphical interface.
- Variance oriented—DW users who are focused on variances in numbers over time. These users mainly want a set of standard reports that they can generate or receive periodically so that they can perform analyses.
- Number crunchers—DW users who are spreadsheet fans. They take whatever data is available and refine it, recategorize it, and derive their own numbers for analyzing and managing. Their needs are best met by providing a spreadsheet extract output format for any reports or ad hoc queries provided.
- Technically oriented—DW users who are already familiar with computers and have sufficient motivation to learn and use everything they can get their hands on. These people want to have complete control

over the way they retrieve and format information. They are often systems analysts who have moved into an education function. They want to have all of the tools the DW development staff uses.

Most school organizations have all of these categories of individuals. This makes it advisable to provide each type of DW user interface.

The final user interface decisive factor is that it be able to support access to the DW. If a user interface is easy to use, allows all potential users to get the information they need in the format they need, and does it in an acceptable amount of time, it is the right interface.

IMPLEMENTING THE DW

Summing up, DW implementation includes loading the right data, designing a user interface look and feel, developing standard queries and reports, and thoroughly training DW users. In the final analyses, the education enterprise is totally responsible for ensuring that its DW is implemented and becomes a school enterprise-wide asset.

BLUEPRINTS FOR BUILDING A DW

"Design engineering" a DW is a lot like "design engineering" a physical warehouse. Both involve a rigorous development cycle and require the right tools. A building is constructed using architectural diagrams (blueprints) that clearly depict the building's infrastructure (foundation, walls, roof, electrical wiring, plumbing, and so on). The DW is also built from architectural models of school enterprise infrastructure (policies, goals, measures, desired outcomes, results, and so on).

Blueprints are also used to enlarge an existing building or to make any significant modifications. Without a diagram of the infrastructure, such changes are difficult and are very costly. The same holds true with DWs. Initially, update an enterprise architecture model so that it reflects changes (e.g., new courses or new services) and then modify the DW to support such changes.

DW engineering change is far easier and less costly when based on an accurate architectural model of the school enterprise. Furthermore, a DW is easier to use and consistently produces desired outcomes when decision makers have access to an enterprise architecture that accurately reflects enterprise-wide infrastructure.

NOTES

1. Some data warehouse details are drawn from Alan Perkins, who is the managing principal of Visible Systems Corporation.
2. W. H. Inmon, *Building the Data Warehouse*, 2nd ed. (New York: Wiley, 1996).

CHAPTER 7

The College of Engineering Helps Bring Education into the Twenty-First Century

Accountability for student learning requires meeting state and federal mandates. To understand such mandates calls for an "engineering mind-set." At its best, engineering fosters ingenuity, creativity, and resourcefulness.

In this chapter, we explore some of the major weaknesses of the colleges of education and why technology seemingly finds it difficult to thrive in education circles. Throughout the United States and around the globe, the engineering schools—and not the colleges of education—include courses in ISO 9000 Education Standards and the Malcolm Baldrige National Quality Program Criteria for Education in their curricula. Community colleges have numerous courses in these same quality processes and standards. We intend to pioneer a discussion on this subject.

Together, the authors enjoy considerable firsthand experience with engineering design and engineering management principles as well as a broad range of subject matter.

APPLYING ENGINEERING PRINCIPLES TO CLASSROOM TEACHING

Is it possible to consider "engineering principles" an important phase of classroom teaching? To the majority of educators who train our classroom teachers and administrators in the colleges of education, engineering might signal a cold, technological, and seemingly dehumanizing process. If pressed, educators might say (because the topic is rarely discussed) that education is really concerned with the keeping and spread of all that is especially human.

To probe one's personal thoughts and feelings, or, more generally, "looking into or under the surface of things," is called introspection. Let us look, in an introspective way, at engineering and engineers to help answer the question.

Today, wide-ranging, thoughtful discussions are heard at engineering conferences, seminars, and meetings about the changing role of engineers in modern society. Such discussions were rarely heard in the past. How could it be otherwise considering the social upheaval of the 1960s, the environmental crisis of the 1970s, the political turmoil of the 1980s, and the progression of a totally altered global, information-driven economy in the 1990s and still today?

Introspection coming from engineers parallels an increasing interest in technology on the part of politicians, historians, ethicists, and social scientists. It is hardly news to report that people in all walks of life are waking up to the importance of science and technology in their daily lives. And it is not much of a stretch to argue that engineering is increasingly becoming central to our lives.

The UN Human Development Index ranks nations on what they do to meet basic needs: keeping persons healthy, raising education standards, and helping persons earn the income needed to make choices. Most technologically advanced nations achieve the highest ratings.

For all the compassion and good will toward others, every nation is engaged in a fierce battle to carve out a stake in world commerce. And in each nation the quality of its schools is on the front lines of that battle (chapter 8 offers ample evidence of the role engineering-type thinking plays in education around the globe).

But here, we make the case that the application of engineering principles to education, particularly its mind-sets for finding solutions to complex problems, is a major factor in the striving of those frontline "fighters." We are aware that this observation may meet with stiff resistance among educators. What we are talking about is linking essential courses from the college of engineering with the training of new teachers. That would come as a revolutionary step for most college of education faculty, and no doubt, for teachers and school administrators. We would dare estimate that less than a negligible percentage of colleges of education faculty have any engineering background or experience. Samuel C. Florman gives perspective on the major reasons for a struggle of acceptance of this powerful new concept in education because ultimately all real change in schooling is dependent on the understanding and acceptance of the general public. He writes:

> Yet engineering is not a word one is likely to hear in our communal discussions—for example, on Sunday morning television interview programs. Everybody agrees that we live in an era of "high tech," and that technology has changed our lives. Multimedia, virtual reality, information highway, genetic engineering—these are buzzwords of the day. But real engineers, the people who conceive of computers, and oversee their manufacture, the people who design and build information systems, cars, bridges, airplanes, and so many other things that are central to our lives, are nameless and obscure.[1]

INSIGHTS INTO THE NATURE OF ENGINEERING

If engineering is one side of a coin, science and technology is the other.

Before anthropologists—humanists and social scientists—even start to identify a particular skull to determine if it may be human, they search the area where it was found for evidence of tools. Along with certain physical measurements, the evidence of tools is the surest way of making an accurate determination.

The definition of the word "technology" helps us understand this reasoning. The word comes from the Greek "techne." It was the word the Greeks used to describe art and skill in making things. "Techne" describes the work of a sculptor, a stonemason, a composer, or an engineer. The suffix "ology" means the study or the lore of something. "Technology" then in its first meaning is the study of the art and skill of making things, things as different as a machine, a piece of music, or a building. There is also a technology of organizing human enterprises—including managing schools. Like all enterprises, schools have people trying to make products or deliver services.

THE ENGINEERING WAY OF THINKING

The engineering cast of mind is a particular way of approaching problems that is sorely needed to solve them. This is the major argument for linking engineering courses as part of the design and execution of classroom teaching. Florman addresses this matter well:

Our public debates are too often characterized by passion, ill will, and distortion of the facts, sometimes intentional and sometimes unwitting. Engineers are trained to solve problems, adhering to facts and truths of experience, shunning personal sentiment, or at least recognizing it for what it is. Engineers do not expect to find perfect solutions, because in their work there usually are none; they seek optimum solutions, given constraints of time, materials, and money. Their objective is to get a product "out the door," on schedule and within budget. They have to take human nature into account.[2]

Engineers challenge assumptions. This is their trained mind-set. They refuse to believe that something is impossible merely because it has not been done before, because someone has said there is no way to do it, or because it could upset established ways. The engineer in the field of education, as elsewhere, starts with a goal to be reached, not with the dead weight of precedent or unexamined beliefs. Like Roger Bannister, the first runner to break the four-minute mile, he knows that pushing from within stretches the limits of possibility, by setting an outside goal and doing what's necessary to reach it. In track and field, the four-minute barrier—once believed to be insurmountable—was surpassed as other runners soon matched and even exceeded this feat. This was achieved because they had learned that it was possible. Each runner had changed his assumptions!

CHANGING TOXIC ASSUMPTIONS ABOUT SCHOOLING

In the field of education, too many teachers and administrators share deeply rooted assumptions about something called "aptitude" or "the ability to learn." It is the major obstacle to poor schooling. It is the classic example of the lack of an engineering mind-set.

After all, what is aptitude? Nearly all educators treat it as a rough predictor of grades like A or F that, in turn, are believed to show how much a child has learned. Then, any discrepancy between this guess and the eventual grade is explained away as "underachievement" or, less often, as "overachievement."

For example, after a given math or English course, test results generally show that some students have learned significantly more than the others, and that a certain group, often quite large, has barely scraped through. According to these test results, teachers then assign grades, with most students falling somewhere in the middle of the scale and, except in rare cases, with relatively few at either extreme. Then, on the basis of these grades some students learn to think of themselves as good students, others as fair, and the remainder as poor or impossible learners. Each of us knows well about this system because each of us went through it, and if we did well enough to be reading this book or working now in a school, few of us give this ancient practice a second thought, except to increase "fairness" or "accuracy" in assigning grades.

After all, none would deny that some students are—or appear to be at the time—brighter or sharper than others or that some students work harder. So it seems reasonable to continue to sort students into the *B* slot or the *F* slot with the impartiality of a postal clerk who separates the dead letters from the first-class mail.

No doubt, school faculty may try to improve the program of the school so that each student learns more, whatever his or her supposed level of "aptitude": for good students they offer advanced placement courses, and for others some form of "enrichment" or "compensatory education," or remedial courses. Whatever the standards of education used, the faculty continues to sort the students into various bins according to what they have been able to learn, as measured by their own tests; and in most cases the students take on these grades and scores as part of their self-definition.

AN ENGINEERING MIND-SET APPROACH TO APTITUDE

This entire approach to aptitude, so ingrained that it seems part of the "natural order" of things is foreign to an "education" engineer assigned to develop solutions. Of course, they might not disagree that students differ in aptitude, but they would argue persuasively that aptitude needs to be defined not as the degree of mastery a student may attain within a given course, but rather as a function of the amount of time and the *quality* of the classroom teaching and support system needed to attain full mastery of a learned task. The engineering characterization of aptitude turns attention away from the routine of sorting students according to how many questions they successfully answer after completing a course of study. Rather, it sets as a goal for the end of an educational cycle each student's mastery of skills, not merely a fair grade. In other words, as applied to the acquisition of basic skills, this definition of aptitude demonstrates that, apart from a very small percentage of students, every student can earn an *A*.

Obviously, some students master a skill such as basic reading more quickly than others, and some will be quite slow. But if the curriculum and use of reliable teaching methods is tailored to these differences, every student can learn to read, calculate, or master the skills essential to a productive life in our society. And when they do master it, they deserve an *A*—or rather, since letter grades are obsolete assumptions, they deserve a certificate of initial mastery describing the skills, which is an accurate reflection of a *competence warranty* the teacher and the school proudly stand behind.

What matters most is not how long a student took to master a particular skill or even the type of teaching received, but the fact that the student now possesses that skill.

What happens when we accept the engineering mind-set definition of aptitude? In place of a fixed program in which each student learns what he or she can, a goal of basic mastery is set for everyone and then they are offered whatever programs are necessary to meet that goal. Instead of, or if necessary along with, grades, teachers give diagnostic tests to help them decide which program each student needs. At the end of this process, teachers might award skill warranties instead of, or together with, the increasingly doubtful "diploma" as a warrantor of completion. With regard to the basic skills, instead of labeling some students as "losers," start with the assumption that every kid will finish every class as a winner. In this sense, the school treats learning to read and to do essential math not as a race to the top of a mountain but as the ability to get there, one way or another, at a variety of paces.

As long as schools cling to the distorted notion of aptitude, teachers will remain satisfied to grade students on whether they can mount from one level of reading to the next in the average time allowed within the standard pattern of instruction. Too often, if a student does poorly he or she is defined as having "low aptitude" or lacking motivation or classified as having a chronic case of "dyslexia" (a fancy way of saying that the school has not taught him or her how to read). Worse yet, the student goes through the rest of life with a "reading problem." This failure is seldom blamed on the school. Somehow the school usually blames it on an external condition outside of its control such as an economic and/or social background.

Whether this has become an institutional cop-out or carried forward with the best of intentions, it is a step toward providing special programs for students who are presumed to have special needs. Thus, in referring to some students, educators speak of the "culturally deprived" or the "socially disadvantaged" student. In practice, however, these labels act less as a descriptive term than as a value judgment that often surfaces, submerges, and then reappears in a new guise. Such labels are useless in dealing with the problem. In fact, they serve to mask the ineptness of some educational programs and provide a rationalization for methods that do not work. If the methods work for some students, we just assume there is something wrong with the others.

The satirist Jules Feiffer depicted the futility of such labeling in a series of drawings of an impoverished, elderly gentleman reflecting to himself:

> I used to think I was poor.
> Then they told me I wasn't poor. I was needy.
> Then they told me it was self-defeating to think of myself as needy. I was deprived.
> Then they told me deprived was a bad image. I was underprivileged.
> Then they told me underprivileged was overused. I was disadvantaged.
> Now, I still don't have a dime. But I have a great vocabulary![3]

MODIFYING EDUCATOR EXPECTATIONS THROUGH THE ENGINEERING MIND-SET

For fear that we lightly dismiss such labeling as a harmless exercise in semantics consider that categorizing certain students and their families as "deprived," "disadvantaged," "uninterested," or "lazy" actually leads, more often than not, to corresponding behavior on the part of both the labeler and the group being labeled. No matter how well meaning the use of such phrases, they too often are taken to imply a chronic condition, a sort of social fate that may well be passed along to the next generation and to the one after that.

Sympathetic terms such as "disadvantaged," no less than doubtful judgments such as "lazy," can work as a self-fulfilling prophecy. Often in subtle ways, we act as if these students will have trouble or will probably fail, and the students become discouraged as they acquire, often without even realizing it, the fear and finally the expectation of defeat.

The tragic consequences of this phenomenon came to our attention by experiments on teacher expectations conducted in south San Francisco by Robert Rosenthal and described in his book *Pygmalion in the Classroom*.[4] In his experiments, teachers were led to believe at the beginning of a school year that certain students could be expected to show considerable academic improvement during that year. The teachers thought these predictions were based on tests that had been administered to the student body at the end of the preceding school year. In fact, the students designated as potential "spurters" were chosen at random without reference to test results or to grades. Nonetheless, intelligence tests given after the experiment had been in progress for several months indicated that, on the whole, the randomly chosen students had improved more than the rest.

Rosenthal's study has been well publicized and widely discussed, but have we taken full account of its findings? Keep in mind that the experimental group was chosen randomly and, thus, contrary to the teachers' belief, was no different from the control group. When teachers were asked to describe students in each group, however, they found members of the experimental group more attractive, better adjusted, more appealing, and less in need of social approval than members of the control group. Naturally, some of this group also gained in intelligence during the year, and Rosenthal discovered that, on average, the more a student in the control group gained, the less favorably he was described by his teacher. This inverse ratio between high rate of unexpected pupil gain and an unfavorable teacher attitude provides us with a devastating portrait of the persistence of low expectations on the part of teachers, regardless of student performance. In other words, the teachers knew that members of the control group were not supposed to do well, and they apparently regarded students who forced an exception to that rule as somehow "uppity."

If we consider this finding about teacher expectations together with the charges that intelligence tests are culture bound and are often failing to detect the full potential of some students, we are faced with the possibility that certain schools, in the words of their sharpest critics, actually make students more stupid.

John Holt, a sharp-eyed schoolteacher, has leveled the much broader charge that students actually decline in enthusiasm, curiosity, and confidence from the very day they start formal school. He sees the present school system as a negative force in learning. This is a striking and terrible indictment.

Our charges are much less broad. We seriously question whether certain schools inadvertently lead many of their students to define themselves as stupid, at least with regard to academic work.

To the extent that this charge is true, the situation is intolerable, but is it so surprising? After all, if teachers are put in frustrating or even frightening situations, they are no less inclined than any of us to welcome a scapegoat. Whether the scapegoat is supposedly the stupid, a headstrong student, or the environment of which he is defined to be a victim, the result comes out the same. The school is excused for the failure. If the student is "disadvantaged," what can the poor helpless school do?

The answer, according to the noted educator and sociologist Kenneth B. Clark, is that with the proper expectations and programs, schools can teach every student what he or she needs to know. In the past few years, more eyes have been opened to this humiliation not only by senior educators such as Clark, but also by a new breed of writers, teachers, and former teachers who'll tell it like it is. Such books as Nat Hentoff's *Our Children Are Dying*, John Holt's *How Children Fail*, Herbert Kohl's *36 Children*, and the award-winning *Death at an Early Age: The Destruction of the Hearts and Minds of Negro Children in the Boston Public Schools* by Jonathan Kozol, offer devastating indictments of current classroom practices.[5] Grindingly dull, irrelevant, and often inexcusable, these outdated classroom practices cry out for remedy. In these and other books, the students are shown to be victims of a cruel system that eats away at their confidence and fails to meet their needs. Is it really the children who are failing in this situation? That is what the grading system would seem to suggest.

CHANGING STUDENT EXPECTATIONS

How can schools stop humiliating the students they are supposed to be teaching? How can they teach these students to expect success in school? First of all, educators need to end their preoccupation with student disabilities. By now we know the litany by heart. Their vocabulary is limited. They cannot think in abstractions. They are not introspective. They prefer physical to mental activity. They lack motivation to succeed in school, and so on.

Instead of always trying to "compensate" for disabilities, why not first identify, develop, and then build on their strengths? In teacher and administrator professional journals, there are numbers of testimonials from teachers who work in the inner city and in isolated rural areas, teachers who discover the vast learning potential of their students. The recurring theme that runs through these stories is that the teacher did away with all of the negative things he or she had been told about the disadvantaged child. The teacher began with an unshakable belief in the youngsters that was soon sustained by student achievement. As one teacher put it: "I'm fed up with people who keep saying the disadvantaged child can't learn. My children do have the ability to learn. They have innate talents just like other children do. If those talents have been smothered by economic, social, and cultural deprivation, it's the teacher's job to discover and nurture them."

CHANGING PUBLIC EXPECTATIONS

This teacher, along with an increasing number of others, now has come to believe that the school has the responsibility not merely to expose each student to a course of instruction, but to give each a real chance to succeed. In the past, schools have not been required to bring about achievement. Schools have too long been thought of as "relatively passive," while being expected to provide free public resources. Yet, the U.S. Supreme Court has recognized that the state does not satisfy its constitutional responsibility if it merely takes people as it finds them, setting equal standards of access. The state must ensure each citizen an *effective utilization* of this fundamental right. The effective utilization standard varies with different rights but the state is obliged to make safe an equal opportunity for an equal educational result.

Like many constitutional legal theories, the effective utilization standard is deliberately vague as well as challenging. It points in a direction and names a goal but leaves the detailed implementation for further negotiation. Ultimately, a citizen has been able to use a right only when he or she has obtained whatever that right is designed to guarantee.

In the case of learning basic skills such as reading, to which every citizen has a right, we know that the school has made possible an effective utilization of this right only when its students can successfully demonstrate their ability to read. If certain students fail this test, a school might argue that it had done everything humanly possible to teach such students. But the burden of proof must henceforth fall on the school and not, as it now does, on the failing student. Moreover, the school needs to have shown not only that it had provided the failing student with instruction that worked with other students who were in some way similar, but also that no program it could reasonably provide would offer substantial promise of teaching that particular student how to read. In order to effectively argue the latter point, a school official would need to have acquainted him- or herself with new and well-researched programs that are often widely ignored.

The point of this approach is not to elicit a new set of ingenious arguments about the alleged ineducability of many students. The point is, rather, to serve clear notice on the schools that society expects all its children to learn at least the basic skills, and that failures are to be regarded less as the fault of the student or of his or her social or cultural background than of the school, and that the proper response to failure (as principals are fond of telling troublemakers) is not excuses but reform, and in this case reform by the schools.

ENGINEERING FOR GREATER CAPABILITY IN THE PUBLIC SCHOOLS

The mind-set of educational engineering starts with the assumption that all students can succeed and that with an adequate technology of instruction teachers can lead them toward mastery and a certified sense of accomplishment. What this offers is not another grand manifesto, but process improvements through which the school can find programs that work, implement them, and measure the results. The end product of this process is not a new program or a new machine or a new report, but a *capability*!

BENEFITS OF AN EDUCATIONAL ENGINEERING MIND-SET

What benefits does this process improvement offer? First, consider in turn its potential for students, for teachers, and for administrators. Since educational engineering is an approach broader than any particular program, it soon affects the way students view their own process of learning.

For example, most classes now begin with a vague preview of the material to be covered and consist of a series of review sessions, assignments, and tests. There is really nothing much to look forward to. In contrast, most successful commercial enterprises promote their products and services in such a way as to arouse interest before the consumer uses them. We read attractive brochures of a foreign country and begin thinking about a trip; we study the investment pages and contemplate the purchase of some stocks; we pour over a brochure for a new model car before deciding to test drive one. The actual experience of using the product or service is positively enhanced by an advanced knowledge and anticipation of it.

STUDENT BENEFITS

In school, where does the student go to find out what is being offered? Most of them enter courses with little notion of what they will study. Little attempt is made to build prior interest in, or to prepare students for, the experience. Why not give them a prospectus setting out the intellectual adventure they are about to undertake? The precourse materials could highlight things they will learn, books they will read, ideas they will encounter, and a sample of the assignments they will be asked to complete. Properly done, such a prospectus could arouse intellectual ambition in the students and help their parents better understand and prepare to support what is going on.

Any school could do this, but the link to educational engineering is plain. If the process of innovation requires school officials to define their goals in operational terms as a first step, the school would then be able to share with students not merely vague and admirable objectives, such as the ability to communicate effectively, but specific sets of useful skills. In fact, the spirit of educational engineering has reached the students when the student begins to say "I can do that task" instead of "I've had that course." In this process, education is less a program of material to be plodded through than a set of useful skills and understandings to be mastered; and that is the way it needs to be treated in planning.

TEACHER BENEFITS

As a frame of reference, educational engineering offers teachers a much wider role. When farmers had nothing more than a horse and a plow, their productivity was limited by their lack of resources and equipment. With a tractor, hybrid seed, modern fertilizers, and a reaper, the farmer sharply increased his yield. In education, we are now reaching this same kind of transition, and just as the old-fashioned farmers viewed all the new machinery with deep suspicion, many of us wonder what effect new media of instruction and use of performance data will have on teachers.

Insofar as the new media produce results, the effect is bound to be good. In certain schools, teachers now are failing not because they are untrained or lazy but because they are severely overburdened. Like the old-fashioned farmer who hardly had a moment to eat, teachers need help; and if some of the duties can be performed as well or better by someone else, teachers would be able to assume versatile and differentiated human roles in the schools. Instead of leading students through the lockstep of a single program, teachers could assist them in the progress of individualized instruction; teachers could help students discover things for themselves instead of trying to tell them everything; teachers could draw on local development capital through local industry-education partnerships to support process improvements tailored to specific needs.

Teachers can become managers of instruction in tandem with their role as the central presenters of information. Through following

Healing Public Schools: The Winning Prescription to Cure Their Chronic Illness,[6] the winning prescription of the ISO 9000–Baldrige guidelines, and the metrics of the BSC, teachers can operate within a flexibility of form that they have never before enjoyed. Schools will then be able to test process improvements locally before adopting them, and teachers will be called on not to initiate untried proposals but rather to take over the operation of processes that are already familiar and successful.

BENEFITS FOR SCHOOL ADMINISTRATORS

The educational engineering frame of reference can finally ease the persistent problems of desegregation and lower the dropout rate. The solution in each case is the same. If students can begin to master a skill, no matter what their pace of learning, they gain a source of satisfaction and self-respect and the opportunity, in time, to join their peers in the normal course of instruction. It's when students feel hopeless and discouraged that they may decide to quit school; and when they lag far behind their peers, they know they are more of a drag on the class than a contributor to it. In each case, what such students need is rapid, esteem-building progress in learning basic skills.

Until and unless school officials can come around to ensure this kind of progress, their level of authority will continue to erode. Student discipline will become even more common, as will the response with the use of various forms of power to try and contain it.

There is a sharp distinction between authority and power. Whereas power is derived from simple force, such as the use of police or disciplinary action, authority is derived from respect for the moral purposes of an institution. A tyrant, of whatever magnitude, relies on power in this sense; a leader relies on his or her authority.

It now seems more clear that, apart from a certain fringe, rebellious youth are demanding that reliance on power be replaced by responsive authority and that our institutions, including our schools, live up to their promises. To win respect as competent educators, schools need to teach students the necessary skills. The educational engineering mindset is designed to help do just that.

BENEFITS OF THE EDUCATIONAL ENGINEERING
FRAME OF REFERENCE

In particular, what will educational engineering help schools to do? What are its advantages?

First, process improvements allow decision makers at every level, from the federal government to the local school board, to govern the school as a system instead of dealing with one crisis after another. They can set firm goals and hold others accountable for results. This is performance management.

Second, it will halt the unnecessary waste of dollars on educational failures. When a government experiments and fails, the bureaucracy continues to grow; but when a business fails, it goes out of business and another takes its place. Under educational engineering, if a program does not meet performance criteria, dollars flow back to the state and federal till, and administrators will know which schools should not receive grants until they make changes. The BSC helps provide educators with measurements to match their strategic objectives.

Third, it will stimulate the creation of a much more advanced technology of instruction. Inflexible and invalidated instructional materials and techniques such as present and traditional textbooks and lectures simply aggravate the problems of a group system of teaching and are clearly inadequate for individual instruction. How could such methods possibly provide the feedback that a student needs to improve? Instead, they keep him or her in a lockstep and expose him or her to failure. The DW offers the means to implement *Healing Public Schools* and ride the BSC platform.

Fourth, it will allow educators to match the talents and resources of private industry to local needs, on local terms, under local control, and through the intermediary of management support. CRM provides the process improvements to facilitate such wider partnerships.

Fifth, it will foster economy by reducing the cost of effective implementation of successful programs and by highlighting the relatively low-cost effectiveness of some programs now widely used. Performance management based on measurable process data saves employees unnecessary angst and taxpayers unnecessary waste.

Sixth, it will give educational personnel greater incentives for performance, such as instructional personnel working under peripheral issues like dress code.

Seventh, it will change the teaching role from mere information transmission to the management of learning. In many classrooms today, the only person actively and consistently engaged is the teacher. What if every student in that classroom were as fully absorbed as the teacher? The teachers' job might not be any easier but they would undoubtedly be more satisfied.

Above all, a process through which good educational practice is forthcoming can become standard practice in a growing number of schools. Some critics say we lack the necessary educational research, and others say the schools are inept even at running the programs they have.

Wherever the truth may lie in such charges, the fact remains that the thorniest education problem resides between the research on learning and the routine administration of schools. It is apparent that schools lack a mechanism for applying much of what is already known. There are isolated examples of good practice all over the country, but states, districts, and local schools have no adequate way of standardizing these practices.

CASE STUDIES IN ENGINEERING AND EDUCATION COLLABORATION

Pennsylvania State University

For Akhlesh Lakhtakia, a professor of engineering science and mechanics at Pennsylvania State University (PSU), the need for effective science and technical education in public schools hit home while watching his daughter attend elementary school. "When my daughter started going to school, I noticed she wasn't being challenged in science." He became concerned his daughter would rule out a career in science and engineering at a very young age. "When a child is eight or nine years old, that's when decisions take place. A child is ready to receive complicated ideas, so long as they feel involved."[7]

Lakhtakia's concerns prompted him to collaborate with the PSU College of Education and team up with Tom Dana, an associate professor

Future elementary school teachers gain content knowledge and confidence in science and engineering through a special program designed in a collaboration between the Colleges of Engineering and Education. Students apply engineering principles and practices and construct their own projects using materials they can use to teach elementary school children.

of science education, Vince Lunetta, a professor of science education, Mehmet Tasar, a doctoral candidate in science education, Johanna Ramos, a graduate assistant in the College of Engineering, and Joe Taylor, a doctoral candidate in science education.

Together, they developed a new course, ENGR/SCIED 497F, that is designed to teach education majors about engineering before they get to the classroom. According to Lakhtakia, the class is supposed to help these future teachers become comfortable with engineering principles and practices, give them confidence in teaching their own students, and allow them to cultivate children's curiosity of the natural world.

This course is a long-term investment with an impact spanning over the next thirty to thirty-five years. The future teachers who take such a course will in turn teach thousands of kids in that time.

To quote Lakhtakia, "Educating our citizenry is an important mission of universities—not just educating experts. We need to establish both a depth and a breadth of science experience in our society. This course is one of many things we should do to make our citizens well-informed, rational consumers, and to give those with interests in science the foundation that can take them, and us, to new frontiers."[8]

University of Colorado at Boulder

The University of Colorado at Boulder College of Engineering and Applied Science offers specialized workshops and other programs for K–12 teachers to assist them in bringing science and engineering concepts into their classrooms through hands-on activities that will stimulate the curiosity of young students. Programs include:

- Space education through the Citizen Explorer Project, which offers classroom activities for teachers as part of its latest National Aeronautics and Space Administration–funded project
- The Engineering in Everyday Life program integrates theoretical engineering concepts with fun classroom applications that teachers can take back into their classrooms
- Graduate teaching fellows send engineering students into local classrooms at the elementary, middle, and high school levels to assist teachers with hands-on science and engineering education[9]

University of Pennsylvania

Over two thousand University of Pennsylvania students tried out new tools for teaching and learning in the fall of 1999. A dozen engineering courses and a dozen arts and sciences courses are experimenting with Blackboard Course info, an easy-to-use Web application that helps professors meet their teaching needs. "It makes course management a snap," states bioengineering professor Mitchell Litt. "I can post all course information, assignments, quizzes, from home via internet."[10]

The largest single course in the pilot program is ECON 1, with enrollment close to 950 in all the sections. Courses from the Graduate School of Education, Dental Medicine, Nursing, and Veterinary Medicine are expected to join the pilot program during the fall of 2000. Blackboard Course info provides online quizzes, online homework hand-ins, group file-sharing areas, chat areas, and much more. Students are automatically loaded into the system based on their registration.

"This isn't a technology project. It's a collaboration among some of Penn's best teachers to find ways to become better teachers and for Penn students to become better, more empowered learners," said James O'Donnell, the vice provost for information systems and computing and a professor of classics and cochair of the New Tools for Teaching Committee. Helen Anderson, the senior director of the Computing and Educational Technology Services program at the School of Engineering and Applied Science and the other New Tools for Teaching Committee cochair, states, "Committee members from school and centers across the university are participating in the ongoing effort to provide top quality support for teaching and learning at Penn."[11]

THE CHALLENGE TO PUBLIC EDUCATION

Educational engineering is linked to school administration, for which it is a method, and to basic research, on which it depends for knowledge. Its main function, however, is to mediate between the school and the sources of innovation.

In discussing "how to combat the almost inevitable movement of an organization toward elaborateness, rigidity and massiveness and away from simplicity, flexibility and manageable size,"[12] John W. Gardner, a veteran of the worlds of the university, foundations, federal bureaucracy, and voluntary associations, observes that a classic bureaucracy can manage to renew itself by calling in a variety of outside servicing organizations. He points out that corporations routinely call on lawyers, auditors, management consultants, and many other specialists who work for a variety of firms in turn. Although their names appear only on contracts, rather than on the organization chart, few corporations could exist without them. In fact, Gardner points out:

> The remarkable range of such professional and technical services that are available, plus the flexibility of the contractual relationship, gives the modern organization a wide range of choice in shaping its own future. Within limits, top management can put its finger on almost any function

within the organization and decree that henceforth that function will be performed by an outside organization on contract. For the organization that wishes to maintain the maneuverability so essential to renewal, this offers priceless opportunities.[13]

Can such wisdom be applied to public education? By now the need for renewal in the schools should be clear. It remains for administrators, teachers, and stakeholders to take advantage of the opportunities extended by understanding and applying the engineering frame of reference as a newly developed process of school improvement.

SCHOOL PERFORMANCE MANAGEMENT THROUGH ENGINEERING THINKING

Too often, articles in administrative management seldom integrate the technical and psychological aspects of school management into a comprehensive picture of the educator–manager role. Such compartmentalization highlights the differences and hides the common threads that underlie both engineering and school management.

The engineer often sees the administrator and teacher as superficial and lacking intellectual rigor and depth, even though the typical educator deals with systems of far greater complexity each day than the engineer could dream of designing. Conversely, the administrator and teacher look on the technical person as narrow and lacking interest in people and social problems, even though the engineer always designs his technical systems on the basis of a body of knowledge, attitude, and theory that helps people live a richer, fuller, and safer life. Bridges, roads, planes, cars, traffic signals, safety belts, and on and on are designed first and foremost with people's needs in mind. Such insights can help the future teacher or administrator to better understand the complexity of the social systems within which he or she works.

We tend to see engineering and school management resting on different foundations—engineering on physics and school management on economics—whereas school management, economics, and much of engineering share common foundations in feedback, system behavior, and psychology.

A new era in preparing teachers and administrators for the growing demands of K–12 schooling builds on the foundations created by its predecessors. At the same time, engineering has in the past five decades provided a basis for a new, general insight into the dynamics of the school as a complex social system. We might consider administrative education and classroom management of the future as "school enterprise engineering." If so, the following are five contributions that engineering thinking can help bring to school enterprise engineering:

1. The concept of understanding and improving the workings of the school as a system
2. The principles of using feedback control and data to manage the school organization and classroom
3. The distinction between policymaking (change) and decision-making (static) performance management
4. The lower cost of electronic communication to strengthen teacher and administrator knowledge
5. The substitution of data reinforcement for pure feeling and intuition to reach better analytic solutions

Engineering thinking can be a "change agent" to hasten improvements in our school systems. To do so, such thinking must help clarify the enduring goals and objectives of education and the school organization. This approach will give more attention to the surrounding system as a whole rather than looking on it as an array of isolated parts to be controlled. Engineering thinking brings to school organizations the courage to experiment with promising new approaches based on a foundation of design for performance improvement.

NOTES

1. Samuel C. Florman, *The Introspective Engineer* (New York: St. Martin's, 1996), 3–4.
2. Florman, *Introspective Engineer*, 7.
3. Leon Lessinger, *Every Kid a Winner: Accountability in Education* (New York: Simon and Schuster, 1970), 25.

4. Robert Rosenthal, *Pygmalion in the Classroom* (New York: Irvington, 1992).

5. Nat Hentoff, *Our Children Are Dying* (New York: Four Winds, 1967); John Holt, *How Children Fail* (New York: Perseus, 1995); Herbert Kohl, *36 Children* (New York: Penguin, 1990); and Jonathan Kozol, *Death at an Early Age: The Destruction of the Hearts and Minds of Negro Children in the Boston Public Schools* (New York: New American Library, 1985).

6. Allen Salowe and Leon Lessinger, *Healing Public Schools: The Winning Prescription to Cure Their Chronic Illness* (Lanham, Md: Scarecrow, 2001).

7. Pennsylvania State College of Engineering, <http://www.eng.psu.edu/> [last accessed: July 30, 2001].

8. Pennsylvania State College of Engineering.

9. University of Colorado at Boulder, <http://www.colorado.edu> [last accessed: July 27, 2001].

10. University of Pennsylvania, New Tools Web site, <http://www.seas.upenn.edu/newtools> [last accessed: September 13, 1999].

11. University of Pennsylvania, New Tools Web site.

12. John W. Gardner, *Self-Renewal* (New York: HarperCollins, 1965), 80.

13. Gardner, *Self-Renewal*, 84.

CHAPTER 8

Quality and Performance Management Initiatives around the Globe

Why is it that we find lots of school quality improvement activities under way in developed nations around the globe but still run into stiff resistance to bringing quality process changes into the mainstream of American education?

In the past, we explored educator thinking and application of ISO 9000 Education Standards, Baldrige National Quality Program Criteria for Education, and TQM in diverse cultures. We found lots of examples in Asia, Europe, the Middle East, Asia Minor, and in North and South America.

- Thailand reports seventy-seven ISO 9000–certified educational institutions
- Malaysia shows that seventeen lower and higher education institutions have gained ISO 9000 certification
- Swinburne University of Technology, the Schools of Mines and Industries, and Deakin University are ISO 9000–certified universities in Australia
- In New Zealand, Massey and Waikato Universities have received ISO 9000 certification
- United Kingdom colleges and universities have pioneered ISO 9000 certification
- Schools in Saudi Arabia, Egypt's Arab Academy for Science and Technology, and Israel's Air Force Technological University have

found something they can easily agree on: the value of ISO 9000–quality schools
- Across India and throughout Ireland there are ISO 9000–quality schools
- Universities in Austria and Belgium are ISO 9001 certified
- Add Canada, Brazil, Taiwan, and the United States to the list

According to the National Center for Education Statistics International Perspective: "U.S. students perform well in comparison with their peers in other countries in reading. They perform less well in science and geography. Their weakest area relative to students in other countries is mathematics on mathematics assessments. Both 9- and 13-year olds scored lower than their counterparts in the vast majority of participating countries. Only about 10 percent of U.S. 13-year olds scored as well as the top 50 percent in Taiwan, the highest performing country."[1]

We used e-mail for direct interviews and did an exhaustive Internet search to share in this chapter what we learned from these educators around the globe.

No single answer popped to the surface but some of what we did uncover may help jolt into action one more American educator or stakeholder who really holds the interest of U.S. school-aged kids at heart. For example, the following statement comes from Saudi Arabia where almost a dozen ISO 9000–school certification projects are under way:

Quality has always been a major issue in education and improving existing internal systems and procedures. The biggest difference between a good school or college and a poor one is the way it is managed. ISO 9000 is a proven, internationally accepted quality management system, already used in a number of institutions.

Contrary to common belief, management systems addressing ISO 9000 should not result in a bureaucratic paper chase. The aim is to develop documentation that will enable the educational institution to operate effectively and efficiently with a degree of flexibility to ensure that the needs of individual customers can be satisfied. More importantly, the system should be accepted internally by staff.[2]

THE PROS AND CONS OF ISO 9000 FOR SCHOOLS

Two extreme arguments are made on the merits of applying quality process improvement to education in general, and ISO 9000 in particular. L. Harvey negatively comments that ISO 9000 is concerned with conformance to *service* standards rather than *academic* standards. Moreover, he states, there is little indication that ISO 9000 has any impact on the quality of teaching and learning, and that improving education with ISO 9000 is the importing of an expensive, bureaucratic, unwieldy, alienating, and managerial approach from industry.[3]

On the other side, J. Peter and G. Wills express the positive view toward ISO 9000 and quality processes. They praise ISO 9000 as a global quality assurance, as an accreditation structure for educational institutions, and as a better way than the existing local accreditation in terms of customer orientation. They perceive that ISO 9000 has "general currency" and familiarity with the wider public.[4]

Today, almost eighty educational institutions in Thailand, including private and nonformal vocational schools, have received ISO 9000 certification. In an interview conducted by the Thai Ministry of Education, an evaluation of the quality impact of ISO 9002 standards toward Thai schools bears a marked similarity to American education goals in four aspects. In their own words:

1. Teachers and staff have a more positive and internationalizing attitude
2. The standards of teaching and learning are enhanced up to the same level even in different classrooms and with different teachers
3. Continuous improvement system is created
4. Services to stakeholders are better improved[5]

Concluding the study, the Thai Ministry of Education states:

ISO 9000 is connected with *how to manage the school system to assure that the stakeholders' requirements are met and students are reaching their full potentialities*. "Stakeholders" are defined as students, community, society and institution/factory/company which students further study or work at; and "student potentialities" means students being able to survive in society, being good people, gaining knowledge on how to learn by themselves, and being creative or having initiative.[6]

AMERICAN SCHOOLS FOLLOW GRADUALLY

Currently, a few U.S. public school districts are gradually pursuing the ISO 9000 certification. Craig Johnson, a Florida State University professor and the chair of the American Society for Quality (ASQ) Education Division and ISO worldwide committee to establish education standards, claims he has identified about two hundred public schools, colleges, universities, and community colleges nationwide. But Johnson also acknowledges it's not all that easy:

> The obstacles revolve around the lack of experience in measuring performance and using data, resulting from those measures, to correct and prevent nonconforming processes. The typical [school] cycle is plan-do-examine-plan for the next cycle or plan [for] some other process. Best practices are seldom disseminated. Root cause analysis is mostly unknown. Continuous improvement is a slogan. This obstacle could be overcome by teaching school personnel to apply statistical thinking and their intuition when taking corrective and preventive action, but that's a hard sell.
>
> The promising opportunities, at the moment, lie in K–12, Vocational, and Technical Education. This is because they are not responsible for creating knowledge, curriculum, and instructional materials. In some cases they are being urged by school boards and state departments of education to move ahead with establishing a quality management system. Once this system is in place, the schools can adapt Baldrige, ISO, and other quality processes to fit their own needs. They can also free their processes from micro-management by the politicians and regulators who control them.[7]

TANGIBLE BENEFITS

Let's take a different tack and see if we can better communicate the benefits of using quality processes. Here are just a few examples to demonstrate that it's more about pursuing process standards than specifying pizza in the school lunchroom.

- In Claymont, Delaware, ISO 9000 is credited with inspiring the school district to create a Web site so any parent and teacher will be able to see what the district is doing about instruction and discipline.
- The school district in Lancaster, Pennsylvania, the nation's first ISO 9000–certified district, reports saving over $500,000 by improving its purchasing processes. The district used to spend $200 in administrative costs to track each $5 teacher purchase.
- The Peel School District in Ontario, Canada, achieved ISO 9002 certification in its Maintenance Services Department. Turnaround time for work-order repairs from its two hundred schools dropped from as much as six months to thirty days. The department handles twenty-two thousand work order requests per year for basic repairs (locks, faucets, switches, and broken windows) and manages one thousand project requests for facilities improvement annually.
- Jefferson County, Colorado, the nation's largest ISO 9000–certified district, expects to save more than $900,000 on purchasing processes alone the first year. It's pilot testing a purchasing credit card to avoid additional expenses on small purchases.

In August 1999, the Public Authority for Applied Education and Training, the higher public education arm of Kuwait that includes four colleges, four institutions, and two intermediate schools, undertook the ISO 9000–quality initiative. Kuwait is bordered by Iraq, Iran, and Saudi Arabia. The Kuwait ISO 9000 facilitation is being pursued in conjunction with Canada's first ISO 9000–certified university, St. Lawrence College of Ontario, the Daytona Beach (Florida) Community College, and the American International Development Council. Together, they dealt with the interpretation of the ISO 9000 standards and its application in education, as well as the subjects of implementation, TQM, and internal quality auditing.

The Ontario Principals' Council (OPC), located in North York, Ontario, is a professional association for practicing principals and vice principals in Ontario's publicly funded school system. The OPC currently links five thousand school administrators in a network that inspires, establishes, and supports the highest standard of public education. Their slogan is "Exemplary Leadership in Public Education, ISO 9001 Registered Quality, Our Principal Product."[8]

We asked Bob Kattman, the past chair of the ASQ Education Division, to help us identify where the most serious land mines are buried when getting ISO 9000 and other quality processes used in U.S. schools on a wider scale. Here's what he wrote us:

> Your question cannot be answered easily. Education is a complex system and like any complex system there are a lot of factors to consider.
>
> Probably the greatest obstacle is the lack of understanding by educators. Very few colleges provide any information about quality principles, the Baldrige or ISO. Therefore, attempts to introduce this information are seen as coming from the outside. This belief is reinforced when information on quality is presented in non-educational terms. The Baldrige is the closest to using the proper terminology. ISO has a long way to go.
>
> Another major factor is the impact of politics on our schools. Schools end up reacting to these mandates, most often in ways, which are antithetical to quality principles.
>
> Another major problem is the lack of financial support for districts that wish to implement any of the quality programs. This lack of funding often spells the end of an effort.[9]

A MATTER OF JUDGMENT—TRUE STORY

Most of us know the old saying, you can't tell a book by its cover. Well, one day a lady wearing a faded gingham dress, and her husband, clad in a homespun threadbare suit, stepped off the train in Boston and walked timidly without an appointment into the Harvard president's outer office. The secretary could tell in a moment that such backwoods, country hicks had no business at Harvard and probably didn't even deserve to be in Cambridge. She frowned.

"We want to see the president," the man said softly.

"He'll be busy all day," the secretary snapped.

"We'll wait," the lady replied.

For hours, the secretary ignored them, hoping that the couple would finally become discouraged and go away. They didn't.

And the secretary grew frustrated and finally decided to disturb the president, even though it was a chore she always regretted doing. "Maybe if they just see you for a few minutes, they'll leave," she told him. And he sighed in exasperation and nodded. Someone of his importance obviously didn't have the time to spend with them, but he detested gingham dresses and homespun suits cluttering up his outer office. The president, stern-faced with dignity, strutted toward the couple.

The lady told him, "We had a son that attended Harvard for one year. He loved Harvard. He was happy here. But about a year ago, he was accidentally killed. And my husband and I would like to erect a memorial to him, somewhere on campus."

The president wasn't touched; he was shocked. "Madam," he said gruffly, "we can't put up a statue for every person who attended Harvard and died. If we did, this place would look like a cemetery."

"Oh, no," the lady explained quickly. "We don't want to erect a statue. We thought we would like to give a building to Harvard."

The president rolled his eyes. He glanced at the gingham dress and homespun suit then exclaimed, "A building! Do you have any earthly idea how much a building costs? We have over seven-and-a-half million dollars in the physical plant at Harvard."

For a moment the lady was silent. The president was pleased. He could get rid of them now. And the lady turned to her husband and said quietly, "Is that all it costs to start a university? Why don't we just start our own?" Her husband nodded.

The president's face wilted in confusion and bewilderment.

And Mr. and Mrs. Leland Stanford walked away, traveling to Palo Alto, California, where they established the university that bears their name, a memorial to a son that Harvard no longer cared about.

You can easily judge the character of others by how they treat those who can do nothing for them or to them.

MAYBE WE'RE STARTING THE ISO 9000 CAMPAIGN AT THE WRONG END

Franklin Schargel, a quality consultant from Albuquerque, New Mexico, answered our question regarding obstacles to wider use of quality processes in schools this way:

First is the lack of awareness about what ISO and the Baldrige can do to help the improvement of learning.

Second is the complacency with what already exists in education. At most, businesses, politicians and educators pay "lip service" about the need to improve education and learning.[10]

FORO, a Spanish think tank, contacted Schargel regarding his work implementing ISO 9000 in public schools. FORO group members met him at New York's Westinghouse High School to see firsthand the school's progress. Schargel then went to Spain, visiting forty-three schools—public, private, and technical—at various competency levels. Eventually, sixteen schools took on the ISO 9000 challenge, three of which are now ISO 9000–certified with the rest expecting certification by year end 2002.

A WHOLE TOWN EARNS ISO 9000 CERTIFICATION

When the cities of Phoenix, Arizona, and Christchurch, New Zealand, won the 1993 Carl Bertelsmann Prize and with it designation as the "Best Run Cities in the World," we didn't hear many complaints from the leaders of Braintree, England.

After all, being the best-managed local government in your home country isn't a bad honor on which to fall back. Although that title for Braintree is unofficial, it appears to fit. In late 1993, the Braintree governing council became the first local unit of government to gain "company-wide" ISO 9000 (or British Standards Institution 5750) registration for the service standards and continuous improvement processes it has established for all seventy services it delivers.

Local government in Great Britain is divided among two levels: counties (providing schools, libraries, social services, police, fire, and other services to an average population of more than five hundred thousand) and districts (providing such services as housing, parks and recreation, development planning and management, and waste management for populations of roughly one hundred thousand).

What makes Braintree, in the county of Essex, special among Great Britain's districts is this:

- Braintree tracks service quality and management performance aggressively using local government performance standards developed by the British Audit Commission.

While dozens of standards are used to track various aspects of service, thirty to forty are used as a barometer of overall organization performance. These measures are discussed and reviewed at least quarterly at the council level. In a 1989 survey of residents in twenty-six districts, Braintree earned the highest marks for its housing, refuse collection, and overall *customer satisfaction*.

- Braintree borders on the obsessive when it comes to communicating with customers about the level of service they should expect. For example, the council publishes a "charter" for citizens, describing the service standards, which the council pledges to provide.

Among other things, the Braintree charter promises that council staff will answer phone calls quickly and courteously, will respond to correspondence promptly (within seven days on letters of complaint, ten days on other correspondence), and do so in plain English.

- The Braintree charter's provisions range from the general to the highly specific. On the one hand, it pledges that customer visits to the council's offices always will be welcome. On a more detailed level, the charter specifies that the council plant at least one tree for each of the district's 130,000 residents by 2000, which it did, as part of the nation's community forests program to regenerate the environment.

Along with a charter describing its service commitments to the district's citizenry as a whole, Braintree has developed separate charters for industrial/commercial customers and public housing tenants.

Braintree District Council Core Values are:
1. We are customer orientated
2. We believe in the abilities of the individual
3. We must be responsive and responsible
4. We believe in quality
5. We are action orientated

- Braintree publishes "contracts" for each of its major services. Each contract describes a service in detail, outlines the council's service standards, and gives customers information about how to lodge a complaint about poor service. In its waste management services contract, for instance, Braintree specifies it will provide each household with fifty-two black garbage bags every six months:

1. Collect waste on the same day each week (barring a holiday)
2. Provide notice of upcoming holidays at the same time the garbage bags are delivered; remove one bag of garden waste per week in addition to the regular household waste
3. Close doors and gates and replace lids on trash bins; and clean up dropped refuse

As with many of the Braintree services, the contract also pledges that a duty officer will be on call twenty-four hours a day, seven days a week to handle customer inquiries. Meanwhile, in its engineering services contract, the council promises to respond to flooding problems within twenty-four hours. In food safety, the council promises to respond to complaints about contaminated food or unsanitary restaurants within three working days.

To give you an idea of the extent to which the council goes to inform citizens of its service standards, Braintree even publishes a contract for its recreational swimming program.

- Braintree disseminates detailed complaint-handling instructions to employees, including step-by-step procedures for responding to a complaint by phone versus a complaint by letter, along with guidelines for how elected councilors should respond to complaints
- Braintree operates an employee suggestion system and a "lookout scheme," in which employees and councilors are encouraged to report any lapses in service quality that they might witness
- Braintree devotes funds equal to 2.5 percent of total payroll in management, communication, and customer awareness training
- Braintree maintains council office hours from 8:30 A.M. to 6 P.M., with emergency service personnel available by phone twenty-four hours a day, seven days a week
- Braintree compensates its employees on a pay-for-performance basis, based on attaining annual personal goals established by each worker and his or her supervisor

- Braintree encourages customer feedback via a suggestion system, and has customer satisfaction survey cards available at all service locations[11]

QUALITY STARTS WITH CARING

Perhaps we need to first come to grips with better recognizing the consequences of not keeping our streets clean and not fixing our broken windows before we are ready to tackle the quality processes of learning needed by schoolchildren. We need to understand what these forms of neglect say about our caring.

In their award-winning book *Fixing Broken Windows: Restoring Order and Reducing Crime in Our Communities*, George L. Kelling and Catherine M. Coles state:

> This model [of petty crime control] restores responsibility to communities and establishes new mechanisms of police and criminal justice accountability to neighborhoods and communities. . . . Order arises out of what [author] Jane Jacobs has called the "small changes" of urban life: the day-to-day respect with which we deal with others and the concern that we exercise for their privacy, welfare, and safety. Such respect and concern does not divide rich from poor, black from white, or one ethnic group from another. Instead, it unites diverse neighborhoods against those who behave in outrageous ways, and who prey on the weak and vulnerable.[12]

Often, kids give us a greater insight into what's wrong than we care to recognize. A common complaint of kids in trouble is "my folks don't care what happens to me." Similarly, a common warning from kids that we are failing in school is "if my teacher doesn't care, why should I care?"

Craig Johnson relates an interesting story about a university president who said to him in frustration: "Don't use the word 'quality' around me any more." It's just possible that the word "quality" is really a word that tugs at our conscience. Is it that we underestimate the importance and value of quality?

The following story from Philip Crosby always comes to mind when we define "quality":

Quality has much in common with sex. Everyone is for it. (Under certain conditions, of course.) Everyone feels they understand it. (Even though they wouldn't want to explain it.) Everyone thinks execution is only a matter of following natural inclinations. (After all, we do get along somehow.) And of course, most people feel that other people cause all the problems in these areas. (If only they would take the time to do things right.) In a world where more than half the marriages end in divorce or separation, such assumptions are open to question.[13]

NOTES

1. National Center for Education Statistics, *Outcome of Learning: Results from 2000 Program for International Assessment of 15-Year-Olds in Mathematics, Science, and Literacy* (Washington, D.C.: U.S. Department of Education, 2001).

2. See <http://www.jawdah.com> [last accessed: May 19, 2001].

3. L. Harvey, *Quality Assurance System, TQM and the New Collegiaism* (Microfile, ERIC Doc. Ed. 401810 [1995]).

4. J. Peter and G. Wills, "ISO 9000 As a Global Educational Structure," *Journal of Quality Assurance* 6, no. 2 (1998): 83–89.

5. Thai Ministry of Education, "ISO 9000 in Private Schools: Case Studies," 27 March 2001.

6. Na Ayuohya quoted by Thai Ministry of Education, "ISO 9000 in Private Schools," emphasis in the original.

7. Craig Johnson, e-mail to authors, July 12, 2001.

8. See <http://www.principals.on.ca> [last accessed: January 7, 2002].

9. Bob Kattman, e-mail to authors, July 25, 2001.

10. Franklin Schargel, e-mail to authors, July 24, 2001.

11. "England's Braintree Earns ISO 9000," *Public Sector Quality Report* (September 1995): 1–2.

12. George L. Kelling and Catherine M. Coles, *Fixing Broken Windows: Restoring Order and Reducing Crime in Our Communities* (New York: Kressler/The Free Press, 1996), 19.

13. Philip Crosby, *Quality Is Free* (New York: McGraw-Hill, 1979), 17–18.

CHAPTER 9

Benchmarking for World-Class Schools

WHAT IS BENCHMARKING FOR SCHOOLS?

Benchmarking has grown in importance led by successes at Xerox and Ford Motor Company. In the early 1980s, Ford had more than five hundred people in its North American accounts payable function. Ford set a targeted 20 percent reduction in head count through improved processes and systems and as part of its analysis, it decided to benchmark the same job function with Mazda, a business partner in a number of ventures. The Ford benchmarking team found that Mazda was doing its accounts payable with five people (noting volume levels were not comparable). Ford totally redesigned its process and ended up doing the same work with hundreds of fewer people.

The most successful U.S. firms share an emphasis on competitive benchmarking. And the trend is moving into higher education with more institutions surveying its administrative and business costs. Unfortunately, as with most new management techniques, many organizations aren't too clear about benchmarking or even how to do it properly. To attempt benchmarking without a clear understanding may actually lead to negative results.

The following chapter sets out the specific steps required for a successful school benchmarking effort, the role of school leadership in launching such an initiative, and how to avoid common mistakes in schools.

WHY BENCHMARK A SCHOOL?

First, strategic planning is now legislated in more states and is widely practiced in even more school districts. Dealing straight up with key questions allows a school district to develop more innovative strategies. But in spite of such forward thinking to use precise planning for strategic thinking, even the most brilliant strategy can fail unless carried through successfully. Still, too many schools do not practice genuine performance improvement, and while costs grow as a percent of budget and schools, faculty in particular have trouble answering the question: What is the value-added benefit of its teaching and administrative functions?

At the core of these issues rest a host of familiar factors: lack of customer focus, slow program development, rising overhead costs, and mediocre quality. Benchmarking, when properly implemented, is a major tool toward uncovering solutions to these problems.

WHAT SCHOOL BENCHMARKING IS

In plain language, "school benchmarking" is a structured approach to creating and driving change into a school organization. Such change comes about by doing process-to-process (or function-to-function) comparisons with other entities (either inside or outside of education) and developing detailed data about performance levels and best practices. In other words, benchmarking is the search for those practices that lead to *superior* performance. Benchmarking addresses three key questions:

1. How good are we? Too frequently school districts are complacent about realistically assessing their effectiveness and efficiency. Many school organizations have an intuitive sense of how well their processes or functions are operating. But what is frequently missing is an in-depth understanding of cost, quality, and response-time performance.
2. How good can we be? When comparing your school to others, the chances are that one or several benchmarking partners will

demonstrate significantly better performance levels than your school. The performance of others can serve as an effective basis for both short- and long-range goal setting.

3. How do we get better? Simply knowing that someone else is much better than you is only part of the challenge. The trick is to determine how these performance levels are achieved. What practices does your school district need to adopt to be as good as the best?

Benchmarking is a change management tool that can broaden the horizons of school leadership and staffs by helping all realize there are proven better ways. The successful benchmarker sheds the "not invented here" condition and rids itself of outmoded notions such as "we're not going to learn anything from other school districts," "this district is as good as you can get," "there is no such district as outstanding," or "we're different and can't be compared to anyone else, especially business."

In its place, the benchmarking mind-set is symbolized by attitudes, such as "we'll borrow good practices shamelessly," "we can learn something from anyone," or "we certainly don't have a corner on all the answers." The benchmarking effort forces colleagues to talk openly with their counterparts in other schools, districts, and communities. Taking stock of how others do things successfully can be very therapeutic.

Benchmarking separates fact from fiction. So finding the better way somewhere else paves the way for new actions. It's much easier to convince the school organization that a better way is doable and not a "pie in the sky" if school leadership can point to another school or district already doing it. It saves reinventing the wheel!

Although advocates of TQM, ISO 9000 Education Standards, or the Baldrige National Quality Program Criteria for Education might say that benchmarking isn't all that necessary (as a matter of fact if done properly it advances each of the three), it greatly spurs continuous improvement. Incessant step-by-step improvement is a sound education strategy—if the starting point lies within a reasonable distance of the goal the school is trying to reach.

Benchmarking propels the school or district to recognize and achieve situations where a *quantum leap* in performance is needed. Quantum leaps usually call for a "clean sheet of paper" and to rethink basic assumptions about how to operate. Continuous improvement is valuable but it cannot get us there if a fundamental change is needed. The key is answering the question: How far do we have to go? Analogous to golf, which club do I need to pull out of my bag to put the ball in the cup (reach the objective)? The answer depends on how far from the cup you are, your lie on the ground, and how skilled you are in using the club.

WHAT SCHOOL BENCHMARKING IS NOT

The best way to better understand benchmarking is to look at what it is not. For starters, benchmarking is not comparative analysis, where an analyst looks at how his or her school stacks up to others in terms of measures like the student–faculty ratio, productivity, cost per student, dropout rates, graduation rates, or student satisfaction. Why? Because this kind of data does not drive change nor does it help us focus on the practices that lead to superior performance.

Neither is benchmarking process reengineering, which is a method for looking at internal processes and making needed improvements. It applies a variety of techniques, such as quality initiatives spelled out in our book *Healing Public Schools: The Winning Prescription to Cure Their Chronic Illness*,[1] BSC, CRM, and DW. For example, the school wants to improve its registration process, so it looks at itself and inwardly works on process steps to fix the problems it finds.

Nor is benchmarking a survey. Schools have traditionally gathered data about their own practices and processes compared to those of others. Surveys are commonly used tools for such data gathering and can be extremely useful. They create the opportunity to compare data points on specific items within and between school organizations and may also provide a useful source for longitudinal trending. But the nature of the data gathering is fundamentally different in these respects:

- Surveys have participants. Benchmarking studies have partners. A survey participant is selected for a variety of reasons such as a common geographic area or type of school (e.g., magnet schools) and may frequently request anonymity. A benchmarking partner expects reciprocity, that is, to learn something in return for sharing information.

- A major purpose of benchmarking is making friends with other people who are doing specific, analogous-to-your-own-school operations in a better way, sharing information, and perhaps helping each other along the way. After all, the other school may not be as proficient as you are in some other areas.
- The output is different. Surveys generally report aggregated, often average, data from numerous participants. Benchmarked output may also include this type of data but will often detail successful scenarios of practices for the process or function.

Many, in fact, completely miss the point of benchmarking. Benchmarking isn't intended as an easily accomplished one-shot effort. Especially, it isn't a three-hour show-and-tell session with another school where it tells you what it's doing and you say, "Gee, that's a good idea. We'll copy it!" Then you come back with one or two ideas and try to make a change. Neither an improvement mechanism has been developed nor has a clear path been laid out for future actions and results. Nor have any measurements of success typically been put in place. The name of the game with benchmarking is to institutionalize the improvement ethic.

Performance measures for classroom teaching practices and school administrative support still remain the exception rather than the rule in most schools. The field of education talks a lot about "exemplary" or "best" practice, without in fact having determined and measured what is in fact "best."

With big changes demanded in schooling to meet accountability for results, schools must develop competently based standards of best organizational, curricular, and classroom teaching practice to match state-mandated learning standards. Only the systematic review of school processes and practices can give educators the ability to self-diagnose the underlying reasons for unacceptable student learning outcomes. The benchmarking question is: What process changes could we adopt that have led elsewhere to better teaching outcomes?

What are needed are mechanisms to make breakthroughs possible to reliable classroom teaching. Benchmarking is a sound tactic. It allows for the free exchange of "best education practices" that have been evaluated in similar situations.

As a standard of comparative excellence, benchmarking is used to measure similar things. The benchmarking process allows the school leadership to compare its practices, processes, and outcomes to other's standards of excellence in a methodical way. Benchmarking also offers a key to gaining support for needed changes. For one thing, a comparison through benchmarking helps identify problems and potential solutions before they negatively impact proposed new programs.

The objective is to aim high, to gain results that other approaches have been unable to reach. Benchmarking yields results far greater than those achieved by less formal approaches. Benchmarking also provides focused and useful data, not just anecdotal information, intuition, or opinion; it creates a culture of continuous improvement; it enhances creativity; it opens minds to new ideas; it overpowers the "not invented here" mentality; and it raises awareness to changes in the outside world.

Benchmarking provides the opportunity for a school organization to see if it really meets its own expectations and to learn why or why not. Possibly, its expectations are set too low or too vague. Benchmarks enable a school organization to think about current operations and where it is going in solid terms; to set measurable goals that benchmarks can help reach; and to consider the costs and benefits of pursuing a given course of action. Benchmarking has a powerful dispersal potential. Others can immediately see *what* has been done, *why* it was done, the results, and the specific actions that produced the result.

Benchmarking has four key steps: (1) determining *whom* to benchmark against, (2) identifying *what* to benchmark and establishing baseline data, (3) determining *how* that standard has been achieved by comparing your school organization's current practices with the way the benchmarked organization does similar things, and (4) deciding *if* to make changes or improvements in order to meet or exceed the benchmark.

DETAILS OF THE BENCHMARKING PROCESS

The following are the key benchmarking steps as part of *Healing Public Schools*:

1. Determine what to benchmark and establish internal baseline data. The first step is to assess current needs of your school. Ask

what results do you want to achieve and by when. Start with a vision of what "doing it well" really means; in other words, what do you consider superior performance? Second, define your own practices and processes down to the smallest detail. For example, when a student fills out a particular form, what becomes of the form? What use is made of the form? Why is a particular piece of information asked for? What is done with each piece of information on that form?

2. What is your benchmark? What standard of excellence are you looking for in this particular practice or process? What other school districts have achieved this excellence? What is the difference between your school's results and the results of the "best" school organization? For example, if you decide to benchmark a school or a company in your area because it handles telephone inquiries faster, cheaper, and with fewer complaints, these are some of the questions to be answered.

3. Determine how that standard has been achieved and compare your school's current practices with the way that "best" organization does similar things. In what ways does the other organization do a similar process or a part of a process better than your school? Why does the way it does the job yield better results, in less time, at less cost? Use analysis to help focus improvement efforts and set expectations for such efforts.

4. Decide to make changes or improvements in order to meet or exceed the benchmark. Benchmarking is most useful when the data is used for more than an academic exercise or comparing one department to another. Data gathering and the entire benchmarking effort is designed to take action and to allow your school to make improvements by thinking about each decision in concrete terms.

These four steps require a background of work to put them into practice. The benchmarking action plan must eventually include monitoring and specifying (1) *how* will we know whether the changes are succeeding, (2) *what* measurements are being used, (3) *why* certain data is to be collected, and (4) *what* time intervals will be used for collecting the data.

The benchmark needs to be reevaluated periodically to determine if it remains the "best standard" now used. If not, determine what becomes the new benchmark and begin the effort to reach the new one. The monitoring phase sheds light on a critical aspect of benchmarking that sets it apart from the usual way organizations try to improve. Benchmarking is not a onetime, quick fix undertaking. It is a continuous learning process.

WHERE TO LOOK FOR BENCHMARK MODELS

Educators normally look only at other schools for "best" practices. This is shortsighted and illustrates another reason for a lack of progress. Successful benchmarking involves looking *outside* of as well as within your own field. In the business world, companies who have successfully benchmarked have liberally borrowed from companies far outside their own industry. For example, Compaq Computer benchmarked Disney World to improve facilities management. Xerox benchmarked L.L. Bean in warehousing and materials handling, Federal Express for billing efficiency, and Cummins Engine for production scheduling—all outside of the Xerox industry. For its manufacturing unit designed to meet customer emergency needs, Corning Glass benchmarked best-in-class hospital emergency wards to understand how such teams are organized for crises.

Confining benchmarking efforts to school organizations like your own limits your goals and creativity. Your own field is too familiar. This makes it all the more difficult to *see* change with a fresh perspective. Conversely, a benchmarking search of organizations outside of your field *stimulates* creativity because it forces the viewer out of habitual patterns of thought and routine ways of doing things.

Most schools have incomplete information about what is the best practice, if in fact they ever even raise the issue. They might note which elementary grade teacher raised reading scores of students the most, but they would probably not move very aggressively to spread that practice. And even if they did, this type of comparison avoids the question of whether *any* of the departments are as effective as they could be. Best-in-class benchmarking lets schools break free of itself and from self-imposed limits on performance.

POSSIBILITIES FOR IMPROVING EDUCATION

In adapting to new demands, schools need the benefits of more research on learning, as three U.S. presidents have noted in their special messages on educational reform. But we must not defer action, or the means to support it, until the day when we may finally understand fully the mystery of the learning process. School leaders already know a great deal more than they are willing—or able—to put into practice. Careful studies and voluminous reports generated by billions of federal, state, and private-sector dollars spent on education research have given educators many examples of proven opportunities to improve school performance:

1. Elementary schools where children have more choice of study
2. Schools where older students tutor younger ones
3. Schools in which each student sets his own pace in prescribed instruction
4. Work-study schools that link education and the world outside
5. Schools with emphasis on learning outside the classroom
6. Schools where parents and community actively participate in planning
7. Parallel programs so students may choose alternatives to reach similar goals

Each example is responsive and more satisfying than in institutions still using rigid and conventional formats to meet the needs of students and teachers.

ON THE SUBJECT OF CHANGE

Benchmarking is still unique to schooling. The process induces culture shock, thereby making the subject of change a pressing matter to tackle. In schools, as in all organizations, change happens when there is an activist, a promoter, a believer, or a sponsor of change.

The first step, the benchmarking breakthrough, comes when followers see that change is both desirable and feasible and school leadership is behind it. The climate has to be right just as it is in biology. Every school system has a "cemetery" full of dead projects. Each change effort was once alive and warmly promoted by some enthusiast. But remember, we are not speaking about projects in this book of tools. We have carefully set forth the cycle of plan-do-act-measure as the clinical methodology of *Healing Public Schools*. Skepticism has become so rampant that many educators (and stakeholders) are wary of *all* proposed improvements, no matter how reasonable and necessary.

The greatest obstacle to change, whether it be via benchmarking other's "best practices" or following quality process improvement criteria, is more psychological than technical. No proposed solution and no set of tools, no matter how strong the evidence, can be adopted and nurtured until school leaders overcome one widespread malady in school life: the *desensitization* of teachers, administrators, and school board members to chronic school problems.

CONDUCTING THE BENCHMARKING SITE VISIT

It's necessary to do more than collect information by phone or survey. Schools need to conduct site visits. This is firsthand feedback. It is on-the-ground information (the afterword by William R. King provides firsthand insights into best practices benchmarking). While site visits are the most time-consuming and expensive method of information gathering, they do provide the highest quality of information. You can witness firsthand work processes, methods, and practices in action. But before you do this, the following nine guidelines, excerpted from Christopher E. Bogan and Michael J. English's *Benchmarking for Best Practices: Winning through Innovative Adaptation*, will help your site-visit teams be more effective:

1. Learn about the partner you are going to visit. Collect information in advance to help the benchmarking team understand the partner's processes.
2. Prepare your questions in advance to guide and structure your team's visit.
3. Prepare the benchmarking partner for your team's visit. Send questions ahead of time and set an agenda.
4. Use the questionnaire to structure your visit and discussions.

5. Travel in pairs or small groups during the site tour.
6. Arrange for follow-up conversation should there be additional questions.
7. Conduct a postsession debriefing to discuss the team's observations and ideas.
8. Prepare a trip report summarizing site-visit findings and conclusions.
9. Send a thank-you note and confirm the accuracy of site-visit notes by describing the benchmarking partner's operations.[2]

Look at the value of effectively benchmarking best practices this way for a moment. For every student failing to be well enough prepared to earn a living or share in the benefits and obligations of American citizenship, *all of us* pay a price in more taxes, greater social unrest, increased crime, and a general vulnerability in a ferociously competitive global economy. At the end of the day, the student is deprived of the realistic chance to reach his or her full potential.

"Insiders" must no longer be allowed to live comfortably with unattended chronic school problems. Perhaps, when "outsiders" finally *see* these chronic problems for the first time they may finally be shocked into action since they have, thus far, not been rendered shockproof.

BENCHMARK: GOOD RESEARCH

There are, literally, thousands of studies dealing with school effects on student learning. We have read hundreds of studies. No doubt, one could find good research we did not include with this book. But this book is intended as a living document that prescribes solutions to greater school effectiveness. Good schools do lots of good things at the same time. Often, these actions are mutually reinforcing. Therefore, it is difficult to isolate the distinct contributions of particular policies and practices. The literature is full of case studies that describe the interdependence of the characteristics of effective schools. But despite the limitations of education research, there appears to be substantial consensus among those who study schools about the consequences of certain policies and practices for student learning. There is less agreement about particular instructional strategies, curricula, and learning resources.

Almost all good benchmarking studies illustrate the effectiveness of different schools and the importance of context in determining the impact of different policies and practices. Thus, much of what we conclude may seem unsurprising. At the same time, what we find in the research is much less often found in schools. One explanation for why policies and practices likely to improve student learning are not more widely used is that these effective policies and practices do not neatly fit the pattern of good schools that dominates popular thinking. One reason why school effectiveness research has had less impact than it might have had is that it rides alongside of, rather than within, the thinking of many educators, policymakers, civic leaders, and parents on why and how schools make a difference. While it is common to criticize many proposals for school improvement as "too theoretical," almost every stakeholder carries around with him or her assumptions, whether they are called mental models or general explanations relating to education. These become the window through which people explain what they see and hear. Often, such imbedded theories influence what we learn and choose to do.

BENCHMARK: RELIABLE TEACHING AND SCHOOL EFFECTIVENESS

Research-based principles have important consequences for teaching and learning. For example, they explain why: (1) effective instruction must actively engage students in problem solving that is meaningful to them, (2) what students can learn is shaped by what they already know and believe, (3) teaching that is unresponsive to student differences is likely to be unproductive, and (4) schools need to engage the full range of influences on student learning. Teachers influence student learning in many ways. A review of research on alternative explanations for student achievement conducted for the U. S. Department of Education in the mid-1980s concluded:

> In virtually every instance in which researchers have examined the factors that account for student performance, teachers prove to have a greater impact than programs. This is true for average students and exceptional students, for normal classrooms and special classrooms. Teachers allocate and manage the student's time, set and communicate

standards and expectations for student performance, and, in a multitude of other ways, enhance or impede what students learn.[3]

BENCHMARK: PROCESSES THAT DRIVE PERFORMANCE

Organizations are ways of structuring, focusing, and facilitating collective human behavior. Some elements of an organization are more central to what makes them successful or effective than others. If these processes do not work well, other elements of the organization will be relatively ineffective. School organizational processes need to be sharpened when one or more of the following conditions exist:

- The relationship between core activities and goal attainment is uncertain. For example, teaching becomes less reliable because the effects of particular instructional practices depend on circumstances the practitioners cannot know about or even affect.
- The task to be performed varies greatly and must be modified in response to its observed effects. For example, students vary in readiness to learn from day to day and from subject to subject in ways difficult to predict.
- Desired outcomes are multiple, diffuse, and difficult to measure. What does it mean, for example, to "prepare students for democratic citizenship"?

Therefore, the processes needed for school organizational effectiveness depend on (1) flexibility and adaptability, (2) the quality of information about the tasks to be performed and the probable consequences of alternatives to perform such tasks, and (3) the competencies, judgment, and collaborative skills of the persons responsible for the core activities.

BENCHMARK: ESSENTIALS OF EFFECTIVE SCHOOLS

To put it simply, school effectiveness is determined by what students learn in school. And solid evidence of student learning and productivity is the way school effectiveness needs to be measured. While advocates for school reform have developed models and long lists to identify conditions, structures, policies, programs, and practices associated with student learning, there appear to be five types of interrelated school-level influences that most powerfully affect student learning:

1. Teacher motivation and capabilities related to effective teaching
2. School-level conditions that support collaborative problem solving
3. Shared values, beliefs, and professional standards of the school
4. School resources that affect student opportunities to learn in school
5. School policies and practices that affect student readiness to learn

So does it all come down to leadership when we talk school effectiveness? Almost every study of achieving more effective schools starts with the importance of leadership. Leaders look first and foremost at the processes used in the school to define and achieve its strategic objectives.

THE SPIRIT OF ORGANIZATIONAL CHANGE

Ready. Fire. Aim! There is a psychological dimension to benchmarking because billions of dollars are wasted on ambitious efforts to alter patterns and practices in businesses, hospitals, and schools. Most of these initiatives start with a bang and shortly sputter, soon ending with things pretty much as they were. The energy created in the beginning is lost or misplaced somewhere along the way. The cause of this sad track record is becoming clearer.

If we approach change in a human enterprise solely from a technical mind-set, assuming that simply changing strategy or restructuring roles is going to do the trick, we're probably doomed to fail. In such cases, everything we try will be quickly absorbed by the very cultural patterns and practices we want to change.

However, if we think about changing behavior as a spiritual undertaking, a different set of opportunities present themselves. First of all, we use a different vocabulary and embrace different, less familiar, assumptions. Second, we pose new questions that are routine in other aspects of our lives but rarely thought about in business or schools. Questions like: How can we beef up our school's spirit? How can our work be uplifted by more spirit? How can we move our people to a new commitment to student success or encourage them to adopt past convictions long since abandoned? How can we reclaim the spiritual underpinnings of the origins of public schooling to create new sources of energy to sustain the demanding journey change requires?

In a prophetic statement quoted for many generations, John Adams wrote: "I must study politics and war that my sons may have the liberty to study mathematics and philosophy. My sons ought to study mathematics and philosophy, geography, natural history, naval architecture, navigation, commerce, and agriculture in order to give their children a right to study paintings, poetry, music, architecture, statuary, tapestry, and porcelain."[4]

We know how modern people create spiritual energy. In a church or synagogue, spirit is beckoned through scripture, liturgy, music, and ritual. It should be possible to tap such energy in a school system.

The solution, at least as a first step, is to recognize that ours is a spiritually, as well as a technically, driven world. Such consciousness fits our knowledge that the path to genuine power also requires the recognition of the nonphysical dimensions of the human being.

Of course, explaining how spirit works in an organization is a tough task. But here is an example that might help us. Spirit is like going to the bank to open a safety-deposit box. It takes two keys to open it, your key and the bank's key. Leaders of change understand that spirit applies to fundamental matters, to what counts most for us, and that it cannot be kept apart from other aspects of our lives.

Spirit, as we have come to understand it, defies rigorous definition. The spirit of a holiday like Thanksgiving, for example, shines brilliantly once each year. It inspires people to experience the magic of the season. It creates plentiful if only a temporary supply of ego energy. As the spirit rises, the world looks and feels different, more sunny and confident. When spirit is removed, only the basic outward appearance remains, while the energy slips away.

Spirit moves us beyond failure. It helps us strive toward setting new goals, developing new attitudes, and achieving new accomplishments. We cannot live and work in a school totally driven by efficiency, productivity, and materialism. One only needs to look at the drive and remarkable comeback of three-time Tour de France winner Lance Armstrong whose testicular cancer had spread to his lungs and brain. Only a few years earlier, Armstrong was given less than a fifty-fifty chance to live. But here he was in 2001, driven by his indomitable spirit, triumphing once again and wearing the winner's yellow jersey.

Must we look for our daily motivation from other sources? Not really. Sure, spirit has some credibility problems. Yet, despite all this, the term "spirit" regularly unites itself into our everyday conversation and experiences. Charles Lindbergh flew *The Spirit of St. Louis* solo to Paris. The American Revolution is immortalized in "The Spirit of '76." Expressions we use all the time include "keep the spirit," "the spirit is willing but the flesh is weak," "team spirit," "esprit de corps," "school spirit," and "his spirits are up." Such phrases are effective motivators.

In the aftermath of September 11, we almost instantly witnessed an unprecedented display of American patriotism—a spirit built around displaying the flag, wearing red, white, and blue pins or ribbons, singing "America the Beautiful," and countless other smaller expressions of the American spirit.

Spirit can be either a constructive or destructive force. Positive spirit spawns hope, ego energy, and confidence—a belief in one's self—a can-do mind-set. But it's easy to spot what happens when an organization's spirit goes sour.

Negative spirit is the root of hopelessness. It saps energy, shatters hope, and drags down performance. If an organization is plagued by an unhealthy spirit, what can be done? Consider what happens when a sports team spirals down into a prolonged slump. It leaves us at the point where tinkering with input and structural features of the organization is not going to get us to where we need to go.

What's needed to break out of the slump? It takes bold, risk-taking leaders that are willing to leave the safety of the status quo, to sail uncharted waters in the quest of finding new spirit. Otherwise, our schools, like the sports team, will continue to lose faith in itself and lose face in meeting the skill demands of intense competition.

IDENTIFYING LOW-PERFORMING SCHOOLS

A central piece in state and district accountability systems, mandated by Title I, is the establishment of procedures and standards (measurements) for defining and identifying low-performing schools. For example:

- Maryland established a school performance index to determine if a school is meeting state expectations. To meet standards, schools must maintain a 94 percent attendance rate, have 70 percent of students scoring at the satisfactory level on the state assessment, and have no more than a 3 percent high school dropout rate.

- In New York, at least 90 percent of students in each school are expected to score at or above state benchmarks. In addition, no school's dropout rate should exceed 5 percent. Schools that fail to achieve minimum performance standards risk having their registration placed under review.

- The Kentucky Instructional Results Information System establishes a baseline starting point and academic goals for each school in the state. The state has projected goals for student performance through the year 2010. Schools that exceed the goals are eligible for financial awards and schools that fall behind are designated "in decline." The lowest-performing schools designated as "schools in crisis" are those whose performance declines by more than 5 percent of their baseline for two consecutive assessment cycles.

- The Texas Education Agency annually collects data on its more than 1,000 school districts and 3.7 million students. In conjunction with results from the Texas Assessment of Academic Skills (TAAS), Texas disaggregates student performance data and measures not only a school's progress, but also student performance across a range of racial/ethnic and income groups. In order to make adequate yearly progress, Texas schools must obtain an "acceptable" rating from the state's accountability system—a rating that requires at least 40 percent of all students and student groups to pass each section of TAAS, a dropout rate of no more than 6 percent, and an attendance rate of at least 94 percent. These standards increase each year.

- The San Francisco Unified School District uses nine performance indicators to identify low-performing schools, including the percentage of students who score below the twenty-fifth percentile on the district assessment; the numbers of suspensions, dropouts, and student absences in schools; the percentage of teachers who are long-term substitutes; and the number of students requesting open enrollment transfers out of certain schools.

As part of this emphasis on accountability, data gathered from state and district assessments are informing the public about school performance. Eighteen states, including Florida, Oklahoma, Maryland, Texas, and Wisconsin, distribute school report cards that display information about student learning in every school in the state. These report cards are helping stakeholders judge how well schools are achieving their long-range goals and how schools measure up to other schools with similar student populations. For example:

- The New York State Education Department issues a report card for every school each year. These report cards allow for comparisons of student achievement results across a cohort of similar schools based on the likeness of the age range served by the school, the resource capacity of the district, and the economic need of the school's students.
- The Charlotte-Mecklenburg school system distributes easy-to-read student learning goals to parents at the beginning of the school year. The district follows up with school report cards on student attendance and performance that are distributed to parents and every household in the district and are published in the newspaper.

The establishment of state and local systems of accountability has been important for leveraging change in low-performing schools. In many cases, being publicly identified as low performing has been a necessary impetus for change. But it is only the first step on the road to improvement. Turning around low-performing schools requires tough choices and a focus on strategies that will improve curriculum, teaching, and learning.

Real school transformation demands changes in the relationships among adults within schools and between educators and parents, school and community leaders, unions, district officials, and partners at all levels of government. School reform requires a willingness to learn, to alter old practices, and to act in new ways.

BENCHMARK PRINCIPLES FOR RELIABLE SCHOOLS

The job of every school is to continually improve the learning experience of each student to master learning, to assume responsibility for student learning, to assess student performance against rising achievement standards, and to assure students are readied to perform quality work in the twenty-first century.

Our list of benchmark principles, which focuses on goals, was created to help guide schools to measure their progress (see appendix D). Adapted from the Baldrige National Quality Program Criteria for Education, they help faculty measure effectiveness. Each benchmark principle identifies expectations for growth and establishes a tool for school self-appraisal. To pursue reliable quality in schools ushers in a new era of caring. By applying Baldrige Education Criteria, the reliable quality school comes into being. The hallmark of the reliable quality school is evaluation and accountability. The education benchmark principles are intended to bring relevant principles and metrics of performance management into schools.

The principles to measure *system-wide* school improvement comprise seven interrelated factors of systemic change:

1. Information and analysis
2. Leadership
3. Student achievement
4. Quality planning
5. Professional development
6. Partnership development
7. Continuous improvement and evaluation

Reliable quality schools measure their progress three times each school year to see their progress. This gives them motivation to keep improving. Equally important, the measurement process brings the staff together to reinforce its shared vision and to plan for other continuous improvement steps for the school. This process strengthens the belief that improvement is continuous and ongoing.

Benchmark principles are not static. The principles themselves help school leaders and stakeholders learn more about school change and the most effective ways to nourish it.

BENCHMARKING CASE STUDIES

The Job That Couldn't Be Done—Guilford County Schools, Greensboro, North Carolina

Results of an international mathematics and science exam released by Boston College ranked Guilford County students above Massachusetts, Connecticut, Pennsylvania, Maryland, North Carolina, and South

Carolina in both mathematics and science achievement. The 1999 Third International Mathematics and Science Study (TIMSS) focused on the mathematics and science achievement of eighth-grade students.

Guilford County school students scored twenty-seven points above the international average in mathematics and forty-six points higher than the international average in science. Guilford County eighth graders scored twelve points above the U.S. average in mathematics and nineteen points above the U.S. average in science. "We are very pleased that the study revealed that our students stack up exceedingly well with students from across the country and around the world," said Terry Grier, the superintendent of schools. "The scores are even more revealing when you compare our spending and population characteristics of those with similar demographics."[5]

Of the thirty-eight participating countries, the United States scored in the middle of the pack. The top-scoring U.S. school systems were in predominantly white areas with a high rate of per-pupil expenditures.

The 1999 data revealed that 37 percent of Guilford County school students were from families who were eligible to receive free or reduced-price meals, which classified them as low income. The top-scoring U.S. systems had only 14 percent of their participants from low-income families. The benchmarking study assessed eighth-grade students' knowledge of mathematics and science and provides an in-depth look at the achievement of districts and states that participated.[6]

Twenty-seven states, districts, and consortia of districts participated in the TIMSS 1999 benchmarking study. The thirteen states were:

Connecticut	Missouri
Idaho	North Carolina
Illinois	Oregon
Indiana	Pennsylvania
Maryland	South Carolina
Massachusetts	Texas
Michigan	

And the fourteen remaining districts and consortia of districts were:

Academy School District #20, Colorado Springs, Colorado
Chicago Public Schools, Illinois

Michigan Invitational Group
Delaware Science Coalition
First in the World Consortium, Illinois
Fremont/Lincoln/West Side Public Schools, Nebraska
Guilford County, North Carolina
Jersey City Public Schools, New Jersey
Miami-Dade County Public Schools, Florida
Montgomery County, Maryland
Naperville Community Unit School District #203, Illinois
Project SMART Consortium, Ohio
Rochester City School District, New York
Southwest Pennsylvania Regional Math and Science Collaborative

U.S. SCHOOLS ACCEPT SINGAPORE MATH BOOKS

Thanks to the TIMSS, one of Singapore's most-talked-about exports these days is neither the computer equipment from its factories nor the rubber from its plantations. It's math textbooks. Elementary and middle school students in this 247-square-mile Southeast Asian nation ranked first in the world on the math portions of the TIMSS assessments, which were given in 1994 and 1995. To earn that title, Singaporeans outpaced their counterparts in thirty-nine other countries, including such educational powerhouses as Japan and Taiwan. They also outscored students in Belgium, Canada, France, Hong Kong, and Switzerland. And they beat the United States!

Now, scattered groups of U.S. educators are hoping the textbooks from that island nation in part hold the secret to Singaporean students' notable success. Sales of the books, published in English, have multiplied since 1998, according to their sole U.S. distributor. It filled orders for "several thousand" of the paperbacks in the 2000–2001 school year. And the volumes are going to a wide range of educators, including home schoolers, private school operators, and public schools from Colorado to Maryland.

Primarily black and white, the books contain none of the colorful, eye-popping graphics that publishers incorporate into many American textbooks to grab students' attention. But admirers of the math books praise them for their clear, simple text, their novel problem-solving approaches, and the complex, multistep problems they give students, beginning in first grade. Students are introduced to algebra concepts early through word problems that seem more at home in high school texts. But rather than use algebraic equations to solve the problems, the books present pictorial strategies that are easily grasped by elementary-level pupils.

There is a great insistence on full understanding and an avoidance of mindless rituals that lead to a solution. The Gabriella and Paul Rosenbaum Foundation, a Chicago-based family philanthropy that promotes math achievement, finances the training of teachers. Whether due to the textbooks or not, students in the program, known as the Ingenuity Project, have gone on to receive honors in local and national mathematics competitions. Two ninth graders, in fact, scored in the top 1 percent on a national mathematics competition in February 2001.

Schools in Chicago, Montgomery County, Maryland, and Paterson, New Jersey, are also piloting the books for a more heterogeneous student population including some children who find school a struggle. One bonus for students using the books is that they are thinner and lighter than most American-made math texts. A drawback is that the books are riddled with unfamiliar names, British-flavored spellings and terms, and metric measurements.

Like the math texts published by Saxon Publishers, a small, Marion, Oklahoma, firm, the Singapore text may buck current American trends in mathematics education and local or national standards for teaching the subject. Though Singaporeans speak a mix of languages, more than 90 percent of the 4.2 million residents of the former British colony are literate. The central Ministry of Education develops textbooks in every subject, and students pay a fee to use them. Singaporean parents, like parents in other Southeast Asian countries, also typically supplement their children's learning with after-school tutoring sessions.[7]

POLICY VOIDS BLOCKING SCHOOL IMPROVEMENT

There are three missing policy initiatives that power or block school improvement and absent these initiatives to power change, current efforts cannot pierce the underlying armor of the school culture. According to E. John Chubb and Terry E. Moe, "[a]ny reform which leaves the basic structure intact will tend to be assimilated and neutralized. In general the

various components of the existing system are so strongly interconnected that any attempt to change one component in isolation will set off
a series of compensating adjustments among all the others, mitigating
the impact of the reform."[8]

Louisiana provides a striking example. It was way ahead of the rest
of the nation in enacting education reform laws and new policies. The
titles to the laws and policies promulgated over a ten-year period read
like a table of contents to a book summarizing the policy reform efforts
of all the other states combined. What has been the result of reform in
Louisiana? The following markers tell the sad story:

- Louisiana has the highest illiteracy rate among the fifty states.
- The average American College Test scores of Louisiana students
  rank twenty-seventh out of the twenty-eight states, trailed only by
  Mississippi. The gap between Louisiana's scores and the national
  average is larger than it was ten years ago.
- Louisiana students scored significantly lower than the national average among southern states (Arkansas, Florida, Louisiana, South
  Carolina, and West Virginia) that participated in the Southern Regional Education Board/National Assessment of Education
  Progress eleventh-grade reading-testing program in 1985–1986.
  Although more than 80 percent of the Louisiana eleventh graders
  tested said their grades were mostly As, Bs, and Cs in school, test
  results indicated only 37 percent read well enough for college-
  level work.
- The program results showed that the reading scores of black
  Louisiana eleventh graders are equivalent to the average reading
  scores of white seventh graders nationally.
- Louisiana has the lowest graduation rate among the states—only
  54.7 percent of the state's ninth graders went on to graduate from
  high school four years later in 1985, according to the U.S. Department of Education. Graduation rate data is not compiled in the
  same manner by every state, and Louisiana officials say many of
  their students who drop out eventually get a General Education
  Diploma.
- Louisiana's college freshmen are so unprepared when they leave
  high school that over half (51.4 percent) of them had to take re-

medial courses in Louisiana's public colleges and universities despite the fact that they were all high school graduates.

The fate of public education reform efforts in Louisiana despite more than a decade of trying to improve the school system bears out Chubb and Moe's observation quoted earlier. Those who have tried to change the system have time and again seen reform measures watered down, ignored, improperly implemented, taken to court by the teacher unions, repealed, mired down in turf battles and power struggles between public bodies, or not funded (often not because the money was not there, but because failing to fund a program is a certain way to kill it).

Regrettably, the Louisiana example is not unique. It is an example of the current state of most education reform efforts. To us, the absence of three highly interdependent education policies account in large part for the poor results of educational reform. Their continued absence and implementation virtually guarantees continued failure. The three education policies center on: (1) the performance management of breakthrough and control, (2) teacher accountability for knowing and using best practice, and (3) administrative logistical support of the teaching and learning process. These policy voids plus the *missing outrage of concern for chronic problems among staff and leaders* must be addressed.

Policy Void #1: The Performance Management of Breakthrough and Control

To restructure education, mastery of breakthrough and control is essential.

"Breakthrough" means change. Its performance management is targeted toward a dynamic, decisive movement to a new and higher attainment. The range of breakthrough events is as broad as the human imagination.

"Control" means staying the course. Its performance management is targeted to sticking to current standards and preventing change.

Breakthrough and control are part of the plan-do-act-revise cycle. The cycle consists of alternating plateaus and gains in performance. Plateaus are the result of control. Gains are the result of breakthrough.

In a dynamic school enterprise, this cycle goes on and on. The differences between breakthrough and control are so great that the decision of whether, at any one time, to embark on breakthrough, or to continue on control, is of cardinal importance. "The choice of breakthrough or control is a decision not only as to the results desired; it is decisive also as to the means."[9]

Policy Void #2: Teacher Accountability for Knowing and Using Best Practice

The "soul" of any profession consists of the tools, processes, and materials its members customarily use to satisfy their duties and task requirements. In short, a profession relies on its technologies. Such professional technologies come to life in the *practice* of its members. Taken together, they represent professional practices. In medicine, law, and engineering, it is possible, and often legally mandated, for the professional to distinguish clearly between good practice, poor practice, and malpractice.

Such has never been the case in education. The word "practice" itself is often reserved for learning, as in practice teaching. It is seldom invoked for the furtherance of professional mastery, as in a *teaching practice*. Until recently, education lacked an agreed on authoritative body of classroom teaching practice; now, however, teaching has such an inventory; it's just not using it.

Whereas the doctor, the lawyer, and the engineer are held personally accountable for knowing and using best practice as their regular practice, the teacher is not. The teacher is free to ignore or to remain ignorant of what works, or to use tools, processes, and materials that do not (or can not) contribute to intended standards for student outcomes. A teacher can repeatedly use inadequate technologies with poor results and still enjoy the same professional status as one who is getting results.

Any profession that cannot or does not describe and use good practice as regular practice and does not distinguish between good and bad practice lacks all possibility for breakthrough. Its members are forced to rely on its folklore and various ideologies. Professional practice calls for the concept and regular use of good practice and constant improvement toward best practice. Absent such insights and policies, its members, supporters, and detractors will continue to seek external explanations to teaching and learning failures that are under their control. It's like Flip Wilson's old comedy routine—"the devil made me do it"—when things go wrong.

The single most effective and proven strategy for using breakthrough and control in school policy is to design, locate, train, install, and support "best practice" as regular practice in schools and classrooms. Following the examples of medicine and agriculture, the teaching profession must be encouraged by benchmarking to hold itself accountable for knowing what is and using best practice.

Policy Void #3: Logistical Support

The profession of education lacks the concept of logistical support, and this goes a long way toward explaining why there is so much unreliability in classroom teaching. The field of logistics is ripe for the picking by education. The teacher, *with logistical support as a fundamental part of management*, can really begin to meet such an epic vision as "no child left behind."

Webster's New Collegiate Dictionary defines *logistics* as "the handling of the details of an operation." Anytime we are involved with people, we are involved with logistics. Logistics is the series of mechanisms that supports the work of people. Logistical support is used, but its nature and importance is often overlooked. In a shift away from Industrial Age individuality and toward Information Age teamwork, the field of logistics plays an ever-increasing role.

Logistics is operational leverage. It is the *service* in the service organization. It provides the opportunity to gain service superiority through the resolution of recurring issues. Wal-Mart built its customer service dominance on logistical support, so, too, did Target stores. Caring is the soul of logistical support.

- In the military the logistical objective is to minimize casualties and maximize campaign effectiveness.
- In space exploration NASA seeks to minimize human risk and maximize man–machine effectiveness. *Apollo 13* is a stirring example of logistical support in action.

- In sports the name of the game is to minimize your own mistakes and capitalize on your opponents errors—create every opportunity to score. The application of new technologies has provided logistical improvements for both players and coaches.
- In healthcare the goal is to minimize health provider time and maximize patient-centered results. To the consumer, more is at stake in healthcare than in almost any service field.
- In manufacturing, the producer seeks to minimize waste and maximize quality output. An entire global standards industry driven by ISO 9000 testifies to a worldwide effort to make the customer's life easier. ATMs and 35mm picture film is standardized throughout the world.
- Food services want to minimize wasted time and maximize customer satisfaction.
- Banking is standardized within nations and already meets international transaction standards. Checks and forms are becoming more uniform worldwide.
- Transportation services are built on logistical support—to minimize time/cost and maximize delivery/satisfaction. American Airlines, Amtrak, and Greyhound use effective logistical support systems. So too Hertz, Avis, National, and Budget rental cars could not deliver customer satisfaction without logistical support. UPS and FedEx build next day and second day delivery services on a logistical support system of dedicated people backed up by planes, trucks, computers, communications, terminals, and tracking systems. The U.S. Postal Service has adapted logistical support to satisfy its waning customer base.
- Emergency services rely on minimizing time and maximizing safety. Behind every 9-1-1 call is a vast array of logistical systems to support dedicated people who dispatch ambulances, police, fire, evacuation orders, storm, and disaster relief. The system is built on the premise of *care for* the caller and victim.
- Research is intended to minimize duplication and maximize the collection of data and information. The University of California at San Francisco has 800,000 volumes and 2,800 subscriptions to current journals to support their medical research technology and people.

In education the need for and the application of logistical support is every bit as vast as any of the previous examples. It is aimed at helping the student select courses, offering and distributing books, fiscal and reporting services, individual and workshop-based assistance to faculty in preparing existing or new course work, instructional design, materials development, teaching strategies, classroom management and evaluation. It means getting assignments back and forth between instructors and students, proctoring exams, taking and reporting attendance. It provides enrollment services and student records. It makes available information and media technologies including Internet, satellite up and down links, AV support of content, library on-line catalogs, and electronic databases. Logistical support involves academic support (administering academic programs), student services (intellectual, cultural, and social development), and institutional support (planning and executive leadership.) Distance education is fast becoming a worldwide service. Logistical support is solutions and strategies for schools.

NOTES

1. Allen Salowe and Leon Lessinger, *Healing Public Schools: The Winning Prescription to Cure Their Chronic Illness* (Lanham, Md: Scarecrow, 2001).

2. Christopher E. Bogan and Michael J. English, *Benchmarking for Best Practices: Winning through Innovative Adaptation* (New York: McGraw-Hill, 1994).

3. W. Hawley and S. Rosenholtz, "Good Schools," *Peabody Journal of Education* (1984), chapters 3 and 7.

4. David McCullough, *John Adams* (New York: Simon and Schuster, 2001), 462.

5. Third International Mathematics and Science Study (TIMSS) Report, 4 April 2001, <http://nces.ed.gov/timss> [last accessed: January 7, 2002].

6. TIMSS Report.

7. Debra Viadero, *Education Week*, 27 September 2000.

8. E. John Chubb and Terry E. Moe, *Politics, Markets, and the Organization of Schools* (Washington, D.C.: Brookings Institution, 1986).

9. Joseph M. Juran, *Managerial Breakthrough* (New York: McGraw-Hill, 1964).

CHAPTER 10

Conclusion: Education and the Future of the Nation

In his best-selling biography of John Adams, the second president of the United States, David McCullough shares with readers Adams's short but profound insight into the role of education:

> The more Adams thought about the future of his country, the more convinced he became that it rested on education. Before any great things are accomplished, he [Adams] wrote to a correspondent,
>
> "A memorable change must be made in the system of education and knowledge must become so general as to raise the lower ranks of society nearer to the higher. The education of a nation instead of being confined to a few schools and universities for the instruction of the few must become the national care and expense for the formation of the many."[1]

Ray Marshall, former U.S. secretary of labor, and Marc Tucker put the issue of the value of education to the nation in more stark terms in their book *Thinking for a Living: Education and the Wealth of Nations*:

> But the threat is clear. If we do not come to a consensus on the need to establish our economy on new principles—the principles of human-resource capitalism—then our prosperity will vanish and our democracy will be under siege. If we can reach beyond our own parochialism to borrow from the most creative and successful policies in the world [benchmark], if we have the will to reexamine the relevance of deeply entrenched institutions, and if we have the courage to take on a multitude of vested interests, then we can leapfrog over the best the world has to offer and build a system for the development and productive use of our human resources that will be without peer.

... The only resources we have is ourselves—our energy, our intellect, our confidence, and our ability to work with one another to common purpose to make American industry and American society the world leaders that they once were, and can be again.[2]

And in *Head to Head*, MIT professor of management Lester C. Thurow minces few words when he states,

Local governments don't want to pay for first-class schools. They know that less than half the population has children in school at any one time, that students will leave home and use their skills in different geographic regions of the country, and that high taxes necessary to pay for good schools would drive industry away. Firms would locate next door and free ride on their well-educated workforce. Someone else should make the necessary investments. . . .

Communities would agree to quit using schools as a dumping ground where they assign social problems that cannot be solved elsewhere. The school's prime responsibility is to insure that their students are educated. The front lines of the war on crime, drugs, teenage pregnancy, or housing desegregation should be established elsewhere. Better nutrition, driver's training, and sports are secondary. The energy of our school systems should be focused on education—not dissipated on other goals, no matter how laudable.[3]

Keynoting the 2001 National Education Summit, Louis V. Gerstner Jr., the chairman of IBM, said:

I want to remind us all why we're here. . . . It's not about books, it's not about buildings, it's not about tests, and it's not about transcripts. . . . [We are] here for one reason, and one reason only.

We're here for the children of America. We're here because we understand, just as the Founding Fathers understood, that absent a healthy, vital system of free public education you can't have an enlightened electorate, which means you can't sustain a working Democracy; you can't build a competitive workforce, which means you can't envision a more prosperous future. It's exactly that clear cut. We have an abiding responsibility to the kids and their future.

. . . If we've learned one thing in this struggle, it is that the schools alone cannot solve this one. This is a national problem. It demands that the entire nation participate in its solution.[4]

PRECIPITATING CHANGE: STARTING AN EPIDEMIC

So where does this leave us? How do we start an epidemic in thinking and action toward improving the quality of schools? Do we wait for another breast-beating speech by a politician?

"The paradox of the epidemic: that in order to get one contagious movement, you often have to create many small movements first," writes Malcolm Gladwell in *The Tipping Point*.[5] It isn't one epidemic focused on one thing. It's thousands of different epidemics, all focused on the groups who have a stake in education.

Diffusion helps understand how an epidemic moves through a population. We have been asked numerous times: How are we going to get everyone to do what you are proposing? Simply stated, you're not. But we do acknowledge certain characteristics about educators (or for that matter other professional groups) that help us predict how things change.

We know that about a one-third of stakeholders will immediately welcome these proposals and tools. These educators are pacesetters, they lead and want to be at the forefront of creating change in schools. These are opinion leaders, respected and thoughtful persons who have analyzed the tools of change.

Another one-third are fence-sitters. This is not all together negative since these are mostly skeptics and deliberate thinkers. They've seen school-change proposals come and go. They prefer to wait and see. They'll tip toward adoption of these new ideas as the pacesetters begin using these new tools to facilitate change. New tools are highly contagious and others want to get on board. Pacesetters and those fence-sitters who are the first to climb down and adopt these tools are, in fact, visionaries. They want revolutionary change.

If the goal of the visionary is to make a quantum leap (breakthrough), forwarding the goal of the pragmatist is to make a measured movement toward change. Innovations do not slide effortlessly from one group to the next. One might picture a wide chasm between the two groups.

The other one-third would just as soon (control) see change go away. These are the most traditional of all. These are the footdraggers. They'll eventually get on board or move on to another school district or career.

What is eventually needed to complete an epidemic are translators, that is, those who can take the new ideas and information from the highly specialized world of education and translate them into a language the rest of the community stakeholders can understand. The message, and the value of the proposed tools for finding solutions to seemingly intractable school problems, needs to eventually make emotional sense to a wider audience. This is the job for the "mavens, connectors and salesmen" as Gladwell puts it.

So at the end of the day, or the end of this book, the reader is left with this question: Where do you fit on the continuum of stakeholders just described?

- Pacesetter?
- Fence-sitter?
- Footdragger?
- Maven, connector, or salesman?
- None of the above?

It's up to you, the reader, to decide.
Now, what are you going to do about it?

NOTES

1. David McCullough, *John Adams* (New York: Simon and Schuster, 2001), 364.

2. Ray Marshall and Marc Tucker, *Thinking for a Living: Education and the Wealth of Nations* (New York: Basic, 1992), 239, 256.

3. Lester C. Thurow, *Head to Head* (New York: Morrow, 1992), 274, 279.

4. Louis V. Gerstner Jr., keynote speech at the 2001 National Education Summit, Palisades, New Jersey, October 9, 2001.

5. Malcolm Gladwell, *The Tipping Point* (Boston: Little, Brown, 2000), 192.

Afterword

When Allen Salowe first asked me to write this afterword, my first thought was, "What does he think I can contribute?" Allen and I have been associates in several projects over the past ten years, and we have written a couple of proposals together. We could never seem to find the right combination of ingredients to realize our shared vision.

Then, he and Leon Lessinger wrote and published their second book, *Healing Public Schools: The Winning Prescription to Cure Their Chronic Illness*, and it was like the flashbulb (okay, for the younger generation, the strobe flash) went off in my head. In *Healing Public Schools*, Allen and Leon outlined a prescription for fixing what's wrong in our system of public education today. In this, their latest effort, they have drilled down to the details. I'm honored to speak about this work in this valuable new book.

The term "benchmarking" originated in the mid-nineteenth century when land surveys were critical to the westward expansion of our country. Without precise surveys, property ownership rights could not be accurately established. The benchmark was "a mark on a permanent object [such as a metal plate affixed to a granite marker] indicating elevation and serving as a reference in topographic surveys."[1] The definition has been expanded today to designate any "point of reference from which measurements may be made."[2]

In chapter 9, the benchmarking process for organizations was laid out in three very simple and basic steps; these are repeated here, with my loose interpretations:

Step 1. Determine: How good are we? (This is called "establishing the baseline." You can't know how well you've done at the end if you don't know where you were at the beginning.)

Step 2. Partner with others to find out how good can we be. (This is how you establish your targets.)

Step 3. Plan: How do we get better? (Or, how do we get from here to there?)

Determining "how good are we" is perhaps the hardest part of benchmarking, because you have to determine *what* to measure. Allen and Leon addressed this phase thoroughly and accurately, so I will not presume to supplement their work, but simply to encourage it. Without doing this critical groundwork, you cannot progress to the next step.

Regarding partnering with others to find out "how good can we be," Allen and Leon state: "Taking stock of how others do things successfully can be very therapeutic." Indeed, it can be very therapeutic for all parties to a benchmarking study—each will find things he or she does very well, which can be shared. The contributor gets a gratifying sense of having helped the recipient(s). But contributors will almost certainly find things they could do better, too, and a better practice flows back to them, in return. It is truly a mutually beneficial (win-win) experience. Hence, the concept of *reciprocity*. It's not data collection for analytical comparative studies. It is evaluating different operative scenarios, identifying the ones among them yielding the best results, and putting them into practice. But this is also not the end of it. The hard part in this step is institutionalizing the change. There will be tremendous resistance to change, and it will take courage and determination on the parts of all concerned to ensure the resistance is met with firm resolve. And finally, the importance of the feedback loop for continuous quality improvement cannot be underestimated. What really must happen here is to change the "organizational state of mind," but without ongoing feedback, you cannot know if that's actually taking place. I like to think of it in the simple terms of the (somewhat dated) TQM initiative: plan-do-check-act. I first learned this when I joined Systems and Computer Technology Corporation (SCT) in 1994, and to this day I think to myself "plan-do-check-act" whenever I'm approaching a new benchmarking activity. It is a handy shorthand way to remember the essential ingredients for any successful organizational endeavor. (I wanted to say "human endeavor" there, but that would be beyond the scope of this piece; however, I encourage the reader to consider the concept.)

As for planning "how do we get better," my favorite phrase for a long time has been "the man with a plan wins." One of my SCT colleagues says it even better: "He who controls the pen controls the situation." This all goes to saying that *something* is better than *nothing*. The person or persons who write down their thoughts, plans, and visions and place them out there for others to critique have put a stake in the ground. This forces the recipients to either take issue with the initial document—and make them come up with something better—or to accept it at face value. (Which rarely happens, human nature being what it is.) At least it gives the larger community a starting point for discussion, which will lead to refinements and buy-in. (And buy-in is *very* important, because it leads to implementation success. Without it, the project stands a better than even chance of failure.)

At this point, a practical definition of the term "benchmarking" in the context of today's business, government, and educational communities bears repeating: Simply put, "steal shamelessly" describes the concept. This doesn't mean "steal criminally"; it means imitate only the best and share your own successes back with them; make best practices out of "pretty good practices."

As my friends Christopher E. Bogan and Michael J. English put it so succinctly and eloquently in their book *Benchmarking for Best Practices: Winning through Innovative Adaptation*:

In a world where common sense prevailed, benchmarking would seem prosaic. It is simply *the systematic process of searching for best practices, innovative ideas, and highly effective operating procedures that lead to superior performance*. What could be more straightforward? No individual, team, or operating unit—no mater how creative or prolific—can possibly parent all innovation. No single department or company [or school] can corner the market on *all* good ideas.

In view of this reality recognizing human limitations, it makes eminently *good sense* to consider the experience of others. Those who always go it alone are doomed to perennially reinvent the wheel, for they do not learn and benefit from others' progress. By systematically studying the best business practices, operating tactics, and winning strategies of others, an individual, team or organization can accelerate its own progress and improvement.[3]

To summarize the process of benchmarking for schools, as Allen and Leon capably describe it in this book, there are four key steps:

1. Determining *who* to benchmark against.
2. Identifying *what* factors to benchmark and establishing internal baseline data.
3. Determining *how* that standard has been achieved and comparing your school organization's current practices with the way that the benchmarked organization does similar things.
4. Deciding *which* changes or improvements are to be made to meet or exceed the benchmark. (If any. It may well be that you'll discover your process is better than any other you've identified. That is a valuable finding, and should encourage you to share your process with your benchmarking partners.)

By following the solutions outlined in this critically important book, educators, administrators, parents, and, most importantly, students will improve their performance. It is a daunting task, but "somebody's gotta do it," and I hope there are many "somebodies" out there who will take this book and run with it. Our future as a great nation is at stake.

Some additional thoughts since our national tragedy on September 11, 2001: A good friend who shall remain anonymous said to me recently, "We must be very careful not to go around as the world's greatest superpower imposing our will on other nations whose values may be different. What happens in fifty years when the Chinese are the world's greatest superpower and *they* want to impose *their* value system on *us*?" I thought this was a very astute and sobering comment, and subsequent events to this point are encouraging. We haven't as yet "bombed Afghanistan back to the Stone Age," but that isn't the point here. The point is, without taking the book you have just finished reading very seriously, the real possibility that the United States could lose its preeminent position as the world's greatest superpower is all too real. That itself should be enough to start an epidemic!
William R. King

NOTES

1. *Merriam-Webster's Online Dictionary*, <http://www.m-w.com/cgi-bin/dictionary> [last accessed: August 15, 2001].

2. *Merriam-Webster's Online Dictionary*.

3. Christopher E. Bogan and Michael J. English, *Benchmarking for Best Practices: Winning through Innovative Adaptation* (New York: McGraw-Hill, 1994), 1, emphasis added.

Benchmarking the Comer School Improvement Process

The goal of the Comer School Improvement Process is to ensure that *all* students are successful in learning the essential curriculum. This process is the outcome of a model that was developed through the collaborative efforts of Dr. James Comer, with his Yale Child Study Center staff, and the New Haven Public School System. It addresses the negative impact of change, social stratification, and conflict and distrust between home and school. The documented results of the implemented process dramatically demonstrate improved student attendance and achievement, as well as a new bonding between parents, teachers, and students.

The Comer School Improvement Process focuses on the knowledge of behavioral and social sciences as applied to every aspect of the school program. Central to this process is the belief that all students can learn and that all the adults involved do their learning best when it is the result of collaborative participation. This approach focuses high expectations for students, a team approach to identifying student and school needs, and parent involvement in school goal setting and planning.

The Comer School Improvement Process requires schools to accept the fact that students enter school at different points along a developmental continuum. Staff, parents, and the school community are actively involved in and committed to an instructional program that recognizes that, although students enter school with different backgrounds and experience, all can be successful when the school accepts them at their current level of development and guides their growth in an appropriate manner.

COMPONENTS AND EFFECTIVENESS INDICATORS

The Comer School Improvement Process is designed to work in all schools. The process, however, may develop differently because of the unique needs of a school and its students. This systems-level, prevention approach is used to plan and manage all activities within the school in a way that promotes desirable staff and parent functioning, and as a consequence, desirable student learning and behavior. It is the process model that allows the school to review its goals and methods and to identify problems and opportunities in a "no fault" atmosphere. It seeks to develop creative ways of dealing with problems and to implement intervention using the collective good judgment of school staff and parents. The program is carried out through regularly scheduled meetings of its major components: a district steering committee, the School Management Team (SMT), the Home/School Services Team (HSST), the Parent Program, and the Comprehensive School Plan (CSP).

District Steering Committee

The Comer School Improvement Process is monitored by a district steering committee comprising district-level staff, building-level administrators, instructional staff, and parents. The committee provides support and direction in the key areas of planning, prioritizing, monitoring, and evaluation. The committee meets regularly with a predetermined agenda. Summary minutes are provided.

The School Management Team

A key program component is the building-level governance and management body commonly referred to as the SMT. The principal or other identified chairperson leads this group. It must be representative of the teachers, administrators, and other employee groups within the school, as well as parents and other members of the school community. A representative from the HSST and the Parent Program should also be included. The SMT should meet regularly and should include an agenda that is distributed in advance of the meeting. Members should be responsible for communicating information and recommendations to their constituents. In order to encourage broad participation, various subcommittees should be formed to work on projects and to deal with issues that affect the overall functioning of the school. The SMT should:

- Establish policy guidelines for all aspects of the school program
- Respond directly to problems and/or opportunities, or delegate this responsibility to other groups or individuals who will report back
- Carry out systematic school planning related to social climate, academics, staff development, and public relations
- Promote effective resource utilization, coordination, and program implementation
- Work closely with parents to plan an annual school calendar that integrates social, academic, and staff development functions
- Monitor program activities
- Conduct other activities related to the ongoing management of the school and its programs

The CSP should be developed by the SMT. Through this plan, the SMT provides yearlong direction and focus to the school in its effort to fulfill its mission. The CSP is monitored and adjusted through SMT meetings. It is aligned with the district's CSP and places specific emphasis on academic and social development, school climate, public relations, and staff development.

1. The SMT consists of representatives from all groups within the school community, that is, parents, grade-level teachers, administrators, and instructional and classified support staff.
2. General operating procedures are developed and adhered to by the SMT. These include identification of a chairperson or facilitator, established meeting times, procedures for agenda development, and dissemination of the minutes.
3. The SMT establishes standing subcommittees as needed that allow all staff members within the building to participate.
4. Additional SMT meetings can be established as the need arises.
5. SMT representatives report to their constituents and gather input for the SMT process.
6. All school planning and decision making is funneled through the SMT process.

7. The CSP is monitored by the SMT on a monthly basis.
8. A structured problem-solving approach is used to address school problems.
9. An SMT meeting is characterized by straight, descriptive talk that is nonjudgmental, meaning, solution talk. Participants do not hedge in identifying problems. They work creatively to solve them.

Home/School Services Team

The HSST is made up of the school principal, counselor, curriculum resource teacher, social worker, psychologist, ESE representative, public health nurse, and other appropriate building-level support staff. The principal or designee leads this group. It works in a diagnostic/prescriptive and preventive fashion. It provides ongoing consultation and services to teachers and to the SMT in matters that pertain to child development. It meets on a regular basis to:

- Facilitate parent and school interaction
- Develop and recommend to the SMT programs and activities that contribute to positive school climate and promote student success
- Consult with classroom teachers to assist them in responding to students in a way that promotes growth and development
- Assist classroom teachers in developing strategies that prevent minor problems from becoming major ones
- Establish individualized programs for children with special needs that may involve the utilization of services outside of the school
- Make recommendations for building-level policy changes designed to prevent problems
- Assist all staff members in bridging the gap between exceptional student education and regular classroom activities
- Recommend to the SMT in-service activities for staff and parents related to child development, human relations, and other home/ school issues
    1. The HSST is composed of the principal, counselor, curriculum resource teacher, social worker, psychologist, special education representative, public health nurse, and other appropriate building-level support staff.

2. The HSST views parents as partners in developing programs for individual students and for the general student population. Consequently, it provides ways in which parents can give input and provide support for interventions and strategies.
3. The HSST develops preventive strategies that modify the school setting in a way that creates optimum conditions for teaching and learning and that develops into class support rather than pull outs.
4. The HSST uses a diagnostic/prescriptive model that is designed to provide interventions for individual students.
5. The HSST recommends and advises the SMT in matters related to child development, human relations, home/school services, and appropriate in-service needs.
6. The HSST develops a process to meet the individual needs of children and promotes student success by utilizing school-based services, school district services, and services provided by the community.

Parent Program

The Comer School Improvement Process views the Parent Program as the cornerstone for success in developing a school environment that stimulates the total development of its students. Parents are expected to:

- Select representatives from their group to serve on the SMT
- Participate in activities initiated by the parent–teacher general membership group and the SMT
- Review the school plan developed by the SMT
- Support the efforts of the school to assist students in their overall development
  1. The school has a parent–teacher organization (PTO/PTA/ Booster Group) that meets with the principal on a monthly basis to discuss relevant issues
  2. The agenda for each meeting is developed in consultation with the principal and is discussed prior to each meeting by the principal and representatives from the executive board of the PTO

3. The minutes of each PTO meeting are distributed to parents and teachers
4. Parents regularly attend school-sponsored programs
5. Parents assist in the planning of child-centered programs and activities
6. Parents volunteer in the school on a day-to-day basis in instructional support positions
7. Parent representative(s) serve on the SMT and act as a liaison between this group and the PTO executive board
8. The HSST facilitator serves as a liaison between parents and the school
9. Parent involvement is reflective of the demographics of the student population

Comprehensive School Plan

The CSP is the document by which the Comer School Improvement Process defines the specific goals and school needs on a yearly basis. The goals are established in four areas: academic, social, public relations, and staff development. Members of the SMT, using input from their constituents, develop the CSP by coordinating and integrating all activities of the school for the entire year. The SMT monitors the CSP on a regular basis to evaluate, assess, and/or modify the components as deemed necessary.

The academic area specifically outlines which subjects will be targeted to maximize student achievement, what outcomes are projected, and a time line for completing instructional objectives. The social area lists any social activities that will be held during the year and indicates in what way these activities relate directly to the assessed needs of the school population. The public relations part of the plan seeks to bring support to the process through continued public exposure to school activities. Through staff development, the CSP addresses the needs of the school staff for in-service activities to successfully support the implementation of the process.

The CSP, utilizing the four components as described, provides the school a vehicle to continually update and monitor the development of the Comer School Improvement Process.

1. The plan addresses the academic, staff development, social, and public relations aspects of the school's operations. Yearlong programs are developed in each of these four areas and are monitored by the SMT on a monthly basis.
2. The CSP is distributed to all staff members and an abbreviated version is sent home to parents.
3. A midyear appraisal of the CSP is conducted by the SMT. Revisions are made if they are seen by the team to be necessary.
4. A comprehensive evaluation of the impact of the plan is made. Results are communicated to staff and parents. Data are used in generating a plan for the following school year.
5. The objectives within the plan are in harmony with the district's CSP.

GUIDING PRINCIPLES OF THE COMER SCHOOL IMPROVEMENT PROCESS

In order to meet the demands of an increasingly complex society, all children must experience a high level of personal development. We must efficiently and effectively use our collective energies and resources to prepare them to enter into the adult world as confident and competent individuals. Hence, schools must endeavor to build working relationships that allow the young to solve the problems that impede their development. By creating a desirable climate or ethos, schools provide models of appropriate human behavior that children can identify with, imitate, internalize, grow, and fully develop academically and socially. These conditions must be generated and nurtured through a process of positive interactions among parents, staff, and students. The SMT, HSST, and Parent Program provide the structure or framework through which the process takes place.

The principal is a key figure in that he or she leads this endeavor and models the appropriate behavior. As teachers, parents, and support staff serve on the respective teams, they assume some responsibility for exhibiting the behaviors that move the school toward a climate that is characterized by collaboration, trust, problem solving, and the recognition of all as important parties in the education of children. The assumption is that virtually any human problem can be solved if people are willing to meet on a consistent basis, explore, and develop solutions without placing blame, develop interventions, and expend the energy necessary to implement and monitor interventions. Hard work and dedication, along with a passionate belief in human growth and potential, must characterize the school improvement effort. Descriptions of the specific goals follow.

High Expectations

Educators and parents hold high expectations with regard to other educational accomplishments and social development of students by building positive interpersonal relationships and by modeling respect for academic achievement. Educators and parents work together to create optimum conditions for student learning and social development.

Child-Centered, Collaborative Decision Making

All decisions in the school are based on the developmental and performance needs of students. Input from parents, teachers, and appropriate school personnel is essential. In all committee work done under the auspices of the SMT, the group shall develop a consensus rather than a "majority rule" vote in arriving at its decisions and recommendations. During meetings, participants make a conscious attempt to focus on problem solving rather than placing blame. Within the Comer School Improvement Process, problems are seen as opportunities to tap the creativity and resourcefulness of the group rather than as crises that immobilize the movement of the school.

Positive, Productive Relationships

The quality of the relationships between adults within the school community directly influences the social development of students. Healthy relationships between adults provide models for students with which to identify, imitate, and internalize. Hence, it is important for educators and parents to work together to identify and solve problems that could adversely impact the overall school climate and student development.

Parental Involvement

Parental involvement promotes accountability—parent to staff and staff to parents. The involvement of parents reduces behavior problems and increases support for academic learning. Parents and school staff share the responsibility for developing children in the key developmental pathways (cognitive, social, psychological, moral, and speech and language).

The first level of parental involvement is in broad-based activities for a large number of parents, such as social events. At the second level, parents volunteer in the school on a day-to-day basis in instructional and support positions. At the third level, parent representatives participate in the SMT.

Planning and Coordination

The planning and introduction of new programs should be facilitated through the SMT. Planning should be conducted from a systems perspective. Any program development or modification should first consider how such change would impact the total system or school community. Planning and coordination should prevent program duplication, fragmentation, and wasted energy and resources and create a sense of direction and purpose.

Effective Material and Resources Allocation

Schools must make maximum and efficient use of people, material, and other resources. Equitable distribution of the same is also essential.

An Instructional Methodology That Is Individualized

The instructional program should contain activities, experiences, and content that allows students to develop academically and socially regardless of their background. It should be stimulating and should have personal meaning and utility for students. Children bring different needs and styles of learning to their respective schools. Professional educators must accommodate these needs and styles by using the most appropriate research-based techniques that will encourage each student to reach his or her highest academic potential.

Relevant Curriculum

The school's curriculum must give each child the opportunity to acquire a well-rounded basic education. There is an emphasis on the processes of reading comprehension, language development, written communication, problem solving, and creative expression at each grade level as well as the core content knowledge of mathematics, social studies, science, and the arts. The curriculum should provide activities that promote creativity, self-expression, and higher-order thinking. Additionally, it should provide for social development and the acquisition for life management skills.

Frequent Monitoring of Instruction

An effective evaluation system is one that is timely, diagnostic, and prescriptive and that gives students immediate and specific feedback regarding their performances. Tests and other forms of evaluation should be used to assist parents and students in identifying strengths and weaknesses and to plan strategies for remediation or enrichment. The school accepts the responsibility for informing parents in a timely fashion as to the academic progress of students.

Effective Staff Development

Staff development programs should be based on what is needed to accomplish the goals set forth in the CSP. Staff development should be a collaborative effort between appropriate individuals at the central office level working with the principal, faculty, staff, and parents at the building level.

Standards of Effectiveness

There is a written statement guiding the principles and goals of the Comer School Improvement Process.

Quality Indicators

1. A copy of the statement is available
2. The statement is consistent with the school district's philosophy

3. The statement has been developed cooperatively, with contributions from groups within the school community
4. The statement reflects staff consensus
5. Staff members can:
   a. Articulate the belief and goals
   b. State specific instructions and provide constructional activities directed toward meeting those beliefs and goals
   c. Cite assessment procedures that monitor student performance
6. The state's goals are used in planning the school's educational objectives and activities
7. The statement is reviewed at least annually

Curriculum

The curriculum is used in planning the instructional program. The district curriculum is adjusted to meet individual school needs if indicated. It is adjusted without reducing standards and expectations.

1. The curriculum specifies all areas of learning that are taught in the school
2. The established learning objectives are appropriate for the growth level of the individual child
3. Academic performance objectives are aligned with those that are in the compendium of the norm-referenced test and any state-mandated mastery test that is used by the school district
4. The principal, teachers, and parents address the psychological, emotional, and social development curriculum cooperatively to meet the social development needs of students
5. All teachers work together to create a continuum of learning
6. The instructional program includes experiences that provide children with basic skills necessary to function effectively in our society
7. Communication skills of reading, writing, speaking, and listening are developed through meaningful, integrated activities
8. Mathematics instruction emphasizes concept development and problem solving through manipulative-based activity and real-life situations

9. Science instruction integrates the development of science concepts with the process of scientific investigation and utilizes an inquiry approach to the study of the natural and physical world

10. Social studies instruction includes study of the interrelationship of peoples and cultures to the historical, geographical, political, and economic factors in the environment, and map and globe skills are developed through meaningful activities in this study

11. Computer literacy is developed through opportunities for students to use the computer as an instructional tool

Staff Relationships

Shared governance recognizes the principal as the key in determining the school's quality, focus, and direction as characterized by the Comer School Improvement Process.

1. The principal conveys high expectations for students, staff, and self

2. The principal is able to communicate effectively with all segments of the school and community, and welcomes communications from these groups

3. The principal encourages leadership by students, teachers, parents, and community members

4. Teachers use instructional techniques that are relevant to the curricular objectives and to research-based principles of learning

5. Teachers use formal and informal evaluation techniques and instruments to measure the curriculum's success

Budgetary Matters

Adequate financial and material resources support the curriculum.

1. Budget allocations are sufficient to meet the needs generated by the curriculum

2. Appropriate and relevant materials are available for each student

3. The school makes use of appropriate resources from other educational institutions, parents, business, industry, and service clubs

4. The SMT recommends the expenditure of funds available to accomplish the school's mission

Teachers' Roles

1. Teachers plan and provide effective instruction to accomplish the school's mission
2. Teachers believe all students can learn and expect them to succeed
3. Teachers use appropriate instructional strategies relevant to the objectives for the curriculum
4. Teachers allow sufficient time to present fully, demonstrate, and explain new content skills
5. Teachers allow adequate opportunity to practice and master new skills
6. Teachers actively monitor student performance, give immediate response, and adjust instruction accordingly
7. Teachers use a variety of instructional grouping patterns, ranging from whole class to one-to-one instruction
8. Teachers continually diagnose academic needs and prescribe appropriate educational activities for individual students, while considering learning styles and rates of learning
9. Teachers identify students with special needs and provide appropriate support in class if possible
10. Teachers use a variety of classroom management skills to create an orderly and comfortable classroom environment conducive to learning

Students' Roles

1. Students are taught how to learn and value learning
2. Students believe they can learn
3. Students understand that they share the responsibility for successful learning
4. Students are held accountable for doing quality work
5. Students give evidence of being able to apply what they have learned

Staff Development

1. Each school has an effective staff development program for all members of the staff
2. The design of the program is based on academic achievement and social development goals; needs assessments include recommendations from both the staff and the parents
3. The staff is routinely provided information regarding valid research and current practice
4. Staff development programs are evaluated for effectiveness
5. The effectiveness of staff development programs is validated through improved teaching practices

General Interests

There is concerted effort on the part of the parents, teachers, administrators, and support staff to aid the social and academic development of students.

Social Development

1. School personnel serve as models and reward appropriate behavior
2. There is a written code of conduct that is cooperatively developed by students, staff, and parents and is followed consistently
3. Students, staff, and parents accept and share responsibility for discipline
4. Discipline is used as a tool for learning rather than for punishment
5. Administrators, classroom teachers, support staff, and parents work cooperatively to address the psychological, emotional, and social development needs of students

Academic Development

1. The accomplishments of students and school personnel are appropriately recognized
2. Student work is attractively displayed
3. Attendance by students and staff is high

4. Students and staff are aware that outstanding performance is expected of them
5. Students and staff expect to be successful, and school personnel believe that all children can learn

Implementation Process

Implementation begins with orientation and overview sessions with the principal initially, and later with the general faculty. After these sessions, the Comer School Improvement Process facilitator works with the principal to:

- Facilitate a process by which representatives are identified for membership on the SMT
- Collaborate with SMT members to set standard operating procedures for the team (i.e., agenda setting, distribution of minutes, problem-solving procedures, and length of meetings)
- Facilitate the development of the CSP by the SMT and a procedure for monitoring it
- Establish the HSST and a time in which the team can meet to review student cases, discuss programs and procedures that affect teacher and student performance, and generally develop programs and activities that contribute to a positive school climate and student success

The work of the SMT and HSST should serve as a model for all committees or work groups established within the school. These groups should be conscious of "no fault" and collaborative problem-solving techniques. The guiding principles become second nature to staff and are seen as the "natural" and "right way" to conduct school affairs. They manifest themselves in the classroom, the guidance office, the playground, the cafeteria, and, under the best of circumstances, in the home and community.

State of Hawaii Act 272 Student-Centered Schools: Summary

WHAT:

To authorize individual schools to implement alternative frameworks with regard to curriculum; facilities management; instructional approach; length of the school day, week or year; and personnel management.

Up to 25 schools may be granted student-centered school status.

HOW:

All public schools may use any available resources.

The school establishes a local school board as its governing body composed of representatives of at least one of each of the following:

- Principal
- Instructional staff members selected by the teachers
- Support staff selected by the support staff
- Parent of student(s) attending the school selected by parents
- Student selected by the students
- Community at large selected by the board

The local school board must develop a detailed implementation plan which includes:

1. Documentation that 3/5 of the administrative, support and teaching personnel, and the parents approve of being a student-centered school.

2. Detailed implementation plan submitted to the Board of Education for review
   - Assures compliance with statewide student performance standards;
   - Description of the administrative and educational framework;
   - Specific student outcome to be achieved;
   - Curriculum, instructional framework, and assessment mechanism to be used to achieve;
   - Student outcomes;
   - Governance structure of the school;
   - Facility management plan; and
   - Annual financial and program audits.

POWERS OF THE LOCAL SCHOOL BOARD:

- Formulate school-based educational policy and goals in accordance with statewide performance standards
- Adopt school performance standards and assessment mechanisms
- Monitor schools success
- Select principal in accordance with Chapter 89

PARAMETERS:

- Exemption from all applicable state laws except those regarding:
  - Collective bargaining
  - State procurement laws
  - Religious, racial or sexual bias
  - Health and safety requirements
- Schools may not charge tuition
- Must meet student performance standards

ROLE OF THE PRINCIPAL:

- Consult and work collaboratively with the board
- Have jurisdiction over the internal organization, operation, and management of the school

FUNDING:

- Allocation from the state general funds on a per student basis which is equal to the statewide per pupil expenditure for average daily attendance
- Allocation for special education to reflect the additional expenses for students in these programs
- Federal and other financial support shall be equal to all other public schools
- Administrative services provided by the Department of Education shall be reimbursed for not more than 6.5 percent of the school's allocation
- All additional funds generated by the boards shall be considered supplemental and may be expended at the discretion of the local school board.

EVALUATION:

- Annual self-evaluation to include but not limited to:
  - Identification and adoption of benchmarks to measure and evaluate administrative programs;
  - Identification and adoption of benchmarks to measure and evaluate instructional programs; and
  - Impact upon the students of the school.
- Fourth year evaluation by the department to assure compliance with the statewide performance standards.

Minneapolis Public Schools' School-Based Management and School Improvement Plans

PREAMBLE

Every employee of the district recognizes the importance of the work of Minneapolis Public Schools. All employees know that their contribution is significant in the achievement of the district's mission to educate all children. Parents and guardians understand that their participation in the education of their children is required as a part of parenting. The community trusts the judgment of the school staff and listens when requests are made for support and understanding. One way of organizing the school community to achieve this ideal is to organize work through site-based management.

Site-based management is a process that can insure maximum support for the teacher and the site staff because the process is based on the democratic discussion of priorities for allocating resources and for making decisions related to student achievement. Through the process of site-based management, all individuals involved in the educating process have an equal voice in the discussion; including district staff, families and students when appropriate.

Further, the benefit of democratizing decision-making is supported by research. Research shows that employees who are involved in the decision making process are healthier and are more successful in achieving the goals of the organization. In addition, research shows that parents and guardians who feel heard by the educational establishment are more active in the education of their children and more supportive of the goals and practices of the institution.

It is possible to educate all students only when the individual school community believes it is possible to do so. Each staff member at each site must share the belief to make the ideal real. This commitment to student achievement cannot be mandated; commitment to the shared ideal requires a process of open discussion and consensus building. Site-based management is the process used by the district.

This document alone will not create learning environments of academic excellence where all stakeholders share in decision making. The easiest part of this task is the development of this agreement. The real work of creating 21st century schools will require an on-going dialogue where progress can be achieved through collegial sharing of perspectives and learning's from the actual experience of trying to operationalize these principles.

SECTION A—GOVERNING PHILOSOPHY:

Site-based management is not an end in itself; is not a game to garner more resources; and is not a "test" of any school. It is a chosen strategy— to move decision making closest to the students served. It is the examination of everything that might be standing in the way of student achievement—be it grade levels, student groupings, materials, or school policies and practices—and keeping what is working and changing what is not.

The ultimate goal is to improve the quality of instruction and learning for students. Through site-based management, it is expected that each school continuously renew itself, and its ability to improve the achievement of each of its students and eliminate gaps in learning between groups of students.

The following philosophical and strategic principles help to shape the concept of shared decision-making and accountability for student learning:

- All students can learn and we have a responsibility to insure that all students do learn. Instruction is rooted in the belief that there are no true differences in ability based on gender, culture, language, economic or family status. There are individual differences in student and teacher talents, learning styles and experiences which need to be addressed in designing instruction and student opportunities for demonstrating proficiency with the learning standards;

- Ours is a vision of shared responsibility—shared among all stake-holders, but particularly among students, staff, families, and community;
- Educators and schools must know, own, and implement the expected standards of learning and instruction;
- Critical interactions affecting student performance take place daily between teachers and students. Teachers, therefore, must be given a shared voice in decisions at the school site. Along with this increased role in the decision-making process, the teachers assume more responsibility and accountability for the success of the school;
- Student progress must be the expectation, not school test-score ranking;
- Effective change begins by taking actions to improve, building on areas of strength and capacity, with an attitude of learning and support, rather than blame.

The Strategic Direction of the Minneapolis Public Schools makes schools the center for initiating and implementing the changes necessary for improving student achievement with support from a service oriented central office. The parties agree that school sites should have as much flexibility as possible in managing their educational programs and be free of unnecessary restraints imposed by central office policies or by collective bargaining agreements.

School and central office efforts must strive to complement each other. The district offices have a responsibility to set high expectations for student learning and the learning environment. Schools must be free to act in ways, which help each of its students reach the learning standards, expecting and receiving support from the district. This district–school relationship was illustrated in the principles of effective schools and effective district support contained in the Site-based Management report of July 1994.

Schools continuously work toward these Minneapolis Standards of an Effective School:

- Have high and rigorous standards for what every student should know and be able to do;

- Promote active, multicultural, gender fair, disability sensitive, and developmentally-appropriate learning tied directly to the Minneapolis learner standards;
- Expect students to share responsibility for their own learning and behavior;
- Have assessments of student achievement linked to learner standards. Provide useful feedback to students, families, staff, and the district about student learning;
- Use instructional methods grounded in educational research and sound professional practice;
- Organize schools and classes to create an environment that is supportive;
- Share decision making and accountability for student success among all stakeholders;
- Provide a safe, respectful, and affirming environment for all; have high expectations for all staff and provide for professional growth and practice improvement;
- Actively involve families in helping students succeed;
- Collaborate with community partners and others in the community to support students and their families.

Complementing the schools' efforts, the responsibility of the district offices are outlined in the standards for District Support of Effective Schools:

- Have high, relevant, future-oriented, and inter-disciplinary standards for student learning in all schools;
- Provide curricular, instructional and assessment leadership in support of the learning standards;
- Set a strategic direction and establish improvement planning processes to support student achievement;
- Provide leadership which is visionary, reflective, focused and consistent;
- Model and support a diverse, safe, respectful, and affirming environment for all;
- Win community-wide support to provide resources for the district and its schools;

- Support and facilitate continuous improvement and learning of all staff;
- Ensure accountability while respecting school autonomy;
- Forge links with the community to advance student success;
- Listen and communicate well;
- Exhibit a service orientation towards the schools;
- Provide an infrastructure necessary to support effective schools;
- Assure that organized stakeholders actively work to produce effective schools.

School site leadership teams and district service units and teams strive to move toward this picture of excellence. This is a dynamic, constant process, which is never finished; success is not a permanent status since perfection is not the goal. The pursuit, however, is critical. The schools and district help each other to improve by providing ongoing feedback about their progress.

SECTION B—GOVERNING PHILOSOPHY:

School Improvement Planning is the primary process used in the Minneapolis Public Schools focus and guide student achievement and staff learning at the site level. While the standards for student performance are set by the Board of Education and are district-wide, the approaches for reaching those standards can and are expected to vary. Each school in the Minneapolis Public School system adopts at least annually a written School Improvement Plan that specifies educational goals, strategies for meeting those goals, and proposed measures of success by which to gauge the achievement of the goals.

Performance improvement can be thought of as a cycle or spiral, and includes these steps in the School Improvement Planning process:

Step 1. Review the District's Strategic Direction and District Improvement Agenda.

Step 2. Review and update the school Mission/Vision Statement.

Step 3. The baseline review of current performance published in the School Information Report from Research, Evaluation and Assessment (REA) Department. The cycle begins with reviewing performance baselines or data collected by the district, state, and school, as a basis for goal setting. Data to be looked at includes but is not limited to:

- Student/Staff demographics;
- Surveys: staff, students, community/parent;
- Behavioral management data, e.g. suspensions;
- Socioeconomic data, free/reduced lunch information;
- Attendance data (student/staff);
- Achievement data;
- Climate and safety data;
- Program data.

Step 4. Identify needs and/or improvement opportunities in each of the following areas:

- Student achievement;
- Learning climate/safety;
- Family involvement in student learning;
- Community confidence;
- Attraction/retention of students and staff;
- Curriculum standards/outcomes;
- Instructional effectiveness;
- Professional climate/support.

Step 5. Prioritize needs and improvement opportunities. Priorities should be based on analysis of School Information Report, the District Improvement Agenda, other collected data and the school team's judgment about what will most contribute to improved student achievement.

Step 6. Goals. Projects clear expectations of the results to be produced, such as reading level expectations for cohorts of students. The results are stated in measurable terms. (Thus, how the goals are to be measured is also determined in this step.)

Step 7. Actions/strategies. Prescribes meaningful changes or actions conducive to achieving the goals. Develop goals and strategies for priority areas to increase student achievement. Develop action steps, staff development plans and evaluation procedures.

Communicate goals, strategies, staff development action plans and the evaluation procedures for each priority area to the whole staff, school, the community and School and Site Services.

Step 8. Initiate action steps, staff development plans and evaluation procedures.

Step 9. Measurement. Monitor and measure progress periodically during the year and adjust actions. The effects of the actions are measured and reported. (Multiple measurements of the same goal and multiple measures of the different goals may occur and need to be reconciled and explained.)

Step 10. Celebrate and report progress to the community. Repeat the process each planning cycle (or more frequently).

The cycle or spiral continues, or begins again, when the process returns to Step 2 as higher expectations (goals) for performance are established.

SECTION C—SCHOOL SITE LEADERSHIP TEAMS:

1. COMPOSITION. Each Minneapolis Public School shall have a site leadership team for the purposes described in this Article. Members of a School leadership team shall be elected or appointed annually and serve until a successor's term begins. (Optimally, teams would be in place when school starts in the fall.) Members of the team should be elected or appointed by major stakeholder segments of the school community, including staff members, families, community members, and students.

   GUIDELINES:

   a. DIVERSITY. The make-up of the team should closely reflect the racial/ethnic and socioeconomic diversity of the student body at the school. Those groups or individuals electing or appointing members should endeavor to meet this diversity standard as well.

   b. STAKEHOLDERS. Major stakeholders of the school need to be represented on the team, including: students (whenever possible), family members, teachers, staff, community, and business representatives.

2. ROLE. The role of the School Site Leadership Team is to lead the school site, including strategy and direction setting; developing and operationalize School Improvement Plans, including

measurement and reporting of progress; communication within the school community; resource management; partnerships with families and others; and/or examining existing policies and practices in order to improve student achievement.

The leadership team in partnership with and inclusion of the principal sets the direction for overall management and operation of the school but may choose to be involved or to delegate any or all of the following areas to individuals, committees, or subgroups. Examples from the Board policy of 1994 may include: the design and scheduling of the instructional approaches, staff development, elective programming, selection of learning materials, budgeting, fund raising, purchasing, disbursement of funds, behavior plans, school-related building use, interviewing staff, staff assignments, parent-teacher relations, use of outside professionals and social service resources, student uniforms or dress codes, and other items covered by the parameters of site based management (July, 1994, and as amended during the life of this agreement).

3. RESPONSIBILITY OF MEMBERSHIP. Any member of the leadership team elected or appointed by a stakeholder group has these obligations of representation:
   - Attending and actively participating on the team;
   - Reaching out to the diversity of the represented group to hear their opinions and ideas;
   - Supporting goals and strategies to implement the School Improvement Plan;
   - Communicating those opinions to others on the team, and
   - Collectively support the School Improvement Process.

4. SUPPORT FOR MEMBERS.
   a. INFORMATION. All information necessary to the decision responsibilities of the team, such as budget and assessment information, is to be provided to all members equally.
   b. INCENTIVES. The team can decide to provide incentives for team membership, including compensatory time, payments of stipends, baby-sitting costs, transportation expenses, and/or workshop registration fees, etc.
   c. TRAINING. Time for team members serving on a leadership team shall be allotted during each year for the purpose of train-

ing or other activities related to site-based management and improvement planning.

d. RESOURCES. It is expected that resources will be available for the team.

SECTION D—DECISION MAKING IN THE LEADERSHIP TEAM:

1. ORIENTATION. The Leadership Team is responsible for maintaining an orientation program on school-based management for all new employees of the school, interested family members, students, and others, which includes an explanation of how decisions are made and what processes exist to provide input.

2. GUIDELINES.
   a. Focuses on meeting academic needs of students;
   b. People most impacted in the decision are involved in the discussions;
   c. How decisions impact student, staff and community;
   d. Promotes professional development of staff at the site and build collegial relationships and foster a professional climate;
   e. Promotes parent and community involvement.

3. OPERATION.
   a. The parties expect the members of a Site Leadership Team to operate as a single decision-making team, not as a group of spokespersons representing constituent groups. Their role is to work together to develop goals and strategies to implement the School Improvement Plan.

   Each site shall have bylaws or operating rules to govern all other aspects of the leadership workings, including how long members serve on the team, how members solicit ideas from others, and how team decisions are communicated to others. These bylaws are in effect until amended by subsequent team action.

   Not all decisions will be made in the same way. There may be times the Team delegates a decision, the Team decides, the Principal decides with participation of others, the Principal decides alone, etc.:

   - The first decision in determining the scope of decisions to be made is WHICH decisions will be made by the team and which will be made by others;

- Secondly, the procedures defining HOW and WHEN decisions will be made should be determined.

This process should be communicated, including the process for participation. While a team may agree initially on specific processes, they may be faced with issues that require them to revisit the scope or process of decision-making.

When the Team is to make a decision together, it is expected that the Site Leadership Team will operate by consensus (where lack of agreement is viewed as a signal that the best option has not yet been put forward). Consensus, however, need not mean unanimity, nor should all decisions require endless discussion, though every effort should be made through thorough discussion and serious efforts to understand the reasoning behind opposing views.

In the event that a Site Leadership team is unable to reach a decision, the Team will have a process in their bylaws to resolve disputes, which may involve a facilitator to help improve the Team's process.

   b. As a part of the bylaws or operating rules, the team will decide how the agenda is developed to insure access and make it inclusive of the school community.

4. SITE TEAM DEVELOPMENT. Team members should receive training as soon as can be arranged to build capacity of the group in at least the concepts and skills of joint problem solving, team building and teamwork, parental involvement, and decision-making by consensus.

Site teams may desire team facilitation or development services from time to time and may access training and facilitation support services via the district's professional development center (within Teacher and Instructional Services), Site Services, leadership teams at other sites, Shared Decisions Minnesota, and/or other vendors.

5. SCOPE OF AUTHORITY.
   a. PARAMETERS. In managing the school, the School Site Leadership Team should make its decisions within these parameters:
- The strategic direction of the Minneapolis Public Schools as a guide;

- Federal and state law, contract language, referendum requirements, and Board of Education policy, unless a waiver has been received;
- EQUITY. We are a public institution, and as a public institution, we serve all students. The actions of the leadership team must embody sound educational policy equitably applied to all students and must assure the education of all students;
- DIVERSITY. Schools site leadership teams will be less effective if any constituency groups are left out of the process. Input or involvement of others who are not members is encouraged as it is believed that decision quality improves with diverse input and participation. The team should be strategic in establishing processes for listening to the diverse opinions of their school communities; these may include such techniques as round tables, park meetings, surveys, and call-ins. There will, of course, be times when decisions will need to be made quickly due to urgency or opportunity;
- ACCOUNTABILITY. Those making decisions are accountable for the results. Accountability means assuring that decisions get made; committing to the decisions; support for implementing; communicating the decision; reporting on the results to others; conducting ongoing evaluation; dealing with the impact by receiving feedback and reporting on results and initiating needed changes;
- NO NEGATIVE EFFECTS ON OTHER SCHOOLS. Site team decisions should consider all effects and not make decisions that negatively impact other schools and communities;
- WITHIN SITE-BASED PARAMETERS. For guidance on issues where schools have primary decision-making responsibilities, see the most recent version of site-based management parameters obtained through School and Site Services. Where a decision is not to be made at the school level, schools should be free to communicate their views and concerns to the relevant decision-maker. (Parameters document as an addendum.)

b. WAIVERS. Our strategic direction makes schools the center for initiating and implementing changes necessary for improving student achievement with support from a service oriented central office. The district level promises to review policies and procedures for their impact on schools and ultimately on students. In addition, however, schools and service units are encouraged to take advantage of the opportunity to mutually find solutions and seek waivers from established district or contractual policies and procedures where such waivers will enhance student achievement.

School sites seeking a waiver from district policy should contact the Executive Director of the service unit responsible for the relevant policy or procedure. The waiver process was approved in Board action, June 1995.

Criteria for Waiver Approval

Waiver approval will depend on demonstrating that:

- The proposers have knowledge of the current policy;
- The proposed waiver will lead to improved student achievement;
- The proposers have considered other options in addition to the waiver in order to achieve their desired goals;
- The waiver request resulted from a process which involved all relevant stakeholders, reports their concerns, and their level of support for the proposal;
- The financial resources necessary to implement the request are available;
- A mechanism exists to measure and report on the success of the recommended alternative procedure supporting and improving student achievement;
- The waiver request considers and ameliorates the impact on other sites or programs;
- Appropriate district-wide committees were relevant and provided feedback and input to the process.

School sites seeking a waiver from this agreement should contact the union steward. Waiver requests will be handled via the union variance process that is different from the district process above.

SECTION E—ASSESSMENT OF SITE-BASED MANAGEMENT:

At least annually, each school team and the district level should undergo a self- or external-assessment of its decision making. While the School Improvement Process (SIP) looks at "Are we doing the right things to improve student achievement?", this assessment would ask "How are the means we are using working?" These evaluations would assess areas such as:

- The efficacy and efficiency of decision making processes;
- The listening to and communicating with various school constituencies;
- The connection of decisions to the District's Strategic direction and the School Improvement Plan;
- The decision parameters themselves: which decisions handled by the district should be moved to the schools, and vice versa; and
- The actions are representing the whole as well as being inclusive of constituencies.

Like quality improvement reviews, the desired result would be feedback for improvement for both site and district decision makers.

SECTION F—EXPANSION AND CHALLENGING THE LIMITS:

To achieve lasting change, the parties realize they must work cooperatively and collaboratively. Significant changes in school governance, instructional practices, staff roles, and community involvement will take time—they will not be accomplished in a single year. Pilot sites and programs and experimentation are envisioned; changes in agreements, policies, and written and unwritten norms will be pursued. The task will require sustained discussions and commitment from teachers, building and central office administrators, families, students, business and corporate community, post-secondary institutions, community organizations, and political leadership in the expansion and enrichment of Minneapolis student capacities. The parties pledge to make this commitment.

Performance Awards

Introduction

A Program to Reward Performance. The State of Minnesota has offered to school districts an opportunity to obtain additional funding in exchange for meeting certain performance goals. The Minneapolis Public Schools is offering to pass these financial incentives along to schools, which meet important goals in support of the following initiatives:

- District Improvement Agenda;
- School Improvement Plan;
- Professional Development Process.

This proposal outlines a procedure by which these funds would be allocated to the successful schools.

It is anticipated that a total of $500,000 could be available for the 1995–96 school year. Approximately $400,000 of this could be distributed in the first round of the performance incentive program for 1995–96.

The proposal involves a "continuous improvement" model in which rewards could be given quarterly. Schools receiving the incentive funds would be expected to "invest" them in activities which will further future progress toward the goals. For example, if the goal is to reduce suspensions, funds could be used to implement programs designed to reduce student conflicts and improve behavior.

Specific Elements

Three Areas of Improvement

District Improvement Agenda (DIA). All schools are encouraged to adopt specific goals listed in the DIA. Each year, the Board of Education establishes a "high priority" goal, such as "Improve reading achievement for all students, and decrease the achievement gap between white students and students of color."

Schools, which make significant improvement toward the priority goal, would be eligible for the incentive grant.

School Improvement Plans (SIP). Since every school is required to have a School Improvement Plan, those plans, which conform to a high standard of expectation would provide a framework for incentive rewards. Again, those objectives, which are aligned with the District Improvement Agenda would receive consideration for an incentive reward. Multiple measures are encouraged, although the summative measure(s) must include the citywide assessment instruments being used to monitor progress toward the District Improvement Agenda.

Professional Development Process (PDP). The percentage of the school staff involved in the PDP activities would determine the amount of the reward. Quality indicators for PDP could be developed for future application, rather than merely the count of the percentage of staff involved in PDP activities.

Reporting and Payment Schedules

Periodic Reporting. Minneapolis Public Schools function on various class cycles, including quarter, trimester and semester. The progress-reporting schedule for each school will be based upon their class cycle.

Steps will be taken to ensure that all indicators in the incentive program are unbiased and free from "inflation." For example, if a school wishes to use course grades as an indicator, plans would have to be implemented to ensure that any improvements in grades reflect genuine improvements in student learning, and not "grade inflation."

The REA Department and School Site Services, or an independent evaluator with suitable qualifications, will be charged with the responsibility for ensuring the integrity of the incentives system.

Payment. Schools will receive payment once a year upon certification that the goals have been accomplished to the necessary degree. A sub-committee of the District Leadership Team, consisting of stakeholder representatives, will work out specific details.

Performance Award Review Board

A Performance Award Review Board will be formed as a sub-committee of the District Leadership Team to include one representative from the teachers, principals, other staff, parents, students, business, with staff from Research, Evaluation and Assessment department, Teacher Services, and Site Support.

The review board will review district indicators for the District Improvement Agenda and the site School Improvement Plans to establish specific criteria and measurements for the three categories. The review board will review the assessment/measurement results and recommend sites that qualify for the awards. Review board members will receive training in bench marking, measurement, and other aspects of Total Quality Improvement.

In the final state of the process, each school applying for an award will provide a staff person and a community person to participate in the award process. The review board will make its recommendations to the District Leadership Team. The District Leadership Team will assure that the process is valid, objective, and fairly executed. The DLT will develop a communication plan with the award schools and their communities to share best practices, quality assessments, and achievement successes of students with other schools.

This article shall not be subject to the grievance procedure.

The School Benchmark Principles

BENCHMARK SCHOOL CATEGORY #1: STUDENT ACHIEVEMENT

A reliable quality school:

1. Identifies essential and required student outcomes on which to base curriculum design and assessment methods.
2. Implements "what works" in classroom teaching, providing relevant learning experiences.
3. Integrates technology to make learning more relevant to student real-life experiences and to take advantage of new methods of instruction using such tools as CD–ROMs and Intranets.
4. Analyzes the needs of its student population, researches innovative instructional and curricular strategies, and pursues one or more of them.
5. Implements a mixture of authentic assessment methods such as student portfolios, exhibitions, and performances to give teachers a better idea of student accomplishments. Many schools provide narratives, in addition to report cards, to deliver specific evidence of student results.
6. Begins to disaggregate and analyze student-learning data over time for diagnostic measures on every student, and compares such information to authentic measures of student learning early in order to prevent student failures.
7. Witnesses the benefits of changes in the classroom, including improved attendance, improved behavior, an increase in student

writing, and students actively participating in their own learning. Teachers believe learning is more relevant when students have greater access to technology and students feel their teachers care more when the work is challenging and fun.

BENCHMARK SCHOOL CATEGORY #2: LEADERSHIP

A reliable quality school:

1. Practices shared decision making as its form of school governance and uses this method to make better decisions about such things as budget, curriculum, professional development, and the selection of new principals and staff. By participating in decision making, school staffs gain a sense of ownership in the process, accept greater responsibility for their actions, and feel a sense of collegiality with their peers.
2. Develops a method to support team building and communication—elements that are necessary for a stronger shared decision-making process.
3. Customizes its own school's shared decision-making structure to fit the staff, the faculty, and the school strategic plan.
4. Shuffles the workweek, thereby allowing teachers more time to collaborate, plan, and make decisions. Absent time to collaborate, the school does not have the opportunity to reach the shared vision so crucial to continuous improvement.
5. Learns how to conduct focused meetings to reach rapid consensus, thus making change possible.
6. Serves as a resource for information and expertise, shares its results with other schools and school districts, hosts benchmarking visitors to campus, and provides in-service training for other schools.

BENCHMARK SCHOOL CATEGORY #3: QUALITY PLANNING

A reliable quality school:

1. Develops a mission, vision, school goals, values, and beliefs about student learning.

2. Develops at least a three-year (five-year is better) action plan to guide its continuous improvement efforts.
3. Learns that a quality plan makes the difference between instigating change and accepting change. Schools find that when their plans outline the school vision, the entire school community (all stakeholders) gain a clearer understanding of what they can do to support the change efforts.

BENCHMARK SCHOOL CATEGORY #4: INFORMATION AND ANALYSIS

A reliable quality school:

1. Keeps in mind its student, faculty, and community demographics, its perceptions, and its needs. Information from such analyses helps each school set its goals to meet the needs of present and future customers and to ensure treating root causes as opposed to symptoms of problems.
2. Measures student achievement by ethnicity and other categories appropriate to each school situation to ensure that *every type— and thus all* of students receive what's needed to increase individual student achievement.
3. Diagnoses individual student achievement subcategories over time and uses such data for decision making and better analysis of the impact of its efforts.

BENCHMARK SCHOOL CATEGORY #5: PROFESSIONAL DEVELOPMENT AND MANAGEMENT

A reliable quality school:

1. Engages staff in professional development and training activities to support the gaining and use of new classroom skills. Such activities raise teacher effectiveness in applying new approaches to student achievement.
2. Teaches staffs do intensive research on the result of new instructional and assessment skills and strategies. This research

helps teachers predict the impact of their actions on student achievement.

3. Commits itself to long-term training related to the school strategic plan, rather than one-day-type in-service that takes a "cafeteria" approach to professional development.

4. Recognizes that professional development and training has the most impact when planned in advance and prioritized on the school calendar.

5. Learns that peer coaching combined with the new skills is the most expedient, positive, and supportive way to implement new performance strategies in the classroom.

BENCHMARK SCHOOL CATEGORY #6: PARTNERSHIP DEVELOPMENT

A reliable quality school:

1. Plans for and establishes partnerships with community groups and local businesses. These partnerships bring real-world examples into classrooms, help schools acquire goods and services, provide support training to staffs, and create case studies that reflect positively on the entire community.

2. Develops partnerships with parents to support student learning. Schools use parents as classroom aides and as community liaisons, and offer special classes to parents; some schools add parents to their shared decision-making council; some schools set up parent rooms at schools where parents know they are welcome.

3. Knows that the best way to increase parent involvement is to get those parents and businesspeople already involved at the school to help recruit others like them.

4. Learns that structuring win-win partnerships so both parties benefit is the most effective way to foster new partnerships.

BENCHMARK SCHOOL CATEGORY #7: CONTINUAL IMPROVEMENT AND EVALUATION

A reliable quality school:

1. Collects school data on an ongoing basis to document the results of current activities and uses the knowledge gained in furthering the school's continuous improvement. Each school also uses responses from parents, students, and teacher questionnaires to modify its processes.
2. Reports positive results from student portfolios as a framework for analyzing continuous improvement. Each school finds that information gathered validates chosen approaches and clarifies the next steps.
3. Receives help to develop and analyze a number of information-collection and evaluation systems to help better understand the impact of its improvement efforts. These systems include:
   • Teacher evaluation systems
   • Control charts of a variety of data on students and teacher
   • Follow-up surveys of graduates
   • Satisfaction surveys from parents
   • Program evaluations

These database systems help identify areas where the school management processes need to be improved or redirected to achieve strategic goals. Schools have generally not used this type data. Reliable quality schools find it extremely helpful and accurate. Some schools now have the ability to generate their own charts to better document student progress, which then can be shared with parents, district offices, and other schools.

New Jersey Permanent Statutes Title 18A 7A14.4: Level I District May Apply for Alternative Program of Monitoring, Evaluation

2. a. Notwithstanding any law to the contrary, a school district at Level I may apply to participate in an alternative program of monitoring and evaluation for the purpose of certification pursuant to section 14 of P.L.1975, c.212 (C.18A: 7A-14). Prior to the application of the school district to the Commissioner of Education for participation in the alternative program of monitoring and evaluation, there shall be consensus between the school district and the majority representative of the school employees in the district concerning the district's participation in the program.

   b. A school district approved to participate in the alternative program of monitoring and evaluation shall conduct ongoing monitoring and evaluation according to criteria established by the Commissioner of Education, in consultation with the Commission on Business Efficiency of the Public Schools. The criteria shall include, but not be limited to, the criteria used in the education eligibility category of the *Malcolm Baldrige National Quality Award* [emphasis added], established pursuant to subsection (a) of section 3 of Pub. L. 100-107 (15 U.S.C. s.3711a), and the New Jersey Quality Achievement Award established pursuant to Executive Order No. 47 of 1991, such as: (1) leadership; (2) information and analysis; (3) strategic and operational planning; (4) human resource development and management; (5) educational and business process management; (6) school performance results; and (7) student focus and stakeholder satisfaction.

c. The commissioner may eliminate a school district from participation in the alternative program of monitoring and evaluation, if the commissioner deems it to be advisable. The commissioner shall inform the school district of its elimination from the alternative program of monitoring and evaluation and shall direct that the school district comply with the program of evaluation provided for in sections 10, 11 and 14 of P.L.1975, c.212 (C.18A: 7A-10, 18A:7A-11 and 18A:7A-14).

L. 1997, c.432, s.2.

State of Washington Quality Initiative 97-03
Executive Order: Quality Improvement

WHEREAS, "quality improvement," as described herein, is a proven approach that has demonstrated improved performance in a wide range of public and private organizations.

WHEREAS, *successful quality efforts require effective leadership, strategic planning, customer focus, employee involvement, continuous improvement, and self-assessment of results* [emphasis added].

WHEREAS, enhanced customer service, efficiency gains and cost savings throughout state government can be best achieved by engaging state agency management and employees in the use of continuous quality improvement management systems, work processes and quality tools.

WHEREAS, *quality improvement can help to deliver the goals and commitments of this Administration* [emphasis added].

NOW THEREFORE, I, Gary Locke, Governor of the State of Washington, by virtue of the power vested in me, hereby order and direct the following action.

QUALITY IMPROVEMENT

1. Each agency shall develop and implement a program to improve the quality, efficiency, and effectiveness of the public services it provides through quality improvement, business process redesign, employee involvement, and other quality improvement

techniques. These efforts shall be conducted with the assistance of the front line employees. Employees shall be provided the training to enable them to successfully implement and complete their efforts in quality improvements. The establishment and operations of these programs shall include the involvement of recognized collective bargaining representatives.

2. Upon the effective date of this executive order, each state agency shall designate a person responsible for improvement of the quality of the systems and work processes within the agency. That person shall report to the agency head and serve as the agency's contact for quality improvement with the Subcabinet on Management Improvement and Results.

3. Each agency shall have a steering committee composed of appropriate senior management, mid-management, front line staff and support staff organizations.

4. Each agency shall identify immediate- and near-term opportunities to improve services and or reduce costs.

5. Agencies should *utilize the tools of strategic business planning and performance measures to establish their priorities and measure their progress toward their stated goals* [emphasis added]. Each agency shall develop performance measures to assess customer satisfaction, progress toward accomplishing outcomes specified in agency budgets per RCW 43.88.090 and necessary to provide feedback on the impact of quality improvement, employee involvement and management improvement initiatives. Those agencies which have already begun quality improvement efforts, shall incorporate the requirements of this executive order into their existing initiatives.

6. *Each agency shall report the results of its quality improvement/employee involvement programs to the Governor on a quarterly basis* [emphasis added]. The reports shall specify improved outcomes for public service, efficiency and effectiveness. The reports may also describe how customer service and stakeholder satisfaction is measured, methods used to engage agency employees in the program and how agency business processes have been changed to improve efficiency, effectiveness and quality.

7. Each agency shall evaluate the results of its quality, service and management improvement programs including, but not limited to, leadership, information and analysis, strategic planning, human resource development and management, process improvement, business results, and customer focus and satisfaction.

8. Each state agency shall develop a plan for quality improvement that documents efforts to date and addresses the above areas. These plans shall be submitted to the Governor no later that July 1, 1997. State agencies shall document the results of their quality efforts and report quarterly to the Subcabinet on their progress.

9. *The Governor's Council on Service Improvement and Performance shall be established to advise the Governor on quality improvements. The membership shall include representatives from the business, labor, media, and higher education communities and the Governor's Executive Cabinet. The council shall be chaired by the Governor or the Governor's Chief of Staff* [emphasis added].

IN WITNESS WHEREOF, I have hereunto set my hand and caused the seal of the State of Washington to be affixed at Olympia this 30th day of April A.D., Nineteen hundred and ninety-seven.

GARY LOCKE
Governor of Washington

BY THE GOVERNOR:

_____

Secretary of State

State of Washington Balanced Scorecard Application: Department of Personnel Scorecard—Overall Priorities FY 2001

DOP Mission

To support and facilitate state government's efforts to attract, develop, and retain a productive and diverse workforce that is capable of delivering quality services to the citizens of Washington State.

Value Perspective

Cost-effective statewide human resource management infrastructure exemplified by: *Customer Focus, Operational Excellence, and Innovation & Leadership*

Customer Perspective
- Responsive accessible service
- Good information readily available and timely

Financial Perspective
- Rates commensurate with services provided
- Increase entrepreneurial revenue

- HR systems, rules, and policies that are efficient, effective, adaptable, understandable
- Progressive, outcome-based programs & services

- Improve cost-efficiency

Business Processes

- Qualified, available, diverse candidates ASAP
- Classification system that easily flexes with business needs
- Knowledgeable, consistent advice, interpretation, consultation
- Menus of service choices to support workforce capacity & development
- Research & development: introduce HR innovations
- Prompt, effective communications, marketing, and information access
- Streamlined internal processes to optimally support service delivery

Internal Capacity

- Clarified performance expectations; aligned competencies and training
- Workplace climate to maximize employee capability, productivity, and success
- Continued improvement of internal communications and teamwork
- Enhanced workforce diversity
- Data-based review and decision making
- Optimized use of technology for HR solutions

October 2000

Eighth-Grade Final Exam—1895

This is the eighth-grade final exam from 1895 from Salina, Kansas. It was taken from the original document on file at the Smoky Valley Genealogical Society and Library in Salina and reprinted by the *Salina Journal*.

EIGHTH-GRADE FINAL EXAM: SALINA, KS—1895

Grammar (Time, one hour)

1. Give nine rules for the use of Capital Letters.
2. Name the Parts of Speech and define those that have no modifications.
3. Define Verse, Stanza and Paragraph.
4. What are the Principal Parts of a verb? Give Principal Parts of do, lie, lay and run.
5. Define Case, Illustrate each Case.
6. What is Punctuation? Give rules for principal marks of Punctuation.
7–10. Write a composition of about 150 words and show therein that you understand the practical use of the rules of grammar.

Arithmetic (Time, 1.25 hours)

1. Name and define the Fundamental Rules of Arithmetic.

2. A wagon box is 2 ft. deep, 10 ft. long, and 3 ft. wide. How many bushels of wheat will it hold?
3. If a load of wheat weighs 3942 lbs., what is it worth at 50 cts. per bu., deducting 1050 lbs. for tare?
4. District No. 33 has a valuation of $35,000. What is the necessary levy to carry on a school seven months at $50 per month, and have $104 or incidentals?
5. Find cost of 6720 lbs. coal at $6.00 per ton.
6. Find the interest of $512.60 for 8 months and 18 days at 7 percent.
7. What is the cost of 40 boards 12 inches wide and 16 ft. long at $20 perm?
8. Find bank discount on $300 for 90 days (no grace) at 10 percent.
9. What is the cost of a square farm at $15 per acre, the distance around which is 640 rods?
10. Write a Bank Check, a Promissory Note, and a Receipt.

U.S. History (Time, 45 minutes)

1. Give the epochs into which U.S. History is divided.
2. Give an account of the discovery of America by Columbus.
3. Relate the causes and results of the Revolutionary War.
4. Show the territorial growth of the United States.
5. Tell what you can of the history of Kansas.
6. Describe three of the most prominent battles of the Rebellion.
7. Who were the following: Morse, Whitney, Fulton, Bell, Lincoln, Penn, and Howe?
8. Name events connected with the following dates: 1607, 1620, 1800, 1849, and 1865?

Orthography (Time, one hour)

1. What is meant by the following: Alphabet, phonetic orthography, etymology, syllabication?
2. What are elementary sounds? How classified?
3. What are the following, and give examples of each: Trigraph, subvocals, diphthong, cognate letters, linguals?

4. Give four substitutes for caret 'u'.
5. Give two rules for spelling words with final 'e'. Name two exceptions under each rule.
6. Give two uses of silent letters in spelling. Illustrate each.
7. Define the following prefixes and use in connection with a word: Bi, dis, mis, pre, semi, post, non, inter, mono, super.
8. Mark diacritically and divide into syllables the following, and name the sign that indicates the sound: Card, ball, mercy, sir, odd, cell, rise, blood, fare, last.
9. Use the following correctly in sentences: Cite, site, sight, fane, fain, feign, vane, vain, vein, raze, raise, rays.
10. Write 10 words frequently mispronounced and indicate pronunciation by use of diacritical marks and by syllabication.

Geography (Time, one hour)

1. What is climate? Upon what does climate depend?
2. How do you account for the extremes of climate in Kansas?
3. Of what use are rivers? Of what use is the ocean?
4. Describe the mountains of N.A.
5. Name and describe the following: Monrovia, Odessa, Denver, Manitoba, Hecla, Yukon, St. Helena, Juan Fernandez, Aspinwall, and Orinoco.
6. Name and locate the principal trade centers of the U.S.
7. Name all the republics of Europe and give capital of each.
8. Why is the Atlantic Coast colder than the Pacific in the same latitude?
9. Describe the process by which the water of the ocean returns to the sources of rivers.
10. Describe the movements of the earth. Give inclination of the earth.

Bibliography

Barrows, H. *Designing a Problem-Based Curriculum for the Pre-Clinical Years*. New York: Springer, 1985.

———. *Practice-Based Learning: Problem-Based Learning Applied to Medical Education*. Springfield: Southern Illinois University School of Medicine, 1994.

Bloom, Benjamin S. "The 2 Sigma Problem: The Search for Methods of Group Instruction As Effective As One-to-One Tutoring." *Educational Researcher* (June–July 1984): 4–16.

Bogan, Christopher E., and Michael J. English. *Benchmarking for Best Practices: Winning through Innovative Adaptation*. New York: McGraw-Hill, 1994.

Boud, David, and Grahame Felleti. *The Challenge of Problem-Based Learning*. London: Kogan Page, 1991.

Bradshaw, L. K. "Technology-Supported Change: A Staff Development Opportunity." *NASSP Bulletin* 81, no. 593 (1997): 86–92.

Buebel, S., M. Freidman, and D. Mankowski. *The Identification of Teacher Competencies: A Job Related Curriculum Project*. Columbia: University of South Carolina, College of Education, 1978.

Carter, D. S. G. "Information and Communication Technology in the Professional Practice of Beginning Teachers." *Journal of Education for Teaching* 23, no. 3 (1997): 294–296.

Center for Policy Research in Education. "Creating School Finance Policies That Facilitate New Goals." (1998), <http://www.cpre.org/> [last accessed: January 30, 2002].

Charters, W. W., and Douglas Waples. *The Commonwealth Teacher Training Study*. Chicago: University of Chicago Press, 1929.

Chubb, E. John, and Terry E. Moe. *Politics, Markets and the Organization of Schools*. Washington, D.C.: Brookings Institution, 1986.

Clowes, George A. "Texas Academic Standards Upheld." *School Reform News* 4, no. 3 (March 2000).

Connors, Eugene T. *Education Tort Liability and Malpractice.* Bloomington, Ind.: Phi Delta Kappa, 1981.

Crosby, Philip. *Quality Is Free.* New York: McGraw-Hill, 1979.

Deming, W. Edwards. *Out of the Crisis.* Cambridge, Mass.: MIT Center for Advanced Engineering Study, 1986.

Donohue v. Copiague Union Free School District (407 N.Y.S. 874 2d 64 A.D. 2d 29, 1978).

Dyrli, O. E. "Stats Making News." *Technology and Learning* 18, no. 8 (1998): 82.

"England's Braintree Earns ISO 9000." *Public Sector Quality Report* (September 1995): 1–2.

Faison, C. L. "Modeling Instructional Technology Use in Teacher Preparation: Why Can't We Wait." *Educational Technology* 36, no. 5 (1996): 57–59.

Florman, Samuel C. *The Introspective Engineer.* New York: St. Martin's, 1996.

Fulton, K. "Technology Fluency." *Milken Exchange* (1998), <http://www.milkenexchange.org> [last accessed: June 19, 1999].

Gardner, John W. *Self-Renewal.* New York: HarperCollins, 1965.

Gerstner, Louis V., Jr. Keynote speech at the 2001 National Education Summit, Palisades, New Jersey, October 9, 2001.

Gilliland v. Board of Education (365 N.E. 2d 322, 1977).

Gladwell, Malcolm. *The Tipping Point.* Boston: Little, Brown, 2000.

Harvey, L. *Quality Assurance System, TQM and the New Collegiaism.* Microfile. ERIC Doc. Ed. 401810 (1995).

Hawley, W., and S. Rosenholtz. "Good Schools." *Peabody Journal of Education* (1984).

Hentoff, Nat. *Our Children Are Dying.* New York: Four Winds, 1967.

Hill, R. B., and J. A. Somers. "A Process for Initiating Change: Developing Technology Goals for a College of Education." *Journal of Teacher Education* 47, no. 4 (1996): 300–306.

Holt, John. *How Children Fail.* New York: Perseus, 1995.

Inmon, W. H. *Building the Data Warehouse.* 2nd ed. New York: Wiley, 1996.

International Society for Technology in Education. "National Educational Technology Standards." (1997), <http://www.iste.org > [last accessed: January 29, 2002].

Johnson, Craig. E-mail to authors. July 12, 2001.

Juran, Joseph M. *Managerial Breakthrough.* New York: McGraw-Hill, 1964.

Kaplan, Robert. The Masters Forum, University of Minnesota, Minneapolis, Minnesota, July 13, 1999.

Kelling, George L., and Catherine M. Coles. *Fixing Broken Windows: Restoring Order and Reducing Crime in Our Communities.* New York: Kressler/The Free Press, 1996.

Kohl, Herbert. *36 Children.* New York: Penguin, 1990.

Kozol, Jonathan. *Death at an Early Age: The Destruction of the Hearts and Minds of Negro Children in the Boston Public Schools.* New York: New American Library, 1985.

KPMG Consulting Services, August 3, 2001, <http://www.kpmgconsulting.com/library> [last accessed: January 7, 2002].

Landis, Andy. *Social Security: The Inside Story.* Menlo Park, Calif.: Crisp Publications, 1997.

Leland, Karen, and Keith Bailey. *Customer Service for Dummies.* 2nd ed. Foster City, Calif.: IDG, 1999.

Lessinger, Leon. *Every Kid a Winner: Accountability in Education.* New York: Simon and Schuster, 1970.

Lessinger, Leon, and Allen Salowe. *Game Time: The Educator's Playbook for the New Global Economy.* Lancaster, Penn.: Technomics, 1997.

Malone, M. N. "Make Them Believers." *Technology and Learning* 18, no. 7 (1998): 44–45.

Marshall, Ray, and Marc Tucker. *Thinking for a Living: Education and the Wealth of Nations.* New York: Basic, 1992.

McCullough, David. *John Adams.* New York: Simon and Schuster, 2001.

McLuhan, Marshall. *Understanding Media.* Cambridge, Mass.: MIT Press, 1968.

National Academy of Science. "Making Money Matter: Financing America's Schools." (1998), <http://www.upenn.edu> [last accessed: January 29, 2002].

National Center for Education Statistics. *Monitoring School Quality: An Indicators Report,* by Daniel P. Mayer, John E. Mullens, Mary T. Moore, and John Ralph. U.S. Department of Education, Office of Educational Research and Improvement. NCES 2001-030, December 2000.

———. *Outcome of Learning: Results from 2000 Program for International Assessment of 15-Year-Olds in Mathematics, Science, and Literacy.* Washington, D.C.: U.S. Department of Education, 2001.

National Council for Accreditation of Teacher Education. "Technology and the New Professional Teacher: Preparing for the 21st Century Classroom Report." (1997). <http://www.ncate.prg/projects/tech/TECH.HTM> [last accessed: May 26, 1999].

National Institute of Child Health and Human Development. "Teaching Children to Read: An Evidence-Based Assessment of the Scientific Research Literature on Reading and Its Implications for Reading Instruction." Report of the National Reading Panel, NIH Publication No. 00-4769. Washington, D.C.: U.S. Government Printing Office, 2000.

National Society for the Study of Education. "Programmed Instruction." In *The Sixty-Sixth Yearbook*, pt. 2. Chicago: National Society for the Study of Education, 1967.

New York Times, 8 December 1999.

Norman, Kent L. "Teaching in the Switched on Classroom: An Introduction to Electronic Education and Hyper-Courseware." (1997), <http://www.lap.umd .edu/SOC/sochome.html> [last accessed: September 28, 1999].

Odden, Allan. "Case Study 3: North America. School-Based Financing in North America." In *Needs-Based Resource Allocation in Schools via Formula-Based Funding*, ed. Kenneth Ross and Rosalind Levacic. Paris: International Institute for Education Planning, UNESCO, 1998.

————. "Creating School Finance Policies That Facilitate New Goals." Paper prepared for the Consortium for Policy Research in Education, University of Wisconsin–Madison, Wisconsin Center for Education Research, 1998.

Odden, Allan, and William Clune. "School Finance Systems: Aging Structures in Need of Renovation." *Educational Evaluation and Policy Analysis* 20, no. 3 (1998).

Peter, J., and G. Wills. "ISO 9000 As a Global Educational Structure." *Journal of Quality Assurance* 6, no. 2 (1998): 83–89.

Peter W. v. San Francisco Unified School District (60 C.A. 3d 814, 131 Cal. Rptr. 854, 1976).

"The Report of the Governor's Commission for Government by the People." Chairman Mayor Bill Frederick. Orlando, Florida, vols. 1 and 2, 1991.

Rosenthal, Robert. *Pygmalion in the Classroom*. New York: Irvington, 1992.

Salowe, Allen, and Leon Lessinger. *Healing Public Schools: The Winning Prescription to Cure Their Chronic Illness*. Lanham, Md: Scarecrow, 2001.

Scalet, Sarah. "Repairing the Trust." *CIO Magazine*, 15 August 2000, <http://www.cio.com/archive> [last accessed: January 7, 2002].

Stepien, W. J., and S. A. Gallagher. "Problem-Based Learning: As Authentic As It Gets." *Educational Leadership* 50, no. 7 (1993): 25–28.

Thai Ministry of Education. "ISO 9000 in Private Schools: Case Studies." 27 March 2001.

Third International Mathematics and Science Study Report, 4 April 2001, <http://nces.ed.gov/timss> [last accessed: January 7, 2002].

Thurow, Lester C. *Head to Head*. New York: Morrow, 1992.

Time, 27 August 2001.

U.S. Department of Education. *Home Schooling in the United States: 1999*. Washington, D.C.: U.S. Department of Education, 2000.

———. *What Works*. Washington, D.C.: U.S. Department of Education, 1986.

Utz, Rick L. E-mail to authors. August 14, 2001.

Viadero, Debra. *Education Week*, 27 September 2000.

Walberg, Herbert J. "Improving the Productivity of America's Schools." *Educational Leadership* (May 1984): 19–27.

"What Matter Most: Teaching for America's Future." National Commission on Teaching and America's Future Summary Report (September 1996).

Woods, Donald R. *Problem-Based Learning: How to Gain the Most from PBL*. Hamilton, Ont.: Woods, 1994.

About the Authors

Allen Salowe is a consultant, educator, and author. He is principal of A. E. Salowe and Associates and has consulted widely to public and private clients. He was formerly an adjunct professor of economics at Webster University. In 1997, he was named a senior fellow of the Florida Institute of Education (a Type I Regents Education Improvement Center) and in 1991 he was named a senior fellow of the Florida Center for Electronic Communication (a Type II University Research Center). He served a three-year term, the last as president, on the Plainfield (New Jersey) School Board immediately following the 1960s' urban riots.

He is formerly senior vice president of planning for ITT Community Development Corporation; senior operations executive for ITT Consumer Services Group; and group planning director for Champion International. Over a thirty-year business career, he has held numerous positions in strategic, tactical, financial, and operations planning. He has served as an economic advisor to over thirty Florida community development districts in their infrastructure planning and financing. During his time with ITT, he helped implement the quality management programs of Philip Crosby.

Salowe received an MBA in management from Nova Southeastern University and a BA in economics from the University of Miami. He holds the coveted certified planner designation from the American Institute of Certified Planners and is a former member of the American Society for Quality. This is his third coauthored publication on improving our schools. He is currently under contract to complete a fourth book on education improvement in the spring of 2002 and an Education Tools Workshop Series. The most recent book (coauthored with Leon Lessinger) *Healing Public Schools: The Prescription to Cure their Chronic Illness* was published in 2001.

Leon Lessinger has received the following degrees and credentials: BS in mechanical engineering from North Carolina State University, BA in Psychology, M. Ed. in educational psychology, and Ed.D. educational administration—all from the University of California at Los Angeles. He is a licensed clinical psychologist in California. He has served as a public school teacher, counselor, principal, assistant superintendent, and superintendent in three California school systems.

He served as an associate U.S. commissioner for elementary and secondary education in Washington, D.C., under Presidents Lyndon B. Johnson and Richard M. Nixon. In his more than fifty-year career in education, he has held endowed chairs as a professor at Georgia State University and the University of North Florida. He was a professor and dean of the College of Education at the University of South Carolina. He has conducted research for the State of California and has been a consultant to state departments of education, school systems, and leading companies.

He is a noted speaker on educational issues and economic development and has extensive publications that span the field from research to curriculum and instruction.